MAKIKO'S DIARY

A Merchant Wife in 1910 Kyoto

Nakano Makiko, ca. 1910. (Nakano Takashi)

MAKIKO'S DIARY

A Merchant Wife in 1910 Kyoto

NAKANO MAKIKO

Translated, with Introduction and Notes,

by KAZUKO SMITH

Stanford University Press, Stanford, California

The text of the diary was originally published in
Japanese under the title *Meiji yonjūsannen Kyōto:
Aru shōka no wakazuma no nikki*,

Stanford University Press, Stanford, California

Printed in the United States of America
CIP data appear at the end of the book

FOREWORD:
On the Occasion of the Publication of the English Edition of Makiko's Diary

Nakano Takashi

When I published my mother's old diary, *Meiji yonjūsannen Kyōto: Aru shōka no wakazuma no nikki* (Kyoto in 1910: The diary of the young wife of a merchant house), along with my editorial comments and annotations in April 1981, I was primarily targeting the younger generation of Japanese. My hope was to give them an opportunity to free themselves from their preconceptions about the life and culture of the Japanese people during the Meiji and Taishō periods and to further their understanding of those times. Now that the English edition is about to be published for a Western readership, it will mean that her diary will also promote increased understanding of Japan in the wider world.

My mother knew that in my doctoral dissertation, which was published in 1964, I had quoted from her diary as well as from the diaries of my great-grandfather. She understood that I thought it important to use personal documents in my research and had been a supporter of my studies from early on, so that when I asked her about the idea of publishing her diary she was not surprised. She was not totally convinced, however, and asked, "Why would a diary of a twenty-year-old woman be of interest to anybody else?" In her characteristically mischievous way, she also said, "Wouldn't our relatives of my generation be surprised and shocked if they found out about this!"—and gave me her permission. She was looking forward to its publication but, sad to say, died at the age of 88, three years short of its appearance. Had she known that her diary was also going to be published in the United States, she would truly have been surprised.

When Kazuko Smith approached me with the idea of translating the diary, I was more than happy to give her my consent. She was born in Japan and taught in the Japanese language program at Cornell University for more than twenty years. She and her husband, Professor Robert J. Smith, an internationally known cultural anthropologist who studies Japan, are old friends of mine. Who could be better qualified to do the translation? I had an opportunity to read a draft of her Introduction, and, struck by her deep understanding of the subject as a Japanese woman herself, I realized how fortunate it was for my mother and myself that she had undertaken the translation. The detailed questions she has raised with me, not only in the course of doing the translation of the diary, but also in writing the extensive Introduction, the description of my mother's social world, and the Epilogue, have required some rethinking of many issues on my part and made me realize that further explanation of some points would have been very helpful to my Japanese readers.

I wish to take this occasion to express my deepest gratitude to Kazuko Smith, from the standpoint of a researcher of modern Japanese social history and life histories—and as Makiko's son.

ACKNOWLEDGMENTS

I owe an enormous debt of gratitude to those who have been so generous with their time in helping me bring Makiko's diary to an English-speaking audience. I am particularly grateful to Professor Nakano Takashi, who offered me encouragement and provided the kind of information and depth of insight that could have come only from Makiko's son. Many people have been kind enough to read the manuscript in its many different states. Carol Kammen, a local historian who has made extensive use of diaries in her research, gave the very first version of the manuscript a characteristically expert and thoughtful reading. William B. Hauser's suggestions and criticisms were informed by his long involvement in the study of the history of the Kyoto-Osaka area. Margery Wolf, one of my oldest American friends, took time out from her own busy schedule to give generously of her expertise as a feminist and anthropologist of East Asia. Anne Walthall encouraged me to complete the task I had started and offered detailed critical comments from the vantage point of a historian of Japan and a specialist in women's studies. Marian Wittink gave me invaluable insight into Japanese women and how they relate to others socially. Arnold Olds helped guide me in the preparation of the maps, charts, and illustrations. The calligraphy at the beginning of each month in the diary is by Kyoko Selden, who literally and figuratively lent me her hand at a critical moment. Muriel Bell and Ellen F. Smith of Stanford University Press have offered expert advice in editing and designing the book. For their generous assistance in my search for appropriate photographs, I am indebted to Professor Shirahata Yōzaburō of Nihon Bunka Kenkyū Center; Okukubo

Atsumu of Tankōsha in Kyoto; the Kyoto Prefectural Archives; Henry D. Smith II of Columbia University; Martie W. Young and Jackie Clark, Herbert F. Johnson Museum of Art, Cornell University; Margarita Winkel and Chris Uhlenbeck of Leiden; and Aaron Martin Cohen and Suga Hiroto of Tokyo. Finally, I must acknowledge the contribution of Robert J. Smith, my sternest and most persistent critic throughout this endeavor in every dimension of the undertaking.

K. S.

CONTENTS

MAPS AND FIGURES

Photographs of Makiko's family and friends and of Kyoto appear throughout the book.

A NOTE ON NAMES AND TERMS

Names are given in the Japanese order, surname first.

A word is in order concerning Makiko's somewhat capricious use of the words affixed to either the surname or the given name. These words are *-san*, *-sama*, *-chan*, *-sensei*, *-don*, *-han*, and *-yan*, and, being gender-blind, they pose something of a problem for the translator. None of these terms makes distinction as to marital status, including the Kyoto localisms *-han* and *-yan*. The term *-chan*, a diminutive of *-san*, is used almost exclusively for children of both sexes. Where it is important to know whether the individual is a boy or girl, I have given the information in a footnote. The term *sensei*, roughly equivalent to "teacher," is used for distinguished individuals and professionals. The term *-don* is used only for servants, male and female.

For the convenience of the reader of English, I have altered some of the names as they appear in the diary. For example, Makiko never referred to her brother by his name, "Manzō," but always as *ani* (elder brother). Similarly, she called her half-sister *Senbon no neesan* (elder sister who lives in Senbon), but for the sake of simplicity, I have used "Elder Sister Kōshima." Kinship usage in Japan forbids use of the first name alone for persons who occupy a status superior to the speaker, even if they are chronologically younger. The reason that Makiko refers to her brother-in-law Hidesaburō by his name even though he is two years older is that, as the wife of his elder brother, she outranks him in the household hierarchy.

Makiko sometimes uses the terms "uncle" (*oji-san*) and "aunt" (*oba-san*) in referring to older relatives, old family friends, and neighbors who are of her parents' generation. As in American English, these terms are used for non-kin to indicate a particular feeling of closeness and a degree of intimacy.

Makiko's style does have one interesting characteristic that probably reflects the usage of the time. She uses *-sama*, today considered more formal than *-san*, for some of her friends and other intimates, such as Matsui Jisuke, who marries her husband's sister. He is invariably referred to as Matsui-sama.

In giving recipes, Makiko uses the Japanese units of measure: 1 *shō* equals 1.8 liters (or 1.9 quarts); there are 10 *gō* in 1 *shō* and 10 *shō* in 1 *to*.

In 1910 the yen was equal to about $0.50. There are 100 *sen* in 1 yen and 10 *rin* in 1 *sen*. There are no reliable statistics for family income or average annual wage in 1910, but I have found figures for the average annual income of certain categories of worker at about this time. In 1907 a male certified primary school teacher's annual income was ¥260; a female earned ¥180. In 1910, a male farm laborer's annual wages were ¥47, and a female's ¥28.50, while male domestic servants earned ¥54.72, and females ¥35.52 (Tōyō Keizai Shinpōsha). In 1909 the annual wage of a female silk-reeler employed by a spinning company in Nagano prefecture was about ¥60 (Tsurumi, p. 72). The only reference to an annual wage in Makiko's diary concerns her father's housekeeper, who was seeking an increase from ¥48 to ¥50.

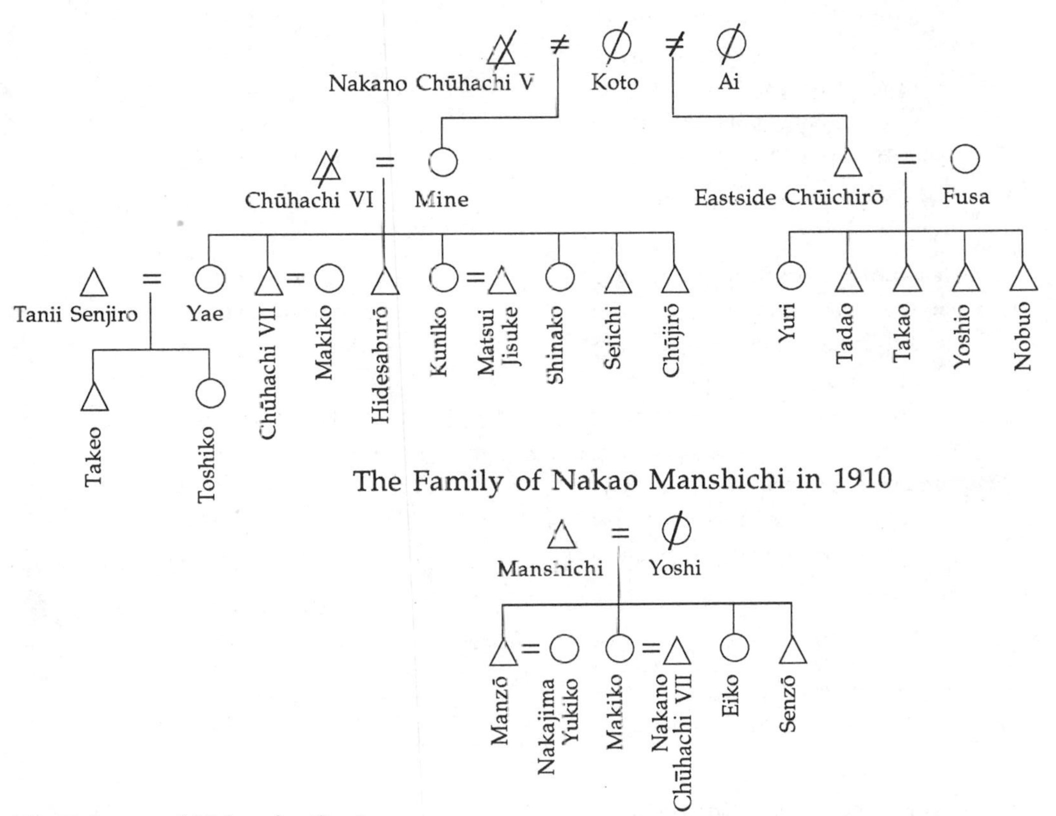

The Nakano and Nakao families in 1910

A Guide to the Most Frequently Mentioned Names

(Listed by family name and, if appropriate, location.)

Names and term(s) used by Makiko in the diary	Name and relationship to Makiko	Age Jan. 1, 1910 (if known)
Nakano family, Gojō		
my husband	Chūhachi VII, husband	26
Mother	Mine, mother-in-law	43
Hide-san	Hidesaburō, husband's younger brother	22
Kuniko-san, Kuni-san, Okuni	Kuniko, husband's younger sister	18
Shinako-san, Shina-san, Oshina	Shinako, husband's younger sister	14
Sei-san	Seiichi, husband's younger brother	13
Chūji-san, Chū-san	Chūjirō, husband's younger brother	8
Moriguchi-san	Moriguchi Seizaburō, head store-manager	48
Yamada-san	Yamada Suekichi, second store-manager	36
Nakano family, Eastside		
Eastside Doctor	Nakano Chūichirō, husband's uncle	36
Fusako-san	Fusako, husband's aunt	
Yuri-san	Yuriko, husband's female cousin	8
Tada-san	Tadao, husband's male cousin	6
Taka-chan	Takao, husband's male cousin	
[not mentioned]	Yoshio, husband's male cousin	
"the baby"	Nobuo, husband's male cousin	

Tanii family

Brother Tanii	Senjirō, brother-in-law by marriage	37
Sister Tanii	Yae, sister-in-law (husband's older sister)	27
Take-chan	Takeo, nephew	8
Toshiko, Toshiko-chan	Toshiko, niece	3 mo

Nakao family, Nijō

my father	Manshichi, father	
my mother	Yoshi, mother (died November 21, 1909)	
Manzō	Manzō, elder brother	28
Yukiko, Oyuki-sama	Yukiko, sister-in-law (Manzō's wife)	
Eiko-san, Eiko	Eiko, younger sister	15
Senzō	Senzō, younger brother	12

Kōshima family

[not mentioned]	Fusajirō, half-sister's husband
Elder Sister Kōshima	Unknown, half-sister
Fumi, Fumiko	Fumiko, half-sister's daughter

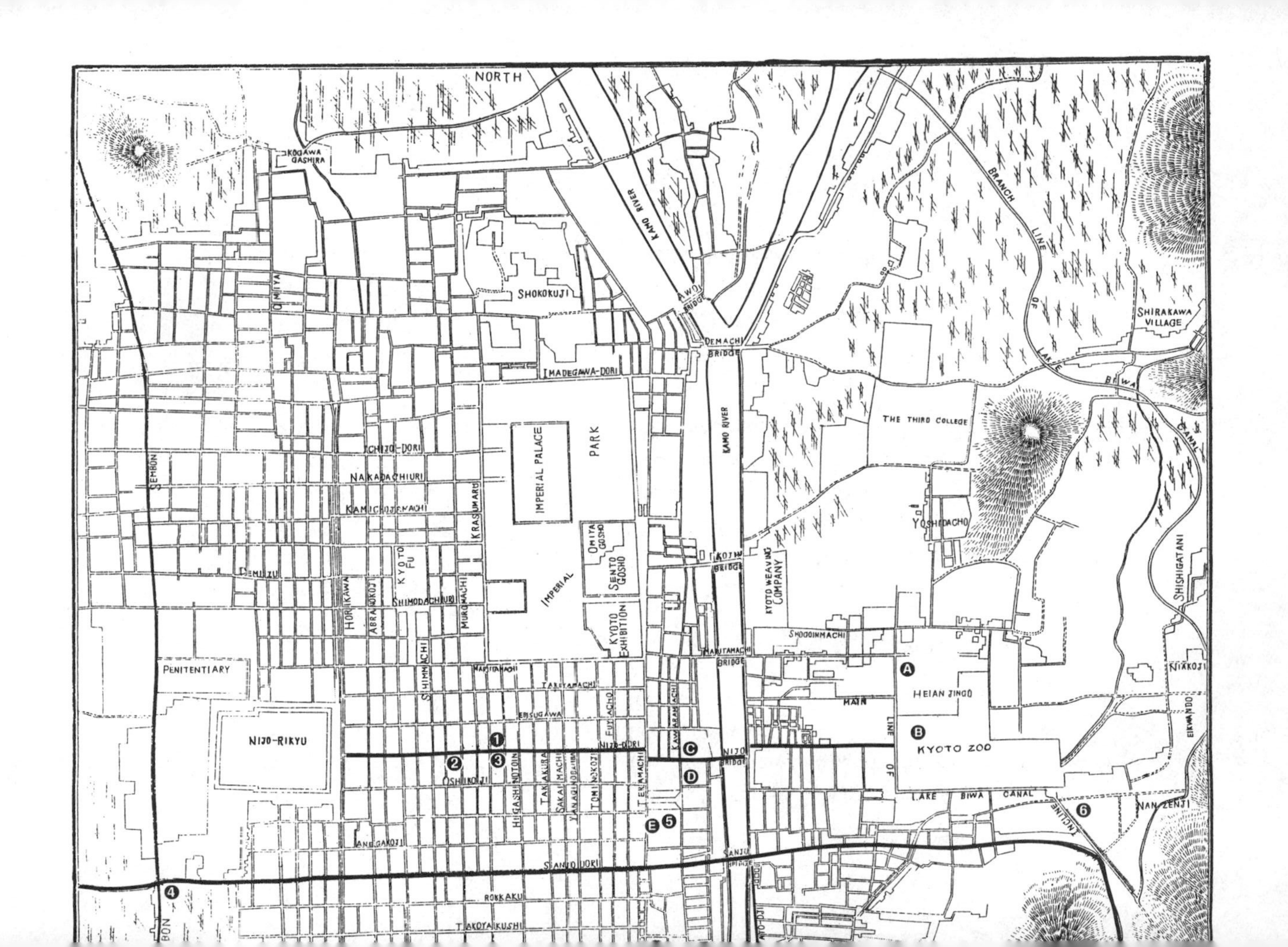

NORTH
KOGAWA GASHIRA
KAMO RIVER
SHOKOKUJI
BRANCH LINE OF LAKE BIWA CANAL
SHIRAKAWA VILLAGE
DEMACHI BRIDGE
IMADEGAWA-DORI
OMIYA
THE THIRD COLLEGE
ICHIJO-DORI
NAKADACHIURI
KAMICHOJEMACHI
SEMBON
IMPERIAL PALACE
PARK
YOSHIDACHO
KRASUMARU
OMIYA GOSHO
SENTO GOSHO
KOJIN BRIDGE
KYOTO WEAVING COMPANY
DEMIZU
KYOTO FU
HORIKAWA
ABRANOKOJI
SHIMODACHIURI
MUROMACHI
IMPERIAL
KYOTO EXHIBITION
SHIGHIGATANI
SHOGOINMACHI
MARUTAMACHI BRIDGE
PENITENTIARY
SHIMMACHI
TAKEYAMACHI
HEIAN JINGO
NIAKOJI
MAIN LINE OF LAKE BIWA CANAL
EBISUGAWA
FUYACHO
KAWARAMACHI
EIKWANDO
NIJO-RIKYU
NIJO-DORI
NIJO BRIDGE
KYOTO ZOO
OSHIKOJI
HIGASHINOTOIN
TAKAKURA
SAKAIMACHI
YANAGINOBABA
TOMINOKOJI
TERAMACHI
INCLINE
NAN ZENJI
ANEGAKOJI
SANJO DORI
SANJO BRIDGE
ROKKAKU
TAKOYAKUSHI
BON

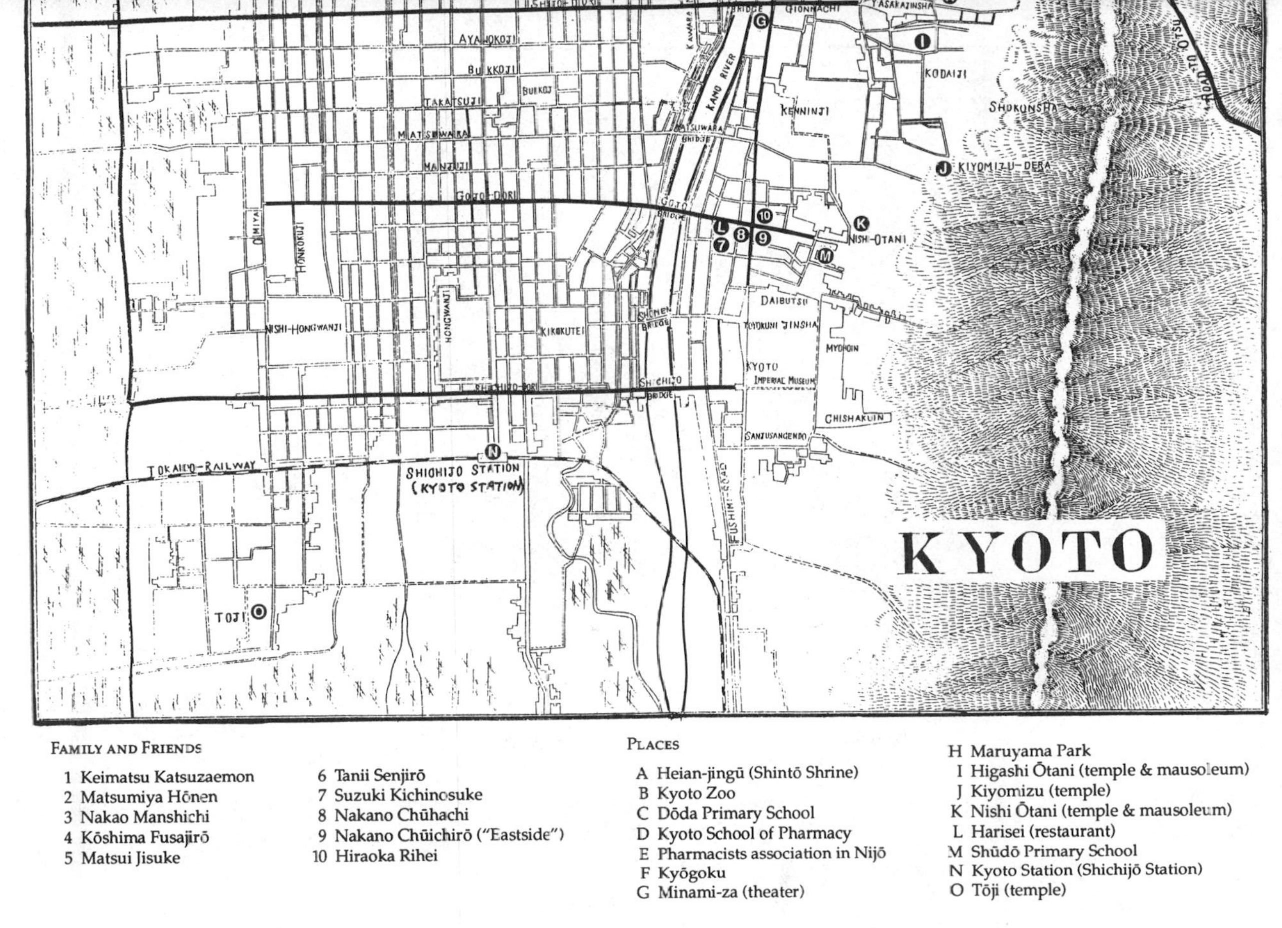

Family and Friends

1 Keimatsu Katsuzaemon
2 Matsumiya Hōnen
3 Nakao Manshichi
4 Kōshima Fusajirō
5 Matsui Jisuke
6 Tanii Senjirō
7 Suzuki Kichinosuke
8 Nakano Chūhachi
9 Nakano Chūichirō ("Eastside")
10 Hiraoka Rihei

Places

A Heian-jingū (Shintō Shrine)
B Kyoto Zoo
C Dōda Primary School
D Kyoto School of Pharmacy
E Pharmacists association in Nijō
F Kyōgoku
G Minami-za (theater)
H Maruyama Park
I Higashi Ōtani (temple & mausoleum)
J Kiyomizu (temple)
K Nishi Ōtani (temple & mausoleum)
L Harisei (restaurant)
M Shūdō Primary School
N Kyoto Station (Shichijō Station)
O Tōji (temple)

Map 1. Kyoto, ca. 1900. (Adapted from M. Ichihara, comp., *The Official Guide-Book to Kyoto and the Allied Prefectures*, 1895)

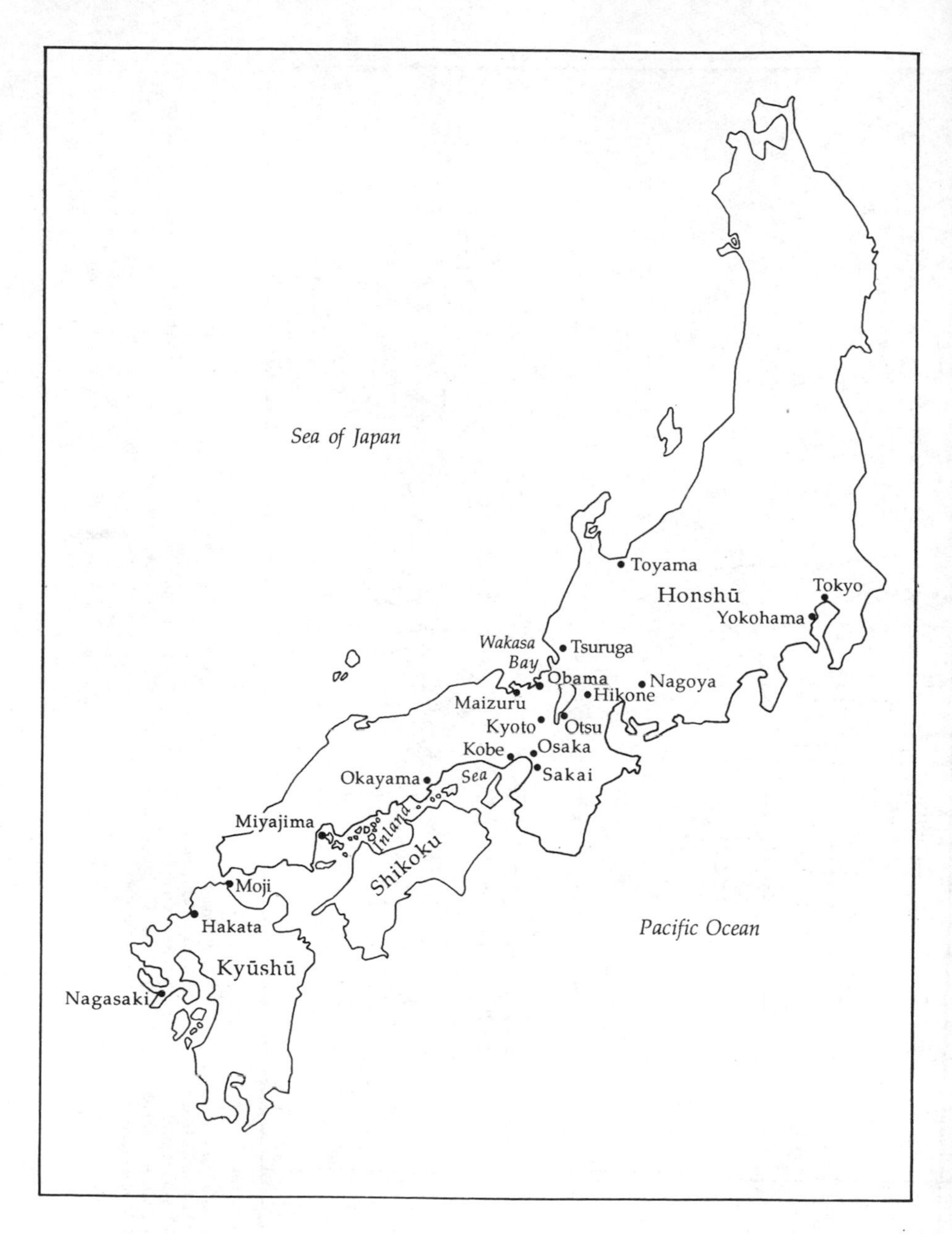

Map 2. Selected sites in Japan

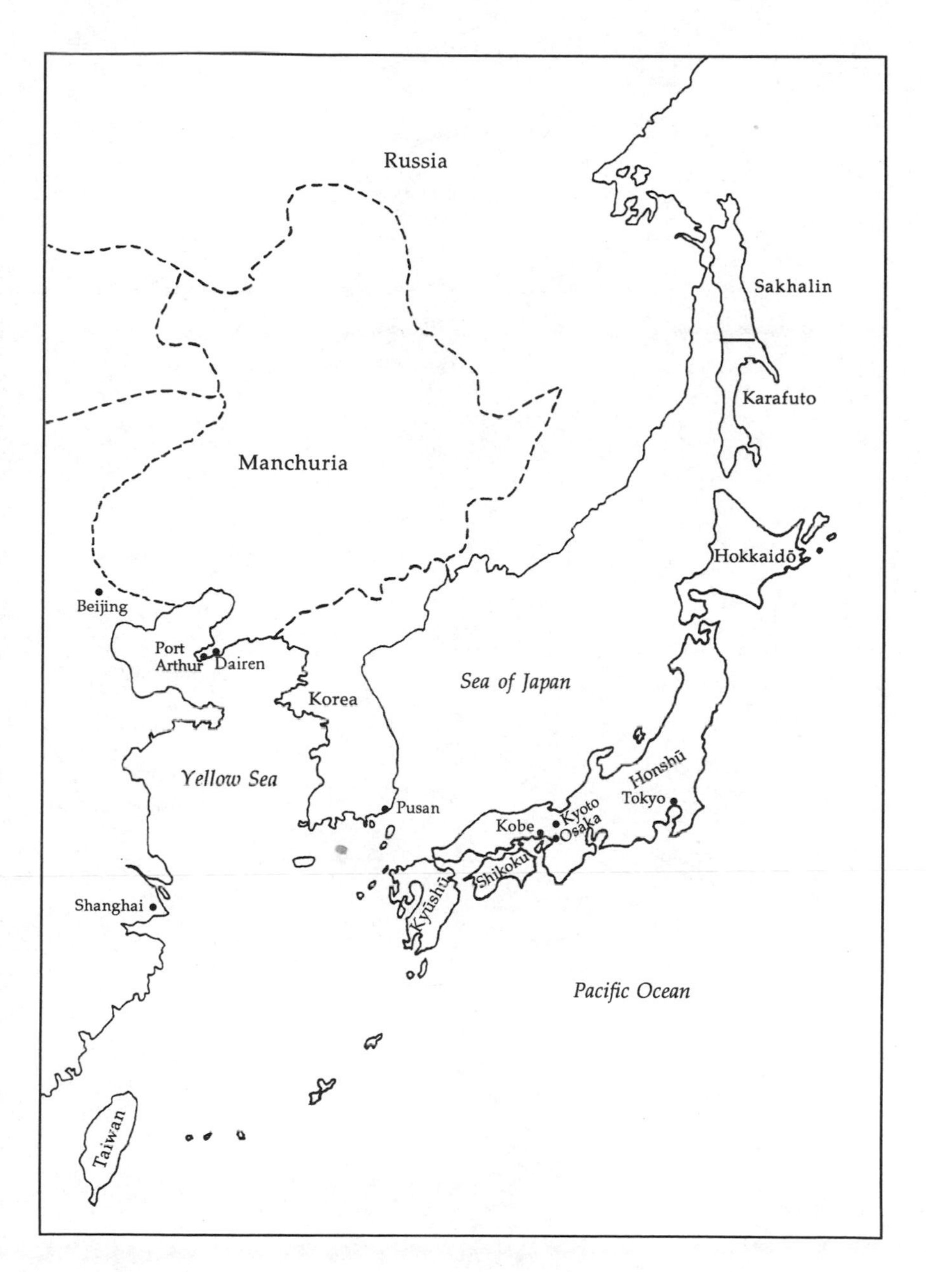

Map 3. Northeast Asia, 1910

MAKIKO'S DIARY

A Merchant Wife in 1910 Kyoto

INTRODUCTION

We owe the publication of one year of Makiko's diary to her son Professor Nakano Takashi.[1] One of Japan's leading sociologists, he has long advocated using personal documents, including diaries and other life-history materials, to contribute to our understanding of society and history. Although Makiko's diary can be read with a social scientist's eye, mine is that of a woman and a general reader. Before I was very far into it, I found myself thoroughly captivated by what Makiko tells us about herself and Japan during its first great modern period of social and cultural transformation. I begin, therefore, with a personal note.

Perhaps any Japanese woman of my age would have had a similar reaction to the diary, for Makiko was younger than my grandmother and just fifteen years older than my mother. I have known many women of her generation, then, but have no personal experience of the culture of the old merchant houses of cities like Kyoto. It follows that, although I found much of what she wrote about quite familiar, some of it struck me as exotic or at least surprising, for more than 80 years have passed since she picked up her brush to write: "First of all, 'Happy New Year!'"

I was born in Japan and lived there as a member of a small nuclear family during the 1930's, 1940's, and early 1950's. There were not many relatives around, and since I did not know any families that were involved in complex kin networks, the so-called traditional Japanese household has always been a mystery to me. The other small

1. See Nakano, *Meiji yonjūsannen Kyōto*, published in 1981.

families in our neighborhood probably were representative of urban middle-class Japanese at that time. Our maternal grandmother did live with us for the last ten years of her life, and because mothers-in-law are assigned virtually demonic character in Japanese folklore, fiction, and drama, I had always assumed that the relationship between my mother and her mother was much more harmonious than would have been the case had they been daughter-in-law and mother-in-law. Now, having read Makiko's diary, I can see that personalities and circumstances have more to do with creating the character of such relationships than does the individual's structural position in the household. This is a particularly important point, for it seems to me that for Western readers the best introduction to the Japanese family is through accounts of its daily life. The Japanese "family system" and the gender inequality it entails have been widely discussed, but it is hard for outsiders to see past the structure to the life within. Makiko's diary provides us with a small window through which to observe the members of a very busy household in action.

Given such limited personal experience of them before I read Makiko's diary, my assumptions about traditional households were based primarily on novels, films, and gossip, which seemed always to emphasize friction, oppression, and complicated emotional tensions. Now I had an opportunity to explore this unknown world, which from the vantage point of today seems more than a little archaic, but nonetheless fascinating. So I began reading, expecting to find confirmation of the discontent, frustration, and humiliation that I simply assumed were the lot of young daughters-in-law of the time. It soon became clear, however, that Makiko lived rather comfortably in a quite orderly and harmonious household, even though, having married the young head of the household only four years earlier, she was its newest member.

Makiko's relationship with her mother-in-law, Mine, appears to have been on a sound footing and was much like what one might expect to find between a real mother and daughter. Probably because of her own mother's recent death and because of Makiko's youth and inexperience, she seems not to have minded terribly even when she was reprimanded by her mother-in-law. In the diary, at least, there is no sign of resentment or any other indication that she held grudges over such incidents. At first this made me suspicious, for I thought that she might have been exercising caution in case someone in the family should happen to read her diary. However, my doubts began to dissolve as I continued to read, for it occurred to me that if she was concerned to conceal her true feelings, she would hardly have bothered to keep a diary at all.

And Makiko was not without feelings. Far from it. For instance, in spite of her diligence in fulfilling the heavy responsibilities of the domestic workload—cooking, cleaning the house, and sewing for the family and all the shop-boys and clerks—she did ask herself, "Why do women seem to be preparing meals all the time?" Occasionally she expressed fleeting unhappiness with her husband, Chūhachi, particularly when he denied her something that she had her heart set on. If the reader begins to have doubts that this equable young woman ever reacted strongly to anything, they will be dispelled by the outburst of emotion over a nasty incident in which the drunken head manager of the store insulted her to her face in the presence of the maids and shop-boys. Makiko poured out her misery and anger in her diary but behaved just as I had always supposed a young wife of the time would—she never said a word to anyone about either the incident or her rage.

If we can view this as a traditional household making a successful transition into a new kind of society, then the obvious question is why this particular one turned out the way it did. I think the key was her mother-in-law, of whom Makiko later told her son, "She was a modern person who understood the situation very well." Nevertheless, Makiko's own personality certainly helped. She was almost unfailingly cheerful, optimistic, and outgoing, and her observations about people and events were often witty. She was gregarious and enjoyed good conversation, and she hated to be left alone in the house when the others went out. At this point in her life she was also trying to learn her responsibilities in a large and complex household, for in her rather repetitive and sometimes boring notes she dutifully recorded in detail what was prepared for lunch and dinner, wrote out many recipes, and recorded who came to the house and what foods they were served. It is still the case that one of the duties of the in-marrying bride in Japan is to learn what are called *kafū*, the "ways of the house," and in her meticulous memos to herself, Makiko's character gradually emerges. It is apparent that one of her purposes in keeping a journal at all was to make a record to which she would be able to refer when needed. Some entries read as though she wrote down verbatim some technique or recipe that her mother-in-law described to her. I should point out that cookbooks were not much used in Japan before World War II; thus, the information about ingredients and their ratios provided here is especially interesting because so many foods that today come commercially packaged were still being made at home.

Perhaps because she was still childless and because her mother-in-law was a young and vigorous 43, Makiko actually led a much more carefree life than one might imagine possible, given the usual stories about the position of women in the household at this period of Japanese history. Later, reflecting back on that time, she told her son, "My mother-in-law was so capable at everything that I had little to do around the house, so I often played jump-rope and other games." Nevertheless, Makiko's diary tells us that she was charged with much sewing, cleaning, cooking, and serving meals for the family and store employees, and on occasion she had to arrange to hire maids. This task seems to have been a real burden to Makiko, for she mentioned frequently in her diary how troublesome it was to find a new maid and how she wished they would not just leave so abruptly. Her negative attitude toward them may well have been a reflection of her anxiety about her ability to manage the domestic help. Even when they were not shorthanded, preparing meals for about twenty people every day was a daunting task that had to be carried out without the assistance of any modern conveniences. Makiko and her mother-in-law supervised the operation and worked along with the maids.

Makiko was also assigned the task of handling correspondence related to domestic matters, probably because she had a particularly fine hand and also perhaps because she liked to write. It is also likely that Mine, who, like most women of her generation, had little formal education, welcomed the chance to pass on the responsibility. According to Makiko, it was easy to get along with her "modern" mother-in-law, "who gave me, a young, inexperienced wife, freedom to explore." True enough, but a very large number of entries in the diary reveal the many specific ways that Mine was training Makiko to be the wife of the head of a household that would have to make its way in a Japan very different from the one she herself had known. For example, she encouraged Makiko to take Western-style cooking lessons from a Japanese chef from the Miyako Hotel. Such a wife would, of course, be expected to assume the responsibility of carrying on the traditions of the household, then in its seventh generation, but at the same time would have to become a suitable spouse for the head of a new type of household, a man of the new age. In fact, Makiko's husband, Chūhachi, did a great deal to move the family pharmacy into the modern business world, and early in his headship introduced many reforms.

Makiko was very young, and perhaps for that reason I found especially affecting the frequent occasions on which she chided herself for being lazy or irresponsible or incompetent and then invariably vowed to improve. Yet, despite the relative lightness of her domestic duties, it is clear that on occasion she found some features of her situation less than wholly satisfactory. The source of her dissatisfaction, not surprisingly to those who have direct experience of the Japanese family, was her husband, Chūhachi. She admired and respected him, worried about him when he was ill, missed him when he was away, and enjoyed the constant stream of visitors who came to see him. Throughout the diary she delights in recounting the conversations between Chūhachi and the small group of male friends who took up so much of his time. Yet it was with these men that Chūhachi went out to dine, attend art exhibitions, see plays, go to meetings, and participate in any number of activities that his wife also found appealing, but that were denied her simply because she was young, married, and a woman.

Chūhachi's friends were forever dropping in unexpectedly and staying for lunch or dinner, which Makiko and her mother-in-law were required to prepare and serve. She enjoyed the lively conversation, which often went on until late at night, and wanted to try her hand at things still new to Japan at the time, such as oil painting, that so intrigued Chūhachi and his circle. Makiko occasionally expressed her envy of these young men for the freedom of action they enjoyed, compared to her own more constrained life, and indeed the lot of them give the impression of being dilettantes. The accounts of Chūhachi's many social activities and those of his friends will inevitably raise the question in the minds of some readers whether he spent much—or any—time actually working. From the evidence of his considerable achievements while head of this business household, it is clear that he worked very hard. We must assume that Makiko ordinarily recorded only those occasions when she was involved personally in the affairs of the store, such as the days when accounts were settled, or emergencies, such as the unusual occasion on which she and her mother-in-law were asked to make up a supply of the small cloth bags used for medicines at the time. For the same reason, the personal friends and acquaintances of the young couple appear in the diary more frequently than do the regular business-related visitors, merchants, and tradesmen with whom the household maintained standing relationships, because they did not touch her life and had little to do with the domestic side of household affairs.

Chūhachi went out to attend all kinds of meetings on an almost daily basis, sometimes more than one on a given day. He bore heavy responsibilities for a 26-year-old, for he had succeeded to the headship of the household when his father died suddenly. It was his duty, therefore, to represent the household not only in business but also in public affairs. Makiko's diary gives few details of her husband's business activities, and, as I have indicated, his day-to-day activities in the store are never mentioned. It seems likely that during this period much of the management of the business was entrusted to the two store managers, both older and far more experienced than he. However, Makiko reports that Chūhachi attended many meetings of the Pharmacists' Cooperative and was very busy with the affairs of the Kyoto Private School of Pharmacy, of which he was a graduate, for 1910 was the year in which efforts to raise the status of the school were under way. The plan involved the creation of a foundation called the Kyoto German Academic Society,[2] and Chūhachi was one of four members of the committee directing the school's expansion. In keeping with his efforts to embrace the modern, Chūhachi was interested in public education and was an active member of the district school board, whose meetings were frequently mentioned by Makiko. In the year of the diary he played an active role in replacing a school principal who was forced to resign in disgrace. Other meetings were of groups in which his membership was determined by his status as head of the household—parishioner (*ujiko*) groups of Shintō shrines and the analogous groups (*danka*) of Buddhist temples, for example. There were also meetings of the neighborhood association (*chōnai*) which, as head of his household, he had to attend as a civic duty.

2. *Kyōto doitsu gakkai*. At this period of Japan's modernization, the influence of German science and medicine was paramount, which probably explains the organization's name.

Although Chūhachi went out almost every day and, as Makiko frequently noted, was likely to return home late at night, he seldom left Kyoto during the year. The only exceptions were two trips to Osaka, once on a social occasion and once to attend a funeral, and two summertime camping trips with friends, not far from Kyoto. Although Chūhachi dreamed about going to England (an ambition inspired by his reading of Sir Robert Baden-Powell's book *Scouting for Boys*, published in 1908), before 1910 he seems to have been abroad only once, on a tour of Korea and Manchuria.

Chūhachi also attended a great many all-male dinners and parties (women customarily were never included—and still are not today for the most part) where the men were entertained by professionals, not necessarily geisha. Such behavior was absolutely routine for Japanese men of the time and to a large extent remains so. However late he stayed out, Makiko dutifully waited up to greet him upon his return, even though the women of the household were expected to rise very early. She would have had no cause for complaint on this score, nor does she, except when he was so late coming home that she was unable to stay awake to let him in.

What to make of Chūhachi as a husband, then? In most ways he seems to me to have been the best kind of husband that a young wife in such a household could have hoped for. His first responsibility was to manage the business in such a way as to enhance its social standing and keep it on a solid financial footing. It is small wonder that he comes across as somewhat authoritarian and not as solicitous of his young wife as a Western reader might expect him to be. This authoritarian style may well have been the result of the suddenness with which he had been thrust into the role of household head, for among his many responsibilities were those of seeing to the education of his younger brothers and sisters and eventually marrying them off. Thus, Chūhachi had to assume the role of surrogate father at an early age. The same was true of Makiko, although the nature of her responsibilities toward her siblings was quite different because she was a woman and their father was still alive. For an older child to take on the role of surrogate parent (both Chūhachi and Makiko were twenty when they did so) was not unusual before World War II, for Japanese life expectancy was short.

It is worth keeping in mind, however, that Chūhachi had been studying the humanities at the best college in Kyoto at the time of his father's sudden death. There he had read Western philosophy and, given the times, is certain to have encountered both democratic and liberal ideas. Makiko's diary reveals very little of Chūhachi's own ethics, philosophy, and ideals directly, but I can point out the importance of what he did not do and what he disapproved of. For example, he disliked parties at which there was heavy drinking, which to any Japanese woman will suggest that he did not run with the crowd that enjoyed the entertainment provided by geisha and other professional women. Instead, Chūhachi's after-hours were spent mostly with his friends at their homes or his, where they painted, played music, and—as Makiko says again and again—talked and talked and talked. I suspect that the discussions tended to center on ideas, the arts, the theater, and education.

In trying to understand the character of marital relations in Japan at that time, the Western reader would be well advised to keep in mind that neither taking a wife, nor going as a bride for that matter, involved particularly personal concerns. I have been asked if all of Chūhachi's late-night outings suggest that he kept a mistress. I think not, mainly because of his distaste for drunken parties and his youthful idealism, but I am obliged to say that it would not have been in the least surprising had he done so, for at that time the practice was accepted by society, by family members, and by the man's wife.

Because household continuity was of such paramount importance, marriages like Chūhachi's and Makiko's tended to be arranged. Particularly in households such as this, the wife was recruited into its service, and Makiko is no exception in this regard. A wife was not only expected to be her husband's lifelong mate, she was also his partner in managing the household enterprise. Nevertheless, Western women are far more likely than contemporary Japanese women to be startled to discover that Makiko had to ask her husband's or mother-in-law's permission to go out, as if she were a child. She appears to have accepted this as quite normal and except for two or three occasions managed to hide her disappointment at being left at home when others went out or at otherwise being denied pleasures she had been counting on. It must be remembered, however, that being left behind to watch after the house and deal with drop-in visitors while others were away was among the many duties of the wife of the merchant-household head at this time. Makiko's mother-in-law would have done the same were her husband still alive, but now that her status had changed, she had handed on the responsibility to her daughter-in-law as part of her training. Ordinarily Makiko cheerfully saw the others off and, when they returned, was eager to hear what they had done or seen.

I cannot leave my characterization of gender relations in the Japanese family in Makiko's day without sharing with my readers a story told me recently by the wife of an American university professor. It is a powerful reminder of how slowly some things change in Japan, despite outward appearances to the contrary. In 1985, when she and her husband were in Tokyo, some of his former students arranged to hold a welcoming party for them. Since she had some free time on the day of the party, she decided to look up the wife of one of the former students, a young woman she had met in the French class they took together. They had become quite friendly during the two years the Japanese couple were at the American university. A telephone call produced an invitation to the young woman's suburban home, and she was waiting at the station with her new baby. It turned out that the young couple were living with his mother, recently widowed. Following common practice in these days of high real estate prices, and also because it is the custom to live with the husband's elderly parents, they had moved in with her after the father-in-law's death. The mother-in-law had lived in England for a time when her late husband was assigned there by his company, and she greeted the visitor in quite good English.

Toward the end of the visit the young husband telephoned from his office to say that he would be unable to attend the party that evening after all because he had to work late. Last-minute changes of plan are routine in Japan, no matter how short the notice, because everyone understands that one's first obligation is to one's company or workplace. Struck by how apologetic the young woman seemed, the American woman said, "Why don't you come to the party representing your husband? I understand I'll be the only woman otherwise. I'd love to have you there, so we can talk." The young woman's face lighted up momentarily, but then she said, "I'll have to ask my husband and mother-in-law." After long consultation on the telephone with her husband and more consultation with her mother-in-law in the back room, she emerged to say that she would be able to go.

She did attend the party, which was held at a club belonging to the company one of the men worked for, because most houses and apartments are too small for such gatherings. The club's staff had set out liquor and a buffet, but did not serve the guests. There were about ten of her husband's former students, all men. Their behavior was quite formal at first, but she did notice that after they had a drink or two they seemed to relax and shift back to the casual style of interaction of their American days. But it was her woman friend's behavior that the American found so striking. Being the only Japanese woman present, she gradually slipped into the role of caretaker. Indeed, she was so busy the entire evening that the two women never got a chance to talk.

Would any part of this story have surprised Makiko? Certainly she would have expected the young woman to ask her husband's and mother-in-law's permission to go out, especially since there was a baby to care for. Finding herself the only woman (especially the only Japanese woman) at a gathering of men, she would with equal certainty have understood that it was her place to serve them. That all the members of the Japanese family in question were well educated would strike her as irrelevant to the issue, but I suspect that even Makiko might have assumed, as I did, that because they had all lived abroad there would have been a less thoroughly "Japanese" outcome to the visit by an old friend from America.

Although Makiko had only the compulsory four years of primary school education of her generation, her diary is that of a bright, open-minded young woman. In the year of the diary, she attended her first performance of the *nō* drama and wrote that it made a powerful impression on her, and indeed she reports having a nightmare influenced by its performance style. Although she hoped to improve her skills at calligraphy and delighted in the gift of a book of instruction, the hand in which the diary is written indicates that she already had developed a flair with the brush. She was also interested in what may loosely be called science and experimentation. She hurried to try to spot the comet that her brother-in-law had told her ought to be visible on a certain night, and shared Chūhachi's interest in finding out whether sea cucumbers would dissolve when placed in contact with straw. (They did not.) She vowed to try to make frozen tofu on her own and, because she failed on the first try, was determined to succeed on the second. (She did.)

According to her son, Makiko was always on the go and something of a tomboy. And indeed, she wrote that when she heard that the cherry blossoms were at their peak, she climbed up onto a small platform on the rooftop[3] with a pair of binoculars and was so entranced by the panorama of Kyoto dotted with clouds of cherry blossoms that she forgot all about her household chores. Apparently the reason that she was still childless after more than three years of marriage was that she had fallen down the stairs on one of her earlier excursions to the rooftop.

She may have been a tomboy, but Makiko was also an obedient wife and daughter-in-law. There is no question that her primary loyalty was to the household she had married into and that one of her goals in life was to learn to manage its domestic affairs. Another goal must have been, in the words of a popular slogan of the time promoted by the Meiji government through the school system, to become a "good wife and wise mother."[4] It was a very common ambition for Japanese women in 1910. In that sense, then, Makiko was not an extraordinary woman at all, but followed the pattern of life expected of the women of her time.

Therefore, the role that she was to play throughout her adult life was already well established and well defined; as long as she fulfilled the requirements of her role, her position in her new home would be secure. She even had two excellent role models whom she admired and respected—her mother-in-law and her own late mother. The household in which she had grown up was very much like the Nakanos, though somewhat smaller in scale in terms of both business and family composition. There were fewer children, fewer store employees, and fewer servants, but she had both caring parents and a grandmother who looked after the family and their employees while she was growing up. When she married and moved into her new home, she acquired not only a husband but also an instant family that was almost identical in composition to her own. This must have been a great comfort to her, since she was only seventeen when she married. Her youth probably also accounts for the character of her relationship with her brothers- and sisters-in-law, who seem more like siblings, since they all live together as a family. From the evidence of the diary, moreover, it seems clear that the care of the younger Na-

3. Used as a lookout to watch for the spread of fires.
4. *Ryōsai kenbo*; see Nolte and Hastings.

kano children was largely the responsibility of their mother, rather than Makiko.

As for Makiko's friends, she either visited or corresponded with a number of women who seem to be friends from school and the neighborhood where she grew up. She often visited one such young woman in Nijō about the time she was to be married, who later paid a return visit to Makiko's home in Gojō. In Japan the worlds of men and women ordinarily are kept quite separate, and so it is hardly surprising that all of Makiko's friends were women. The reader will notice that she never entertained her friends at her home, with the exception of the one instance just mentioned, and even that occasion seems not to have been purely personal. Not only was the young woman Makiko's friend, but she was also the daughter of an old family friend in the pharmaceutical business. The single visit hardly offsets the constant stream of her husband's friends to their home. My own feeling is that it was not that Makiko was forbidden to have her friends in, but that she felt it inappropriate to do so at this point in her life when she was not yet firmly established in the household into which she had married.

In Japan, a person must always be aware how she presents herself and how she looks in the eyes of others,[5] particularly if she is a member of a traditional household. Because Makiko knew what her role was—for she had been brought up in such a household—and what was expected of her, she would have understood that she must refrain from inviting her friends into a house to which she was so new. A young wife in a large complex merchant household was expected to be loyal to the household, to work hard and play little. It is only natural, therefore, that when Makiko did see her friends, she preferred to do so away from the eyes of the Nakano family and the store employees. And on one occasion, she reports her embarrassment at running into several acquaintances of the family at the theater just before New Year's, a time when women ordinarily would be busy at home with preparations for the festivities.

Moreover, at this juncture Makiko probably did not need many young female friends with whom to go out shopping or to the theater, for she got along very well with Kuniko, her husband's eighteen-year-old sister. Their close relationship seemed to continue even after Kuniko's marriage in the fall. On the evidence in the diary, I take it that

5. The word commonly used to refer to society, the public, or people is *seken*.

her closest female confidante was her half-sister, "Elder Sister Kōshima," as I call her in the diary. They took long walks and went shopping and to the theater together. Makiko rarely failed to visit her when she returned to Nijō, and it seems clear that following her mother's death, Makiko came to depend on her elder half-sister for comfort and support. However, close as the two were, "Elder Sister Kōshima" never dropped in to see Makiko at her home in Gojō unless the visit were made on some formal occasion. Given Makiko's outgoing personality, it is safe to assume that she acquired more friends as she grew older, particularly through her children; today this remains one of the most common ways for Japanese women to build their networks. However, it seems that her large family and the networks of the branch-families and the business branch-families kept her very busy and provided all the support and trust she needed for most of her life.

Clearly, Makiko's situation was somewhat different from that of the ordinary bride. Because of his father's sudden death, her husband had left college and succeeded to the headship of the household at the age of twenty and not yet married. His mother, Mine, was the daughter of the Nakano household, which lacked a suitable male heir. She had provided continuity for her family line and business by taking an adopted husband, and she was just 38 when her husband died. Because she had served as the link between the two generations of Nakano household heads and because her son was young, it is safe to assume that she continued to exercise considerable authority in household domestic affairs, including holding the purse strings, for some time after Makiko entered the Nakano house. Yet so considerate was she of her son's young wife that Makiko once lamented when her mother-in-law was away overnight how empty and cold the house seemed without her and then, when she returned home, noted how the house had come alive once again. This incident suggests to me that Makiko was still very dependent on her mother-in-law at this stage and not yet entirely conscious that *she* was the wife of the household head. Consequently, Makiko's mother-in-law treated her more like her own child, a daughter who needed more time to finish growing up.

Makiko did not find all aspects of the life of a large merchant family congenial, however. After visiting the house recently rented by Chūhachi's married older sister in a residential section of Kyoto, she wrote, "It is a very nice house, better than I had expected, and I thought that it would be nice to live in a house like that just once, quietly and orderly, by myself." That she was always surrounded by family members and never at home alone did not mean she was never lonely. She sorely missed her mother, who had died suddenly only a little more than a month before Makiko started to keep her diary. Her deep grief over her mother's death is evident throughout the diary. In one particularly poignant passage, she laments that her mother is not still there to slip her some money to buy small notions like pretty hair ornaments and kimono accessories, as she apparently had continued to do even after Makiko married. This childish emotional reaction shows clearly how dependent she had been on her mother. But as a young wife she often concealed her true feelings and never displayed raw emotions, in accord with accepted behavior in her society. She even hid her occasional disappointments and frustrations from her husband when obviously she needed an outlet. On such occasions I strongly felt her loss and sadness at not having a mother to turn to when she needed her. Her mother would have been the one person she could confide in and ask for advice, the one thing she would and could not do with her mother-in-law, no matter how close she felt to her.

The irony of her mother's death was that Makiko was forced to become something of a surrogate mother to her younger sister and brother and sometimes fill the role of housewife for her father. The three of them were her constant concern, and more than most young married women in her position probably would have done, she shuttled back and forth between her two households in Gojō and in Nijō. Her father and siblings sometimes came to visit her, but more often than not it was she who went to them. At times her visits extended so late into the evening hours that she stayed overnight. It is a good indication of her conflicting loyalties that on such occasions, she worried about being away from her new home, where she might be needed. Nevertheless, whenever there was a domestic crisis at his house, Makiko was called on to help out her father, doing many things for him that she did not yet have to do even in the house into which she had married. I found it fascinating that Makiko actually seems more grown up when she was visiting her father and siblings.

She also missed her older brother Manzō, who had a job in Manchuria. Although he returned to Kyoto only twice during the year (once to get married) Makiko seemed to feel more relaxed with Manzō than she was with her husband. Perhaps she felt that she could tell her elder brother things that she could not tell her husband. Actually, the two men had been close friends since their days together at the Third Higher School, and their fathers had maintained long-standing business and personal relationships. In fact, arrangements for the marriage of Makiko and Chūhachi had been greatly facilitated by the friendship between their two sons. Makiko later said that when she saw her future husband for the first time at an arranged meeting, "I could not see him well and could not figure out what type of person he was." She added that she did not know what to do, but after her brother reassured her, saying, "I can guarantee that he is a good guy, and you should have no hesitation about marrying him," she decided to follow his advice. When Manzō and his bride were leaving for Manchuria, Makiko desperately begged her husband for permission to go with them for a visit. That she would make so unreasonable a request is a good indication of the pain of separation from someone she loved and had depended on for many years.

If she suffered any anxiety about her own situation, it must have been that she had not yet borne a child. An infertile wife, especially one in her position who was expected to produce an heir, posed a grave threat to the succession and therefore to the future of the house.[6] Still childless after more than three years of marriage to the seventh-generation head of a merchant house, Makiko might well have begun to feel uneasy had she been an old-fashioned woman. Characteristically, however, she wrote only, "Why don't I get pregnant like other women do?" and left it at that. I suspect that she was so self-assured in part because she realized that she had a long child-bearing period ahead of her. Fortunately, Chūhachi appears to have been a "modern" man, who placed little stock in traditional beliefs and practices, for Makiko's first child was not born until the seventh year of their marriage![7]

If, as I firmly believe, many Japanese women still follow the pattern of life that Makiko led, albeit somewhat altered in detail, they may

6. The requirement that a married woman bear a child within a reasonable period of time or risk being sent back to her parents derives from a practice that was more common among the old warrior class of the Tokugawa period than among merchant-class families like the Nakanos.

7. She eventually bore him three sons and a daughter, the first in 1913, the last in 1923.

well find in the pages of her diary a model—a woman who seems to have been generally content with her married life. They may also find a more contemporary variant in Makiko's sister-in-law Tanii Yae, Chūhachi's elder sister. This woman, referred to throughout the diary as "Sister Tanii," led a very different kind of life, even though she was a housewife. Yae had married a man who was the prototype of the post–World War II company man, a "salaryman" (*sarariiman*). A graduate of Toyko Imperial University, then as now Japan's most prestigious institution of higher learning, Makiko's "Brother Tanii" was obviously a bright and energetic individual who was rapidly climbing the corporate ladder. He traveled frequently between Dairi in Kyushu, where the company had assigned him to work in a plant, and the main office in Tokyo. On these trips he often stopped over to visit the family in Kyoto, bringing everyone gifts and sometimes taking them out to dinner. When he was transferred to Taiwan, he moved his family to Kyoto to be near his wife's family, having already sent their son Takeo ahead to live with the Nakanos. It was they who rented the house that Makiko admired, not far from the Nakanos and therefore in easy reach should an emergency arise and Yae need help. Her mother-in-law did not live with them.

Like Makiko, then, Yae was raised in a Kyoto merchant house and had led a similar kind of life until she married. But because she did not marry into a merchant family, their lives diverged dramatically. Yae became the typical wife of a busy, successful company man who was often away from home, and as a result she had to learn to be self-sufficient and quite independent. Because her husband traveled almost constantly on company business, it was Yae who was charged with moving all the family possessions and settling into the rental house, and Makiko comments admiringly on her capabilities.

Readers who know contemporary Japan will recognize the Taniis at once, for the pattern of their lives is today a very common one. Indeed, it is very like the life my own family led from the 1920's through the 1940's. My father, a second son and therefore not the heir, was a graduate of Kyoto Imperial University, generally thought to be the second most prestigious in Japan. He went to work for a large bank, married my mother, and in the course of their married life was assigned to bank offices both abroad and in Japan. Because he was reassigned every few years, we always lived in rented houses, and my sisters and I attended many different schools. Since he was so busy with his work, the tasks of packing and moving our possessions always fell to my mother. Like Yae, she was in effect pioneering a new kind of woman's life and faced constant challenges of a sort never dreamed of by her own mother and grandmother. Like Makiko, my mother lived to see the emergence of the role of the salaryman's wife as the dominant model for the middle class in Japan in the period since the end of World War II. Yae, however, died the year the war ended.

For her part, Makiko spent all her adult life in the far more traditional environment of the old merchant house, with all its virtues and shortcomings. She later told her son that she had wanted to attend middle school but her parents would not allow it, for in Makiko's time it was felt especially desirable that the eldest daughter marry as early as possible. Given an opportunity for more education or training or a less restricted environment, she might well have become a different kind of woman, but that option was available to few Japanese women of her generation. I have asked myself whether she would have been happier in such a role, but of course it is a question that cannot be answered with any certainty. What is certain is that in recording the details of her life Makiko has left us a precious legacy. It is my hope that my readers will find in the pages of her diary a better understanding of Japanese women and family life.

Although much of what Makiko has to tell us is universal in its appeal, her diary is nonetheless firmly rooted in a specific time and place. It is important, therefore, to look back to 1910, to see what life was like in Japan, and especially in Kyoto.[8]

The city that Makiko surveyed from her vantage point on the rooftop had been founded more than a thousand years before and remained the imperial capital until the Meiji Restoration in 1868.

8. By an extraordinary coincidence, while I was working on this translation, I came across an English-language travel guide to Kyoto published in 1895 on the occasion of the 1100th anniversary of its founding. The information on hotels, restaurants, and places of interest was extremely helpful in my effort to orient myself to Makiko's Kyoto, but an unexpected dividend was the number of familiar names that cropped up. The editor acknowledges the assistance of the Reverend and Mrs. Otis Cary, for example; see entry for May 30. Narui, the studio where the family had photographs taken on January 16, is mentioned, as are some of the restaurants and inns patronized by the Nakanos and their associates—Nakamura-rō, Kyōraku-kan, and Sawabun. The reader will soon discover why I was so delighted by the entry on page 9, where the author gives the names of the three "druggists" where English is spoken: Keimatsu in Nijō, Koizumi in Sanjō, and Nakano in Gojō. See Ichihara.

When Edo, seat of the shōguns during the Tokugawa period (1615–1868), was renamed Tokyo and made the new capital, Kyoto was left to contemplate what survived of its ancient heritage. Despite its repeated physical destruction by fire and civil war, the city is rich in history and tradition. It is also beautifully situated, with graceful hills and mountains to the north, east, and west, but open to the Osaka plain to the south. The Kamo River runs through the middle of the city from north to south. Across the mountains to the northeast lies Lake Biwa, the largest in Japan, from which in the late nineteenth century a canal was built to bring water and generate electricity for the city.

Although its center of gravity has shifted eastward over the centuries, Kyoto's layout has not changed greatly since its founding in 794. Like Nara, Japan's first imperial capital, Kyoto was modeled after the capital of T'ang China, and both are unique in Japan for the grid pattern of their streets. The periodic destruction of large sections of the city I have referred to has affected all of its great temples and shrines, but Kyoto's principal streets still form a grid and for the most part bear their ancient names (see Map 1). The numbered avenues run east and west, starting with the first (*ichijō*), second (*nijō*), third (*sanjō*), fourth (*shijō*), fifth (*gojō*) and so on, up to the ninth (*kujō*). These street names are also applied to districts of the city, and readers of Makiko's diary will learn that she and her husband lived in Gojō, and that her father's house and store were in Nijō. In Japan, residential place-names often are used in referring to families and people, so that Makiko sometimes called her natal family simply "Nijō" and her own "Gojō." There are many references to Shijō Avenue, in Makiko's day as now, one of Kyoto's liveliest shopping streets.

Makiko's Kyoto was a city of low buildings—a sea of one- and two-story rooflines punctuated by the immense roofs of the temples, shrines, and palaces, and the occasional five-storied pagoda. It was also famed for its gardens, designed by renowned artists and priests, which are still among the major attractions of the city. The beauty of the hills surrounding the Kamo River basin, which has inspired generations of writers and poets, many of the most famous of them women, is extolled in the literature of the Heian Period (794–1185 A.D.). Around 1000 A.D. Sei Shōnagon, who served for about ten years in the imperial court, wrote in her *Pillow Book* (*Makura no sōshi*) of Kyoto:

In spring it is the dawn that is most beautiful. As the light creeps over the hills, their outlines are dyed a faint red and wisps of purplish cloud trail over them. In summer the nights. Not only when the moon shines, but on dark nights, too, as the fireflies flit to and fro, and even when it rains, how beautiful it is! In autumn the evenings, when the glittering sun sinks close to the edge of the hills and the crows fly back to their nests. . . . When the sun has set, one's heart is moved by the sound of the wind and the hum of insects. In winter the early mornings. It is beautiful indeed when snow has fallen during the night, but splendid too when the ground is white with frost. (Abridged from Morris, p. 1)

It was at the court in Kyoto that Lady Murasaki wrote *The Tale of Genji* (*Genji monogatari*) in the eleventh century; this sprawling novel is one of our few windows onto that world of palace intrigue, amorous dalliance, and aesthetic pursuits. The diaries written by the court ladies of the Heian capital are counted among the literary treasures of Japan.

During the Tokugawa period, the merchants of Kyoto and Osaka enjoyed far more autonomy than those of Edo, where the warrior class was the dominant power. Kyoto merchants were well organized and in the Meiji period had considerable influence in shaping the government of their city. The merchant households of neighboring Osaka, for centuries Japan's major commercial center, operated on a scale unmatched elsewhere; their city was known as the "Kitchen of the Empire." Kyoto's pharmacists in particular profited from their proximity to Osaka, whose wholesale houses dealt in the Chinese herbal medicines that entered Japan through the port of Nagasaki throughout the Tokugawa period.

When the capital of the new Japan was moved to Tokyo, Kyoto's decline was precipitate. No longer the center of power—real or symbolic—the revenues of the city shrank disastrously, and in the early years of Meiji its population fell by almost half from that of its heyday. When Makiko wrote her diary, Kyoto was just beginning to pull itself out of this economic slump by developing new small businesses and light industries, and reviving old ones. These ranged from the weaving of brocade silk in Nishijin, the dyeing of silk cloth, the design and manufacture of dolls and fans, and ceramics, to name but a few.

The life that Makiko describes seems remote even to contemporary Japanese. Of course, the life described by an American woman in a diary written in 1910 would strike a contemporary American as improbably distant, too, but for very different reasons. In 1868, the first year of the Meiji era, Japan ended 250 years of almost total isolation from the rest of the world. During the long Tokugawa period, the lives of Japan's ordinary people had been neither much disturbed nor enhanced by foreign influences. Makiko herself was born only 23 years after the overthrow of the Tokugawa and the restoration of imperial rule. Thus, the older people whom Makiko wrote about had been born into a society that from the beginning of the Meiji era they had been urged to transform—to make Japan "modern." The first word of the most popular of the many slogans of the time, "Civilization and Enlightenment" (*bunmei kaika*) meant Western.

Most Japanese readers of Makiko's diary would assume, as I did, that the life of an old merchant household at the end of the Meiji period would mirror the conservatism of Kyoto, for so long the imperial capital. It certainly was more "Japanese" than any household is today, which is why it seems so remote even to members of my generation and will seem even more so to young Japanese. Nonetheless, one of the diary's more interesting revelations is the degree to which "modern" and "Western" things had already become part of everyday life. Indeed, Makiko herself remarked on occasion that they were doing something "modern," like replacing a sliding door with a hinged one, or "going Western" by serving their guests beer and bananas rather than the customary *sake* and snacks.

The pace at which new things and practices had been introduced into Japan after 1868 was uneven, of course. Throughout the diary, there are passing references to any number of new things, some of which were still novelties, such as rubber-tired *rikisha* and rubber-soled sandals. (The latter are not the all-rubber thonged sandals now called *zōri* in the United States, by the way, for although the soles of Makiko's new sandals were made of rubber, then a new material, the upper part was made of cloth or covered with a tightly woven rush matting.) Today's Japanese would find nothing remarkable in encountering most of the other new things mentioned by Makiko, and few now would even think of them as foreign. These include the camera, phonograph, binoculars, sewing machine, baby carriage, piano, organ, violin, billiards, the movies (mentioned only once), oil paints, and the zoo.

Because the Nakanos obviously were quite accustomed to using the telephone at a time when the instrument was far from common,

I was surprised to find that the kitchen got its first electric light in the year of Makiko's diary.[9] Late in the year, lines were being laid that would make it possible for the first time to have water piped into the house. People got about on the city's unpaved streets and roads on foot or by *rikisha*, then a fairly recent invention, and made longer trips by train or boat. Makiko does not mention bicycles, which were not uncommon by this time, although her sister-in-law Kuniko used one to commute to and from school. She only once mentions the Kyoto streetcar, the first in Japan, which like the horse-drawn buses had begun operating many years before.

One striking aspect of their lives is the eagerness with which her husband and his friends sought to experience what was new and not yet fully Japanese. Their interest extended well beyond just "new things" like those mentioned above, but included Western ideas and philosophies as well. One of the many reforms introduced into the Nakano household by Chūhachi, for example, was that family members, store employees, and servants ate the same food. Western readers may find it difficult to believe that this constitutes solid evidence for the claim that Makiko's husband was actively introducing democratic reforms into his business and household arrangements alike, but it was nonetheless a step forward. His deep involvement with the Otogi Club, an organization that promoted stories and storytelling for children, suggests that he was eager to introduce new ideas to Kyoto's younger generations.

It was a time when a sentiment called *kaigai yūhi* was very much in the air. The term is difficult to translate: *kaigai* means "overseas" and *yūhi* "launching out." Thus, it means something like "Seek opportunity abroad!" Perhaps for American readers the well-known injunction, "Go West, young man!" is a useful analogy. In any event, we find much evidence for the expansiveness of the Japanese sense of possibilities in this period, which followed the country's rise into the ranks of military and economic powers to be reckoned with. Japan's victories in two major wars, one with China in 1894–95 and the other with Russia in 1904–5, had greatly strengthened her position on the Asian continent. Makiko's brother Manzō was employed in Manchuria, where Japan had secured special treaty rights in 1905 following the end of the Russo-Japanese War. He returned to Kyoto

9. According to Professor Nakano, the store already had electric lights, but the family quarters did not.

to marry and left for Dairen almost at once with his bride. His superior there was an old neighbor of their family, named Dr. Keimatsu, who on one occasion returned to Kyoto accompanied by another neighbor who had been there on business. The diary mentions two visitors who stopped by on their way to Manchuria, apparently intending to settle there. Her brother-in-law by marriage, Tanii Senjirō, was assigned to a Japanese enterprise in Taiwan toward the end of the year. And one of her husband's good friends emigrated to Brazil, just two years after the first official emigrant ship from Japan arrived at the port of Santos. She wrote admiringly of his courage: "Modern men have to be brave sometimes."

Despite these ventures overseas, I found it surprising how little most of the central figures in Makiko's world traveled, except for the Taniis. During the year of the diary, Makiko herself never left the Kyoto area, and I think it unlikely that she had traveled at all at this point in her life. She also seems not to have been particularly interested in what one might call current events. Indeed, she mentioned almost no national or international news items, a circumstance that puzzled and disturbed me for a long time. I was perplexed because I simply could not understand how a young woman who seemed so curious about so many things could display such a total lack of interest in the larger world around her. The only explanation that strikes me as satisfactory is that people who keep personal diaries tend to record almost exclusively what touches their lives directly; the entries thus concern people with whom the writer has some close association and report activities in which she herself has engaged. This is certainly the case with Makiko as a diarist.

In fact, Makiko mentioned two international events. One was the annexation of Korea on September 1, 1910, about which she wrote this one short line: "There was a celebration of the consolidation of Japan and Korea today." My guess is that a ceremony of some kind had been organized by the neighborhood association and that she heard about it from her husband or someone else who had attended it. The other reference was to Halley's Comet, whose appearance created an international sensation in 1910. When her brother-in-law told the family that they ought to be able to see a comet in the sky, she remarked that whatever it was they saw, it was not Halley's. As for national news, there is only one mention of severe flooding in Tokyo—and that only because of the sharp contrast with a very dry spell in Kyoto.

As I thought about the very limited horizons implied by what Makiko did not record in her diary, it occurred to me that there might well be more to the matter than the alleged usual selectivity of the keepers of diaries. In 1910, before both radio and television, daily newspapers flourished in Japan, and "extras" were on the streets whenever major events seemed to warrant them. But the majority of newspaper readers were men, even though almost all Japanese women of Makiko's age were literate. Better-educated women might express an interest in what was going on outside their domestic realm, but for a busy housewife like Makiko to take the time to read the paper during the day would have been unthinkable.

Having charged Makiko with a lack of interest in current events, however, it is only fair that I point out that 1910 was a rather uneventful year in Japan. Had the diary been written in 1904 or 1905 instead, I have no doubt that it would have contained many references to the course of the Russo-Japanese War, Meiji Japan's last great military adventure. I think it highly unlikely that Makiko would have failed to mention the string of spectacular Japanese victories, the periodic flag-waving patriotic demonstrations and military parades, and the news of acquaintances and neighborhood men who were conscripted and fought in battle.

To give my readers some perspective on the diary's historical context, in 1909, the year before it was written, she surely would have heard about the assassination of Itō Hirobumi, former prime minister and key political figure in Japan's drive to expand on the continent, in Harbin, Manchuria. In June 1910, the major domestic story, which received wide publicity and shook the nation, was the arrest of the anarchist Kōtoku Shūsui and seven members of his circle, among them his lover, Sugano Suga. Charged with high treason, they were eventually convicted of *lèse-majesté* and executed in January 1911. The Kōtoku "incident" was only the most sensational of a number of developments that showed clearly how intolerant of political opposition the government had become, but all of this social and political ferment seems to have escaped Makiko. There could hardly be better evidence for the kind of life she was leading, well protected within her small world at a time when Japanese women were not expected to participate fully in society and the country was at peace. I should note, however, that a small group of active feminists had appeared by this time, and that the first issue of their magazine *Blue-Stocking* (*Seitō*) was published in 1911.

Returning to what *is* in the diary, let me comment on the several matters it deals with extensively, including diet, clothing, and housing. Food is mentioned almost daily. It is tempting to say that the diet that Makiko described was far more traditionally Japanese than is now the case, but in fact the foods that she mentioned still form the core of the Japanese diet. What has happened is that an enormous variety of other foods—Western, Chinese, and Indian—has been added to it. It follows, then, that the diet she described seems quite limited by contemporary standards, featuring as it did rice in several forms, tofu and beans prepared in many ways (both were main sources of protein at the time), fresh and pickled vegetables, and fish. Kyoto is known for its bountiful variety of vegetables and fruits in every season: bamboo shoots, watercress, bracken (*warabi*), butterbur (*fuki*), and lotus root in spring; cucumber, eggplant, plums, and melons of all kinds in summer; sweet potatoes, squash, mushrooms, chestnuts, persimmons, and pears in autumn; and radishes, cabbage, turnips, and a variety of green leafy vegetables in winter. In fairness, I must add that Kyoto is famous for the great variety of its pickles, which combine vegetables in season with spices of many kinds. Pickle recipes were an important piece of household tradition to be passed down from mother-in-law to daughter-in-law, for every family took pride in the uniqueness of the flavor and consistency of its specialties. Makiko probably neglects to mention them simply because they would have been served with every meal. Similarly unmentioned are the many different kinds of bean-paste used in preparing miso soup, variations that made their meals far more interesting than they may seem at first reading. The fish consumed in Kyoto at this time was mostly fresh-water fish taken from local lakes and rivers. That brought in from the Wakasa Bay area on the Japan Sea coast or other distant places often was dried or lightly salted. Beef was used only in sukiyaki, and Professor Nakano says that it was Chūhachi's idea to have beef once a month, so that the family would get used to it gradually.[10] Chicken was served in a variety of dishes, but there is no mention at all of pork, which is now very popular in Japan. Milk had been introduced by this time, but not as a part of the regular diet of adults or children.[11]

10. It is often forgotten that, being Buddhist, the Japanese were largely if not exclusively vegetarian until the Meiji Restoration. Professor Nakano also reports that sukiyaki often was served to young, drop-in guests because they had big appetites.

11. The contemporary reader will conclude that the diet was not well balanced

It is often said that Kyoto people are frugal and eat poorly, preferring to spend their money on clothes, whereas Osaka people spend all their money on food.[12] Makiko seems to provide evidence in support of at least the first half of the old saying, but I think it more likely that her family's diet was not particularly Kyoto-style, but rather that of average city dwellers of the time. On festive occasions—and there were many—and whenever there were guests, special dishes such as the more expensive fish, vegetables, sushi, and sweet red-bean cakes were served. Since sushi was served at so many meals described in Makiko's diary, I ought to explain that it probably was mostly a kind called *chirashi*, vinegared rice mixed with several kinds of chopped and diced vegetables, garnished with strips of plain omelet and thin dried sheets of seaweed called *nori*, rather than *nigiri-zushi* (small balls of rice topped with a slice of raw fish), which is the Kantō (Tokyo) style more familiar to Western readers. *Chirashi-zushi* is easily made at home, as is the popular *inari-zushi*, which is made by stuffing a pouch of fried tofu with a mixture of vinegared rice and chopped and diced carrots, bamboo shoots, mushrooms, and the like. There are many other varieties of sushi as well, some of them made with seasonal fish such as trout, sardine, sea bream, and mackerel, a Kyoto specialty. There is, by the way, one strong indication of continuity in the diet—the festival foods that Makiko mentioned could as easily be found in a Japanese diary written only last year.

The clothing that people wear at home and in public has changed a great deal more, for during the Meiji period the average Japanese did not wear Western-style clothing, despite the early efforts of the Meiji government to encourage its adoption. The men who did wear suits, hats, and shoes were largely members of the middle and upper classes, who were regarded as embodying the popular image of the "enlightened." Civilian clothing was worn primarily by professionals, bureaucrats, and members of the imperial court; uniforms by the military, police, and some high school, college, and university students. Merchants, tradesmen, farmers, laborers, and fishermen still wore kimono. Makiko reports a heated debate between her husband and his friends about which garments were preferable.

Although Chūhachi himself apparently preferred Western-style

---

nutritionally, as indeed it was not. It was particularly short on fat, which is essential for a population that consumes a large number of calories in routine daily activities.

12. The old saying is *Kyō no ki-daore Ōsaka no kui-daore*: Kyoto people's financial ruin is clothes; Osaka people's financial ruin is food.

clothing and may have worn it on occasion, in most of the photographs from this period he is wearing kimono, still the common dress among men of his profession. His brother Hide-san is seen wearing a Western-style college student uniform in the photographs. The brother who was in middle school wore either a Western-style school uniform or kimono with *hakama*, and the youngest wore kimono without *hakama* to primary school.[13] For the majority of men, Western-style clothing not only seemed tight and too confining, but also was beyond the reach of all but the well-off. I should point out that even those men who adopted Western dress for work or public appearances usually wore kimono at home.

Only a handful of elite women, including those of the imperial court, and those who had lived abroad wore Western dress. In photographs from this period, all the women in the Nakano household are wearing kimono. Even girls in primary school wore kimono both at school and in the home. Middle-school girls wore *hakama* to distinguish them from non-students. Like other young women of her age and time, Makiko expressed keen interest in kimono designs and accessories in her diary. The only articles of women's Western dress mentioned are shawls and gloves, both of which were worn with kimono as well.

The change in Japanese houses since Makiko wrote has been quite remarkable, particularly with respect to the building materials used and furnishings. Houses then were largely of wood with tile roofs. The combined house and store typical of downtown Kyoto, where the Nakanos lived at the time the diary was written, still exists;[14] one of its characteristics is that the frontage on the street is narrow in comparison to the depth. Naturally, the storefront of a merchant house faced on the street, and the family quarters were located in the rear. To enter, one passed through the shop curtain (*noren*) and stepped into the store, whose floor was of hard-packed earth (*doma*). In the front of the store, merchandise was stacked in wooden boxes or displayed in glass cases on wooden platforms and shelves. Herbal medicines were classified and laid out in glass cases and jars. In the back of the store was an elevated area covered with tatami mats

13. *Hakama*, a kind of long trousers for men and long skirt for women, were at this period worn over kimono only in public on formal occasions.

14. A good example of this style of house can be seen in the Children's Museum in Boston.

Panorama of Kyoto with tile roof in foreground. (Asian Collection, Herbert F. Johnson Museum of Art, Cornell University)

The Nakano pharmacy, ca. 1910, based on a sketch by Nakano Takashi

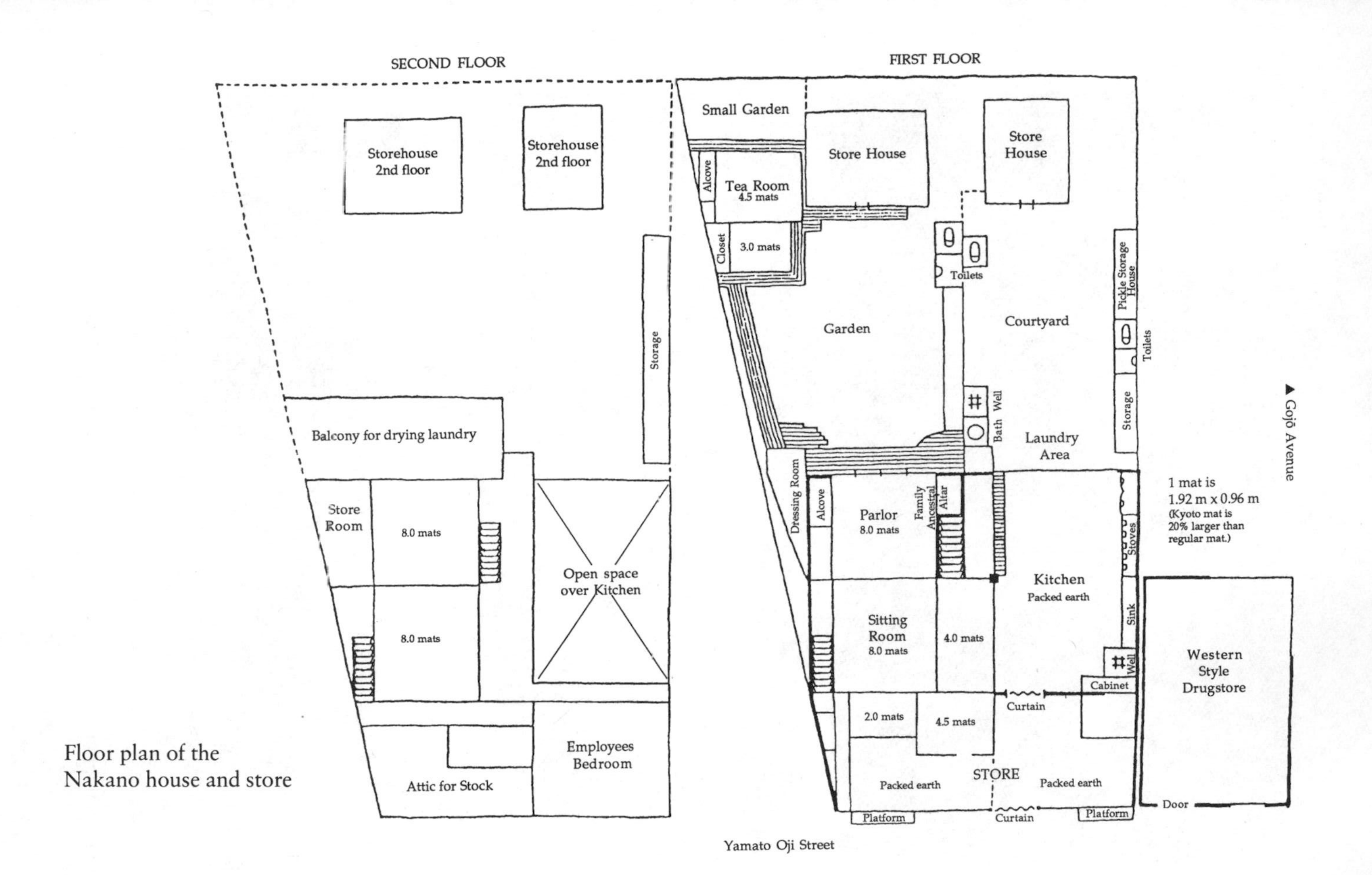

Floor plan of the
Nakano house and store

where the bookkeeper worked. In Makiko's day, this is where the cash box, credit records, and inventory ledgers were kept. In modern times, most shops have replaced all of this with an electronic cash register, but one may still see the layout just described in some old Kyoto stores.

Just ahead was a second curtain separating the family quarters from the place of business. Beyond this curtain was the kitchen, whose floor was a continuation of the shop's earthen one. Although the entire floor eventually was covered with cement, footgear—usually wooden clogs—was worn in this part of the kitchen. However, before one stepped up to the raised floor, which was on the left, footgear had to be removed. In the kitchen the well, sink, and wood-burning stoves were lined up along the right wall, where all the cooking was done.

The description of the rooms that follows is reconstructed from the memories of Professor Nakano and some of the members of his family. Because the house was remodeled piecemeal over the years, the information about the size of rooms and the uses to which they were put may not be entirely accurate. I offer it anyway, in order to orient readers to Makiko's spatial world.

To the left of the kitchen directly opposite the stoves was a long, narrow area with a wooden floor, where the employees ate at two wooden tables that almost completely filled the space. One was for the two head managers and the head clerk, who sat on the floor facing the kitchen. The rest of the employees ate at the second table, sitting on stools in the kitchen itself. There was always plenty of steamed rice for these hungry young people, who served themselves from covered wooden containers placed between the tables. The store employees took turns eating so that business could be carried on without interruption. The maids ate after everyone else had finished.

Family meals ordinarily were taken in the sitting room. Makiko always sat nearest to the door so that she could pass on the food brought from the kitchen by the maids. In the parlor (*zashiki*), the main room of the house, was the household's ancestral altar. Visitors were led into either the sitting room or the parlor, depending on their status and the nature of the visit. On special occasions, such as the New Year's festivities, the family ate in the parlor and all meals for guests were served there as well.

The triangular room to the left of the parlor was a dressing room. Off the second floor in the back of the house was a balcony used for drying laundry or bedding on sunny days. The small four-mat room on the left after one passed through the second curtain (this is the area called *oku*) is where visitors who had come to see the family removed their footgear. A four-mat room is about 72 square feet; the Japanese customarily describe a room by how many mats are required to cover the floor. A four-mat room is an unusual layout, the standard small room being 4½ mats. In Kyoto one tatami floor mat measures approximately 3.15 × 6.3 feet; Tokyo tatami are slightly smaller in both dimensions (Shimizu and Shibata, p. 54).

Beyond the parlor in the back was a courtyard with a small garden. A corridor to the left of the garden led to another part of the family quarters called *inkyo* (retired person), where the grandparents lived if there was a senior generation. Mine, Makiko's widowed mother-in-law, lived there from the time her son married until her death. It had its own tiny garden off the room that could be used for the tea ceremony.[15] Although both gardens were small, they were tended by gardeners who came regularly to trim and shape the trees and shrubs and the luxuriant moss for which Kyoto is famous. Far removed from the store and the rest of the family quarters, this was the quietest part of the house.

To the right, behind the *inkyo* quarters, was the family's fireproof storehouse (*dozō* or *kura*); its thick earthen walls were finished in white plaster and it had a heavy iron door. In this secure building were kept the good lacquer- and chinaware, folding screens, hanging scrolls, dolls for Girls' Day, and other works of art. Large chests held kimono worn only on special occasions, as well as extra bedding (*futon*) for guests. There was another storehouse at the back of the courtyard that probably was used for the same purpose. Several toilets were located in the backyard away from the living quarters. The bath was outside the kitchen area to the left, with a second well right next to it, a convenient arrangement for drawing bath water. On the opposite side of the courtyard behind the kitchen there was a long, narrow building where casks of homemade pickles, miso, grains, and

15. Although Makiko never mentioned the tea ceremony, it must have been part of their lives, since she did mention tea implements and the tea room (*chashitsu*) in the house. The art of tea was developed in Kyoto in the sixteenth century and has continued to flourish there.

other foodstuffs for this large household were stored. The courtyard itself was a kind of outdoor work space, and it was here that a communal gathering of more than twenty people took place on December 27 to make glutinous rice cakes for the coming New Year. Makiko reported that it was so crowded it was hard to work.

There was no second story above the kitchen. Rather the room had a high ceiling with exposed rafters and a small opening in the roof to allow the smoke from the wood-burning stoves to escape. There was a second story above the rest of the main house, however, reached by one of two staircases. In one part of the area right over the store, where the ceiling was low, were the bedrooms of the young clerks and shop-boys. When there were too many of them to be accommodated here, the overflow slept in two small rooms downstairs that were actually part of the store. The other part of this area on the second floor was used for the storage of the store's stock. Over the family quarters was the room the family sometimes called the "music room," where there was an organ; this probably doubled as a bedroom for the older children. The maids' bedroom was also in this part of the house. It is not clear where Chūhachi and Makiko slept, but the normal pattern was for the household head and his wife to sleep in the parlor, and the children in the sitting or other rooms.

Actually none of these rooms can properly be called a bedroom; during the day, since there were few pieces of furniture and all bedding was folded and stowed in closets, it was possible to use any room for any purpose. Moreover, the size of the rooms was quite flexible because sliding doors between rooms could be kept open or even removed to provide more space. On occasions such as weddings, festivities, or funerals and memorial services, the partitions were removed to make it easier to accommodate many people. During the hot season sliding doors were replaced by screens. Kyoto is well known for its summer heat and high humidity, situated as it is in a basin surrounded on three sides by mountains. Makiko comments frequently on the cold in winter and the heat in summer. Winter temperatures are quite mild, in fact, but since houses lacked insulation, a heating system, and tightly fitted windows and doors, the indoor temperature usually matched that of the out-of-doors.

One characteristic of this type of house was the striking contrasts of light and dark. Many of the rooms had no windows at all, so that, moving through the house, one stepped from cavern-like interiors into the light. The gardens of these houses were usually small, but strategically placed to give light and a feeling of openness in what otherwise would have been an extremely oppressive environment.[16]

The small building to the right of the main house was the pharmacy, which the Nakanos formerly had rented out, but in 1889 refurbished to house their expanding dispensary. The exterior was redesigned in the Western style, with a hinged door and glazed windows. As one faces the main store, the right half was devoted to the display and sale of traditional Chinese medicines, and the left to cosmetics and food items such as sugar, imported liquors, and soft drinks.

Even at the remove of more than 80 years, contemporary Japanese will not be unfamiliar with much of what Makiko wrote about the house they lived in, the food they ate, and the clothing they wore. It is left, then, to consider changes that have occurred in one of the most important characteristics of Japanese life—the rhythm of the annual cycle of festivals, rituals, and ceremonies. In Makiko's day, as now, the passage of time was marked by an impressive number of such events. Among them, the New Year's observances are still by far the most important. The occasion for renewal and new beginnings, the dawning of New Year's Day has strong symbolic meaning for all Japanese.[17] The official preparations for the New Year (*koto hajime*) began much earlier than they do today, when the branch-families and business branch-families brought the ceremonial rice cakes called *kagami-mochi* to the main house on December 13.

During the closing days of December, the women prepared the many special dishes associated with the holiday, so that there would be no need to work during the festivities. The men were busy putting up the New Year's decorations and cleaning in and around the store, which would be closed to business on the first three days of the new year. Much of the last day of the old year was devoted to clearing up everything still undone—cleaning the house top to bottom, settling accounts literally and figuratively by paying off bills, collecting debts,

16. The origin of this long and narrow house-style is said to lie in the inflexible grid pattern of streets laid out in the eighth century when the city was founded, which became a problem as the population increased. As the number of houses grew, it was necessary to reduce the frontage of each in order to provide direct access to the street for all.

17. For a beautifully illustrated survey of virtually every aspect of the spiritual and symbolic meaning of the New Year's observances in Japan, see Brandon et al.

and returning borrowed items. In the Nakano household, as Makiko tells us, this custom of cleaning and preparation went on all night on New Year's Eve. The adults literally worked right through the night without sleep. A snack of noodles, which symbolize long life, was served at midnight, just as all the temple bells began tolling 108 times—the number of beads in the Buddhist rosary. Because there are hundreds of temples in Kyoto and the surrounding hills, the solemn booming of their great bells coming from all directions echoes throughout the city. Both in Makiko's time and today, this is the moment to reflect soberly on all that has happened during the old year that is ending, and at the same time to eagerly anticipate the promise of the new year with renewed hope and vitality. Above all, it remains a family-centered observance, despite the many changes in society and the family itself.[18]

Professor Nakano, born ten years after Makiko's diary was written, has given me an account of his memories of the New Year's observances in his home when he was growing up. Apparently the children were put to bed on New Year's Eve, but were awakened in the early hours of New Year's morning and bathed with their father, who had been up all night. The first bath[19] is only one of many ritual responsibilities performed by the household head. Another that Makiko mentions specifically was her husband's final task of the old year—writing the name of each of the family members on individual New Year's chopsticks envelopes with ink and brush. These new chopsticks were to be used at the first meal of the new year and throughout the festivities. Just before dawn the household head drew fresh water from the well—it is called "young water" (*wakamizu*).

According to Professor Nakano, the sacred atmosphere of the welcoming in of the new year was created partly by the long wait in anticipation and partly by the participants' lack of sleep, which created a kind of ecstatic state and something very like a spiritual experience. The first thing the family did after everyone had bathed was to assemble in the parlor where the household's ancestral altar was located and, starting with the household head, to pay their respects to the ancestors of the house. He remembers that the altar was so

18. The New Year's holiday still dominates the annual cycle, and is rivaled in importance only by mid-summer's *o-bon*, that other great family-centered observance, when the spirits of the ancestors are welcomed back to the world of the living for a short time.

19. Called *hatsu-buro*. *Hatsu* means first, and is prefixed to many activities to indicate that it is the first time one has done them in the new year.

brightly lit with candles reflecting off the highly polished brass paraphernalia that it was almost blinding.

Afterward they all took their places in the parlor, the household head in the seat of honor and the rest seated according to their position in the family.[20] Then all bowed and exchanged New Year's greetings, "*Shin-nen omedetō gozaimasu*," first in unison to the household head, and in return, he to them. The New Year's main festive dish, *o-zōni*,[21] was served next. Each person ate from an individual lacquer table, using the new chopsticks for the first time. All of the first three days of the year began with paying respects to the ancestors and breakfasting on *o-zōni*. Readers will discover much more information about the New Year's observances in the diary, but there is one important observation to be made about her many references to festivals, rituals, and ceremonies. I am indebted to Professor Nakano for pointing out that those marked by the preparation or purchase of special food items are the ones that the family really observed. Those not associated with special dishes were for the most part national holidays—many of them quite recently established by the Meiji government—or the festivals of shrines and temples that did not involve the family directly. It is clear that communal eating of foods especially associated with particular festivals by members of the household lay at the heart of the rituals of the Nakanos, which was the pattern found in Kyoto merchant households of the time.

At the beginning of the Meiji Period, when the question of meshing Japan's calendar with that used in the West had to be resolved, the scheduling of indigenous rites and ceremonies began to change. The Gregorian calendar was officially launched on the third day of the twelfth month of Meiji 5, which was declared to be January 1, 1873. By 1910 many rituals and festival days had already shifted from the old lunar calendar to the new one. The Nakanos celebrated New Year's Day on January 1 by the new calendar and "little New Year" on January 15. The dates of the vernal and autumnal equinoxes (March 21 and September 23, respectively) had already been shifted to the new calendar and converted into national holidays. Traditional observances that were not officially recognized could be scheduled by

20. After the household head, his mother, the eldest son (the heir), the eldest daughter, followed by the other children in descending birth order without regard to sex. Makiko, responsible for serving the others with the help of the maids, sat near the doorway.

21. See entry for January 1.

either calendar, however. For example, the great outdoor markets of the Buddhist Tō-ji and Shintō Kitano Tenman-gū were now held on the new calendar's 21st and 25th of each month, respectively. But Girls' Day (*Hina-matsuri*, literally the Doll Festival), which falls on the third day of the third lunar month, was celebrated by some on the traditional date and by others on the arbitrarily assigned date of March 3. Similarly, Boys' Day was observed on either the fifth day of the fifth lunar month or on May 5. The Nakanos continued to follow the old calendar for both.

It had become necessary to move many other crucial dates from the lunar to the new calendar simply because Japan had adopted the system of reckoning time in general use in the West. Thus, the day now was divided into 24 hours rather than the old twelve units, and the month that had been divided into three ten-day periods now had four weeks. Adoption of the seven-day week and, as we shall see, the special status consequently accorded Sunday had a profound effect on the scheduling of domestic rites such as weddings and funerals.

The store's accounts were settled twice a month, on the fifth and the last day—so, March 5 and 31, September 5 and 30. This odd schedule is easily explained. On the last day of the month, every effort was made to pay outstanding bills and collect what one was owed. On the fifth day following, it was the practice to pay or collect whatever accounts remained unsettled.

Although the Nakano household faithfully followed the rituals of tradition, there is little evidence that what many contemporary Japanese would call "superstition" played a significant part in their lives. Makiko never once mentioned the almanac or the zodiacal reckonings that still are widely used to set the dates for weddings, funerals, and important undertakings of many kinds in Japan today. Among the many possible explanations for this, the one I favor is that she simply did not pay much attention to such things because she was not yet in a position to make decisions for which such a calculation might be required.[22]

As for the domestic rites, it is not at all surprising that the households Makiko wrote about conducted Buddhist memorial rites for

22. Professor Nakano offers other explanations. One, and perhaps the more compelling, is that both Chūhachi and Makiko's brother Manzō invariably laughed at what they regarded as superstitious practices. Both men were trained in pharmacology and natural science. Another is that both the Nakanos and Nakaos were followers of the Jōdo Shinshū sect of Buddhism whose teachings explicitly reject such practices.

their ancestors, visited the graves of family members, belonged to parishioner groups of both Buddhist temples and Shintō shrines, and enjoyed the festivals of both religious establishments, all of which are equally characteristic of Japanese religious behavior today. Often, for the convenience of relatives and friends, ancestral memorial services and the public portion of funerals were rescheduled around the work week. I had thought this was a relatively new phenomenon in Japan, probably originating in the post–World War II period, but clearly I was wrong. Perhaps these merchant households were rational and "progressive" in not allowing anything to interfere with business, or perhaps they were simply following what had already been established as an acceptable new custom.

Weddings were held either in the home of the groom (or in that of the bride if, like Makiko's mother-in-law, her household was taking an adopted husband), without the services of a priest of any kind, or at a shrine, at which a Shintō priest officiated, followed by a banquet at a restaurant. There are two weddings in Makiko's diary, one of each kind. The shrine wedding was a very recent innovation, the first having been that of the Crown Prince (later the Taishō emperor) in 1900, only ten years before the diary was written. Today it is considered to be the "traditional" form, but in fact at that time the most common type of wedding ceremony among Kyoto's merchant households was that held in the home. Indeed, such purely domestic rituals were common in rural Japan until well after World War II. But when city dwellers began to hold wedding banquets in hotel dining rooms and wedding halls offering full service sprang up all over the country, the newly disestablished Shintō shrines moved to replenish their depleted treasuries by going into the wedding business themselves.

There is one remarkable difference in wedding customs that puzzled me until I asked Professor Nakano about it—the domestic ceremony Makiko wrote about was held in the evening, and the party following it went on all night, which is never the case today. I found it even stranger that the bride's trousseau was carried to the house of the groom after dark, presumably by lantern-light. His explanation is that merchant households held the wedding ceremony at night because they were reluctant to lose a whole day's business. It seems that Makiko's and Chūhachi's wedding was held at night, for she told her son how the bride and groom sat in front of a gold folding screen, with a large candle stand on either side, and took their wedding vows by the ritual exchange of cups of *sake*. To contemporary Japanese ears, the scene described sounds as though it might have come from a book of fairy tales.

Today, few Japanese think of the lives of women in the Meiji period as a fairy tale. Yet, as Makiko's diary makes quite clear, her life was not one of unrelieved drudgery, nor was it at all joyless. It seems to me that, restricted though she was to the house and nearby neighborhoods, Makiko found family get-togethers to be among life's most enjoyable occasions, so pleasant, indeed, that she sometimes reminded herself not to complain about the hard work they entailed. To anyone who knows contemporary Japan, it is astonishing how many leisure-time activities took place in the Nakano home and how many of them involved a mix of family members, visitors, and business associates. In pursuit of the old, the new, and the interesting, her husband and his friends tried their hands at *sumi* ink painting, painting in oils, painting on ceramics, and calligraphy—all at home. They played both traditional and new card games, sang old (Japanese) and new (Japanese and Western) songs, and listened to phonograph records.

The range of entertainment and amusements they enjoyed outside the home is equally impressive and again an interesting mix of old and new. Makiko or Chūhachi, with some combination of relatives and friends, went to exhibitions of Western and Japanese paintings, attended kabuki, *nō*, and *kyōgen* theatrical performances,[23] went to a Western song recital by a Japanese opera singer and concerts of purely Japanese music, enjoyed vaudeville performances and the latest in stage productions that combined Japanese and Western dramatic forms, took visitors to the only recently created dance performances by Kyoto geisha, and once, at least, one of the children was taken to the zoo and to a movie. They also went to storytelling performances sponsored by the Otogi Club, to which Chūhachi belonged. In addition to all these activities, there were seemingly innumerable festivals, and for the men, entertaining and being entertained at restaurants. The fact that the members of the Nakano household were able to enjoy such a variety of leisure and cultural pursuits shows clearly that they were relatively well off financially.

Let me turn now to how the diary came to be published. Professor Nakano's decision to open his own mother's diary to public scrutiny

23. Both *nō* and *kyōgen* originated in Kyoto, and it was only after the Meiji Restoration that some of the major schools moved to Tokyo.

was not taken lightly, for he was concerned that it might reveal too much of the private affairs of his family. Outweighing such considerations, however, was the opportunity to offer insight into the lives of women of Makiko's generation. With the exception of the autobiographies and reminiscences of a small number of well-known women, such as the heroic ones who were involved in political and feminist movements or became writers, artists, and educators, little has been published about the reality of the lives of more ordinary women, most of whom after all were housewives like Makiko.

Shortly after Makiko's diary was published in Japan, another diary written by an ordinary young woman in 1936 appeared in English translation, *The Diary of a Japanese Innkeeper's Daughter*. She was an unmarried 18-year-old, the daughter of the owner of a small inn in a rural town in Kumamoto prefecture in Kyushu. The circumstances that led to her keeping a diary are unusual. In 1935, the American anthropologist John F. Embree and his wife, Ella, were staying at her family's inn while they looked for a place to live in a nearby village where they were to conduct field research. John Embree found the young woman lively and attractive, and asked her to keep a diary for him, with the promise that it would be translated into English and published. She delivered the diary, which begins on January 1 but is far from complete, to the Embrees in October, just before they left the village. It was finally published in 1984,[24] and it was my small part in bringing it out that not only brought home to me the importance of personal documents in shedding light on the life and thought of people of another time and place, but also persuaded me of the value of translating Makiko's diary. To a far greater extent than the innkeeper's daughter's diary, Makiko's offers a detailed account of the changes taking place in domestic life around the turn of the century.

Because she understood her son's reasons for his interest in her diary, Makiko gave him permission to edit it for publication and looked forward eagerly to its appearance. As she passed through her seventies and into her eighties, he made every effort to get as much information about the household from her as he could. She died on November 23, 1978, at the age of 88, before the diary was published. Professor Nakano used the occasion of the Buddhist memorial ser-

24. An account of how the diary came to be written and the vicissitudes of the English translation is given in Kai, pp. 11–12.

vice held to mark the third anniversary of her death in 1980 to make his final decision to go ahead with the publication plans. At memorial services of this kind, it is the practice to make offerings to the spirits of the dead. His own offering was intended not only for his mother, but also for his father, for the grandmother whom he never knew, and for the many other relatives and friends of his mother whose names appear in her diary.

MAKIKO'S SOCIAL WORLD

For the original publication on which this book is based, Professor Nakano wrote an introduction designed to provide contemporary Japanese readers with a guide to the complex relationships among the people we shall meet. Most of what follows is based on that introduction. So great have been the changes in the world of Japanese commerce that the business organization he describes is almost as unfamiliar to Japanese as to Western readers. It seemed important to me, therefore, to summarize his major points in order to sketch in the system of relationships within which much of what Makiko wrote about took place.

The time of Makiko's diary was a transitional one, the real beginning of Japan's entry into the twentieth century. The long reign of the Meiji emperor, which had begun with the fall of the Tokugawa shogunate and the imperial restoration in 1868, would end with his death in 1912. For Japanese of the time, it was truly the end of an era, the breaking of the last strong link between old and new Japan. The Nakano household is a prime example of a kind of domestic unit that was beginning to emerge at this period. Its most notable feature is that its kin relationships were far more thoroughly bilateral than is usually thought to be characteristic of the time. That is, members of both the husband's and wife's families were on intimate terms and interacted frequently. It is widely believed that, in what contemporary Japanese think of as the traditional family system, once a woman married out, she was obliged to sever contact with her natal family. The constant interaction between the Nakano and Nakao families demonstrates clearly that although descent may have been reckoned unilineally, bilaterality was the rule socially. At the center of the domestic unit of the time was a conjugal family consisting of the household head, his wife, and their children. It is only natural that the diary focuses on Makiko's new family, but as the reader will discover, their daily lives involved interaction within a highly complex network of households. Some of these were kin, both consanguineal and affinal; others were quasi-kin; and still others belonged entirely outside the private, domestic domain, in the public world of business.

At the time the diary was written, the household (*ie*) was legally defined by the civil code of 1898. Unlike the Western conjugal family, which effectively self-destructs in every generation as its children marry and create their own families, the *ie* was conceived to exist in perpetuity. As a rule, its head was a male, one of whose principal duties was to produce an heir to succeed to the headship after him. Because so much was at stake, it follows that marriages ordinarily were arranged. The process was far from mechanical, however. Although it is true that as late as the early 1920's, some couples (my own parents among them) actually saw each other for the first time at their wedding ceremony, there were many ways in which informal relationships played a role in matchmaking. In Makiko's diary, for example, we find several such instances. Her older brother Manzō and Makiko's husband had been classmates, and their fathers had been business associates for many years. Manzō himself married a woman from his grandfather's native town. Makiko's sister Eiko later married one of Manzō's colleagues. Kuniko, Makiko's husband's younger sister, married her brother's close friend and constant companion, Matsui Jisuke. Japanese often say that marriage arrangements made through personal relationships are likely to provide more security, especially for the woman, than those contracted exclusively with the help of outsiders. However the marriage was arranged, the in-marrying bride was ordinarily expected to loosen and eventually sever ties with her natal household. The death of the household head and her husband's succession to the headship automatically elevated her status as well. At her death her memorial tablet was placed in the domestic Buddhist altar along with those of the ancestors of her husband's household.

In the following brief accounts of the history of some of the households whose members we shall meet in the diary, one feature that is certain to strike the Western reader is the number of adoptive marriages, in which the bride has taken an in-marrying groom (*mukoyōshi*) who was adopted by her family to be made heir and successor, and the number of outright adoptions of children. Both were resorted to in order to maintain the continuity of the household when there were no sons. Households that had businesses and assets, like most of those we encounter in Makiko's diary, were particularly concerned to secure the succession. Chūhachi's father was an adopted husband, and Makiko's father was an adopted son. Indeed, in the heyday of the household system, the Japanese engaged in what was virtually free adoption, seeking by almost any means available to secure an heir. A household without sons would try to find a male, preferably consanguineal kin, to adopt directly. Failing that, they might seek a husband for their daughter, adopt him, and make him heir and successor. They often had to go further, adopting a female for whom they then adopted a husband, or even (unusual, but not rare) adopting an already married couple as successor and wife. Arrangements made for adoptions, like those for marriages, were likely to involve personal relationships.

Merchant Households

The character of the relationships among many of the households we encounter in the diary was determined by the fact that they were components of a system of linked households called *dōzoku*.[1] A *dōzoku* was composed of three kinds of household, which merchants of the Kyoto-Osaka area called *honke* (main house), *bunke* (kin branch houses), and *bekke* (non-kin branch houses). *Bunke* were established for persons who bore the same surname as that of the main house, whether consanguineal kin or adopted. *Bekke*, households of former employees who bore different surnames, were capitalized by the main house and set up in businesses on their own. A serviceable English term for *bekke* is "business branch-family," which I have used throughout this book. Non-kin members of the *dōzoku* who maintained their own separate residences might either continue to work in the main house's store or set up one of their own. In the former case they were called *kayoi bekke* (commuting *bekke*), in the latter *mise mochi bekke* (shop-owning *bekke*).[2] The linkages among

1. The merchant *dōzoku* are dealt with extensively in Nakano, *Shōka dozokudan*.

2. The distinction between branch houses established by kin and those established by non-kin is emphasized by Professor Nakano in many of his publications. The latter are not limited to merchant *dōzoku*, but are found also among those engaged in agriculture and fishing.

these kin and quasi-kin groups were extremely complex and overlapped in many areas.

It was the custom for the heads of the branch families of both types, or their wives, to call at the main house on the first day of every month. Early in the morning, the wife of the head of the main house opened the ancestral altar, cleaned and polished the brass paraphernalia, and offered flowers, food, and water or tea to the ancestors of the house. The head of the main house and his wife ordinarily stayed at home to receive the visitors all morning and into the early afternoon, but if he had to go out on business, she would fill in for him. The visitors were first shown into the sitting room and exchanged standard greetings reflecting their hopes for good business in the coming month.[3] Moving on into the parlor, they paid their respects to the ancestors of the main house, who by extension were considered to be the ancestors of the branch houses as well, were served tea and cakes, and discussed family and business matters. They were joined by the commuting business branch-family heads, who on this day usually came dressed in formal attire, affirming the superior status of the main house. On this clearly ceremonial occasion, the heads of all the households were served a lunch of red-bean rice (*seki-han*), a fixture of all ritual meals, miso soup, broiled fish, and a salad made of dried radish. As I have already remarked, in Japan the sharing of food is a very common way of marking the importance of relationships among the living and to the ancestral dead. Although the relationships among the various categories of houses were hierarchical, these first-of-the-month ceremonial visits permitted relaxed interaction among the constituent households of the *dōzoku* after the hard work of settling accounts the night before. News and opinions were exchanged and the solidarity of the group reaffirmed.

The residential pattern of merchant households of the time was to have the residence and the place of business under one roof. Thus, there was constant interaction between family members and those employed in the store, but there was never any doubt as to the hierarchical character of the relationship between owners and workers. Although the contribution of all employees was recognized as crucial to the success of the enterprise, store managers, as well as clerks, shop-boys, and maids, clearly occupied a subordinate status.

3. The expressions used were *Yoi o-tsuitachi de gozaimasu* and *Nani tozo kongetsu mo yoroshū*, meaning roughly, "It's a fine first day of the month" and "May things go well in the coming month."

The daily life of the Nakano household was loosely divided between two closely related domains, private and public. The private one, called *oku* ("in the back"), encompassed all domestic activities. In practice the day-to-day management of household affairs was in the hands of its women. In the Nakano household, its smooth operation was primarily the responsibility of Makiko's mother-in-law, Mine, the widow of the sixth-generation household head. She was assisted by Makiko in her role as the young wife of the current head, of course, and by a number of female domestic servants.

The public domain, called *mise* ("store" or "shop"), was the business itself, which was run by Chūhachi with the assistance of the two store managers, who commuted daily from their respective residences. It was their responsibility to supervise the other workers in the store, the young male live-in clerks and shop-boys. Because of Chūhachi's youth and lack of experience in the business, the store managers seem to have exercised considerable authority.

One of the things that Makiko's diary makes clear is that networks of amicable mutual assistance and personal friendships were by no means based exclusively on the household as a legal entity or the household system (*ie-seido*) as the sociologists tend to define it structurally. Important relationships developed over time out of convenience, often were based on friendly feeling, and changed readily according to need and circumstance. Thus, in the diary we encounter a network of friends, kin, and quasi-kin as well as close ties with neighbors and families that share some common interest. Because so many people throng the pages of Makiko's diary, I offer the reader the following capsule accounts of the households she mentioned most frequently, their business associates, and friends.[4]

Nakano Chūhachi Household

In 1907 Makiko married Nakano Chūhachi VII, head of the main household of the *dōzoku*, whose house-name was Yamatoya. Its business consisted primarily of wholesale and retail sales of pharmaceutical products—both Chinese and Western—sugar and other food items, and cosmetics.

4. The factual information in this section is adapted from Professor Nakano's Introduction to his mother's diary; see Nakano, *Meiji yonjūsannen Kyōto*, pp. 1–26. See also "A Note on Names and Terms," on p. xi, "A Guide to the Most Frequently Mentioned Names," on pp. xiv–xv, and the genealogical chart on p. xiii.

Chūhachi was born in 1884. He attended Shūdō Primary School and Kyoto Second Middle School. Upon graduating, he entered the Third Higher School,[5] majoring in the humanities. However, his studies were interrupted by the sudden death of his father, Chūhachi VI, in 1904. Having succeeded to the headship of the household and the business, he transferred to the Kyoto Private School of Pharmacy and completed the requirements for the degree in April 1906. He passed the government examination for the pharmacist's license prior to graduation and at the time of his marriage had been owner-operator of the household business for only about two years.

Chūhachi VI, who had been active in politics and served as a councilman in the Kyoto prefectural government, had so neglected the business that young Chūhachi VII had to struggle to arrest the decline and restore the enterprise. At the same time, in his role of household head he bore the responsibility for the care and education of his younger siblings. By 1917, seven years after the diary was written, he was in a sufficiently strong financial position to expand the store by incorporating a building fronting on Gojō Avenue, one of the main streets of Kyoto.

In 1910, then, the Nakano household members were Makiko, 20 years old; Chūhachi, 26; his mother Mine, 43; and Chūhachi's five younger siblings: his brother Hidesaburō, a 22-year-old college student; a sister Kuniko, 18 years old; another sister, Shinako, a 14-year-old student at a girls' middle school; and two brothers, Seiichi and Chūjirō, 13 and 8 years old, respectively.[6] In addition, there were a number of live-in employees: four store clerks (*tedai*), six shop-boys (*detchi*), and two or three maids. There were also the heads of two commuting business branch-families: Moriguchi Seizaburō, who oversaw the pharmaceutical end of the business, and Yamada Suekichi, who was responsible for the sugar department, which handled foodstuffs and soft drinks. These two men commuted to the store from their homes in Kyoto, but ate lunch and dinner, and sometimes even breakfast, with family members and the live-in employees.

The business branch-family heads who called on the Nakanos on a regular basis, notably for a formal lunch on the first of every month,

5. One of the top-ranked public higher schools in pre-war Japan. These higher schools are roughly comparable to U.S. colleges.

6. All ages given in this section are calculated as of January 1, 1910. Chūhachi also had an older sister, Yae, who married Tanii Senjirō. See below.

The Nakano family, ca. 1910: (*from left*) Makiko, Seiichi, Mine, Nakao Eiko, Kuniko, Shinako, Matsui Jisuke, and Chūhachi; (*in front*) Chūjirō and "Eastside" Tadao. (Nakano Takashi)

Chūhachi reading, ca. 1910. (Nakano Takashi)

The Eastside family, ca. 1910: (*standing*) Nakano Chūichirō ("the Eastside Doctor"); (*front, from left*) Tadao, Fusa holding Yoshio, Takao. (Nakano Takashi)

Tanii Yae ("Sister Tanii") and her two children, Toshiko (*left*) and Takeo, ca. 1911. (Nakano Takashi)

included former employees who had become independent store owners. The most frequent visitors of this kind were Yamamoto Matsu, who operated a candle store in Kawara-machi, and Ōkita Toyosaburō, whose pharmacy was located in front of the Wakamiya Hachiman-*jinja*, a neighborhood Shintō shrine not far from the Nakano store.

The Nakano Relatives

Nakano Chūichirō Branch Household (Eastside)

The branch household headed by Nakano Chūichirō lived on the east side of the street, opposite the Nakano Chūhachi residence and store on Yamato-Ōji Avenue. Makiko calls them Higashigawa (Eastside) throughout the diary. Its 36-year-old head Chūichirō (the Eastside Doctor) was the eldest son of Chūhachi V and his second wife Ai, whom he later divorced. Mine, Makiko's mother-in-law, was Chūhachi V's only child by his first wife, Koto, who died young. Chūichirō, therefore, is Mine's half-brother and Makiko's husband's uncle.

Ordinarily Chūichirō would have succeeded to the household headship, but the family decided instead to adopt 15-year-old Akazawa Tokugorō with a view to marrying him to Mine and installing him as Chūhachi VI. They chose a young man whose association with the Nakano household is worthy of note. Akazawa Tokugorō came from Sakai, a city south of Osaka, and was an employee of the Nakanos. When Chūhachi V decided to study at the Academy of Chemistry in Kyoto,[7] he realized that he would not be able to learn English easily, so he took Akazawa with him as a kind of surrogate student. Tokugorō then was probably still in his teens, the age at which acquiring a foreign language is not too difficult. The Nakanos must have had considerable confidence in his abilities, for he was made heir and successor just as the business was being forced to adapt to changes caused by the rapid modernization of the Japanese medical system.

7. *Seimi-kyoku*. The first such academy was established in Osaka in 1868; the Kyoto Academy was opened in 1870, the third year of Meiji. *Seimi* is from the Dutch word for chemistry; Dutch, which had been the language of science during the Tokugawa period, was displaced by German in the Meiji. See Introduction and entries for April 23 and July 29.

For his part, young Chūichirō, instead of becoming head of the main house, was made head of a newly created branch household. He graduated from a medical school in Okayama[8] and became Kyoto's first ophthalmologist, with his practice across from the main household.[9] From the beginning his office and the pharmacy operated independently, so that the ophthalmologist's patients had to take their prescriptions across the street to the Nakano pharmacy to be filled. Chūichirō married Fusa, the eldest daughter of the younger brother of Chūhachi VI. The couple had five children in all: a daughter, Yuriko, and four sons, Tadao, Takao, Yoshio, and Nobuo, whose birth in September 1910 is reported in the diary.

Nakano Chūbei Branch Household

Nakano Chūbei III heads another, older branch household, which was established prior to the Nakano Chūichirō (Eastside) household, but whose fortunes had declined during the headship of his predecessor Chūbei II. The other members of this household are Kimi, who was the widowed daughter of Chūbei I, and the children of Chūbei III: an eldest son who died young without succeeding to the headship, a wandering second son, and a daughter, all of whom had to be cared for by the main household. They lived not far from the other Nakanos, but appear only sporadically in Makiko's diary.

Tanii Senjirō Household

The Nakanos considered the Taniis to be close affines, even though they lived far from Kyoto, in Dairi near Moji, a port city at the northern tip of the island of Kyushu. Makiko's husband's 27-year-old sister, Yae, was the wife of Tanii Senjirō, who was 37 and an employee of the Japan Sugar Company[10] in Moji. The son of a policeman in Sakai, a city south of Osaka, Senjirō had been adopted by a woman named Tanii Nui when his own father died. He was taken into the Nakano family as a houseboy and allowed to study while helping out in the pharmacy; this was after Akazawa Tokugorō (later Chūhachi

8. A city 120 miles to the southwest of Kyoto. Although the medical school was located so far away, it was established as a unit of Kyoto's Third Higher School.

9. Given the interest in new, foreign things among Chūhachi and his friends, it will come as no surprise that the Eastside Doctor pioneered the introduction of Esperanto to Kyoto.

10. *Dai nippon seitō kaisha*, one of a number of companies engaged in sugar production and trade after Japan acquired Taiwan in 1895, following the Sino-Japanese War.

VI) left Sakai to become the adopted husband of Nakano Mine. Senjirō eventually entered the Third Higher School, later transferred to the First Higher School in Tokyo,[11] and advanced to Tokyo Imperial University, where he graduated from the School of Pharmacy. Presumably because they recognized his brilliance and promise, Chūhachi VI and his wife arranged his marriage to their eldest daughter, Yae. As we have already seen, Senjirō appears in the diary as a busy, successful company man whose job demands that he travel constantly. The Taniis, always called Brother Tanii and Sister Tanii by Makiko, had a son, Takeo, and a daughter, Toshiko.

Hiraoka Rihei Household

The Nakanos' most highly regarded affinal household was that of Hiraoka Rihei VI. Originally he had worked as a store clerk in a kimono shop, where his abilities brought him to the attention of Rihei V, who adopted him as his successor and heir. He managed the Hiraoka Tōkiten (Hiraoka Ceramic Store), changed its name to the more upscale Hiraoka Manjudō in 1897, and won acclaim for its rapid expansion and evident prosperity. The business occupied a prime location on the northeast corner of the intersection of Yamato-Ōji Avenue and Gojō Avenue, directly across the street from the Nakano pharmacy. In earlier times the Hiraokas had been moneylenders to the poverty-stricken court nobility, but that business declined. It is said that, realizing that something had to be done, Rihei III's wife Iku had suggested opening a ceramics store. Iku was the elder sister of Chūhachi III.

When the Nakano pharmacy faced a severe financial crisis after the death of Chūhachi V, it was Hiraoka who saved the business by extending financial aid. Well aware of their invaluable help in the past, Makiko's husband always took care to acknowledge the importance of the relationship and maintain it. Even though their kin ties had become rather attenuated, the fact that they lived across the street from each other facilitated frequent interaction and the maintenance of close relations.

Akazawa Manzō Household

The Akazawas were the natal family of Chūhachi VI and thus distant affines of the Nakanos. Manzō was the son of Chūhachi VI's

11. Until the end of World War II, this was Japan's top-ranked higher school.

brother. Following financial reverses, the family had moved from Sakai to Kyoto, probably in order to receive assistance from Chūhachi VII. They appear only sporadically in the pages of the diary.

Nishimura Ishinosuke Household

The Nishimuras, the only rural relatives of the Nakano household, lived in Tonoshō village, some four or five miles south of Kyoto. Nishimura Tokusaburō was the son of Shio, the daughter of Chūhachi V's sister, Yone. Shio married, but after she was divorced because of her persistent ill health, she was adopted as a younger sister to Chūhachi VI. Since it was the responsibility of someone in the family to look after its less fortunate members, adoption was a common solution to the problem. Tokusaburō himself was adopted by Chūhachi VI as a younger brother of Makiko's husband. Later, while he was still young, he was adopted for a second time to be the successor of Nishimura Ishinosuke, a farmer in Tonoshō village.[12] At the time the diary was written, he was 21 years old. The frequency of visits by members of this family suggests that the relationship was quite close.

Nakao Manshichi Household

From Makiko's point of view the closest "family" was her own natal household in Nijō, headed by her widowed father, Nakao Manshichi.[13] As a child, he had gone to work as a shop-boy for a merchant named Nakao Mansuke, who later adopted him as his son and heir. Mansuke, who had risen from shop-boy to store manager at an established pharmaceutical firm, became a business branch-family of that firm. He opened his own store in Nijō, where, as we have seen, many such firms were located at that time. Upon Mansuke's death, Makiko's father succeeded to the headship of the business and the

12. Makiko's use of the term *otōto-bun* (younger brother "part" or "role") rather than simply *otōto* (younger brother) for Tokusaburō suggests that the adoption into the Nakano family was never formalized. It is not clear what circumstances led to this complicated pattern of adoption for Tokusaburō. One possibility is the Nakano household wanted to put him somewhere safe but away from the family business in order to avoid any future conflicts about the succession.

13. The reader is cautioned to distinguish the two surnames—Nakao (Makiko's natal household) and Nakano (the household into which she married)—which differ by only one letter in their romanized forms.

household, and eventually moved the store to Niōmon-chō, one of the major cross streets of Nijō Avenue.

Manshichi became a certified pharmacist of Western medicine and expanded his business to include both modern pharmaceuticals and traditional Chinese medicines. Both he and his adoptive father Mansuke were leaders in the pharmaceutical business in Kyoto in the Meiji era, as were Nakano Chūhachi V and VI. Nakao Mansuke had established and administered a school called Kyūsei-sha[14] for shop-boys and store clerks employed by the pharmaceutical wholesalers located in the Nijō district. He and Nakano Chūhachi V studied at the Academy of Chemistry, and in 1875 both passed the examination required for those wishing to open a pharmacy. In 1889 their sons, Nakao Manshichi and Nakano Chūhachi VI, passed the first examination held in Japan under the revised medical law to qualify as licensed pharmacists in Western medicine. Both men were instrumental in developing and supporting the Kyoto Private School of Pharmacy.[15]

Makiko's mother, Yoshi, died on November 21, 1909, and her father was getting old. Having given his eldest son, Manzō, permission to pursue a scientific career, there was no one to succeed to the headship of the business in the foreseeable future. At the time the diary was written, the household consisted of Makiko's father, her 15-year-old sister Eiko, who was in girls' middle school, her 12-year-old brother Senzō, who was in boys' middle school, and a few store employees and maids. Manzō, then 28, and his wife, Yukiko, lived in Dairen, Manchuria.

The Nakao Relatives

Kōshima Fusajirō Household

The relationship between the Nakaos and the Kōshima Fusajirō household, located in the Senbon district on the western side of Kyoto, but not far from Nijō, was quite close. The woman referred to in the diary as "Elder Sister Kōshima" appears to have been the daughter of Makiko's mother by her first husband. Although she was

14. The name of this institution suggests that its aim was the improvement and advancement of underprivileged youth.

15. *Kyōto shiritsu yaku gakkō*; later known as the Kyoto College of Pharmacy, its founding was supported by the Academy of Chemistry.

Makiko's half-sister, they grew up in different households. She and her daughter, Fumiko, appear frequently in connection with activities involving Makiko's natal house, for after their mother's death Elder Sister Kōshima seems to have been Makiko's closest older female relative.

Nakamura Satoru Household

The Nakaos' kinship connection with the Nakamura Satoru household was more direct. Makiko's maternal grandfather, Nakamura Kogorō, had been a samurai in the Hikone domain, one of the fiefs of the Tokugawa period. His son, Makiko's maternal uncle, was Nakamura Satoru, an army general who had sustained injuries in the Russo-Japanese War, and who was now living in Tokyo, serving as head priest of Yasukuni Shrine, where the spirits of Japan's war dead are enshrined. Makiko's brother Manzō had lived with the Nakamuras while studying at Tokyo Imperial University, but in 1910 contact between the two families was infrequent.

Keimatsu Katsuzaemon Household

Across from the Nakao store and residence in Niōmon-chō on the north side of Nijō Avenue was located the store and residence of Keimatsu Katsuzaemon, an important figure among the group of pharmaceutical businessmen in the Nijō district. The Keimatsu and Nakao families had been business associates for two generations. Although it was much later that they became related through marriage, even at the time of Makiko's diary their relationship was very close. The tenth-generation head, Keimatsu Katsuzaemon X, born in 1876, had been a member of the first graduating class of the Department of Pharmaceutical Medicine in the Medical School of Tokyo Imperial University. After graduating, he joined the Central Experimental Laboratory of the South Manchuria Railway Company[16] and later became its director. He played a pivotal role in the career of Makiko's

16. The South Manchuria Railway Company (*Mantetsu* for short) was formed in 1906, just after the end of the Russo-Japanese War. It was established by the Japanese government in cooperation with the military as one of the measures taken to promote the economic development of this strategically important territory. Mantetsu's work involved not only constructing and operating the railroads, but also governing Manchuria. The company founded, owned, and operated numerous research institutions, among them the Central Experimental Laboratory, which conducted scientific research in a variety of fields. One of them was Chinese herbal medicine, the particular interest of Dr. Keimatsu and Makiko's brother Manzō.

brother Manzō, for after his graduation from the same department in the same university, he was offered a job in Dr. Keimatsu's laboratory.

Nakajima Sōbei Household

In 1910, Makiko's brother Manzō married Nakajima Yukiko, the oldest daughter of Nakajima Sōbei from Obama in Wakasa Province, which was also the hometown of the wife of Nakao Mansuke, Makiko's father's adoptive father. The marriage established an affinal relationship between the Nakao and the Nakajima households, but since they lived far apart the relationship remained rather distant.

Chūhachi's Circle

Matsui Jisuke married Chūhachi's younger sister Kuniko in October 1910. The Matsuis had operated a *sake* brewery in Kawaramachi, Kyoto, for generations. Jisuke was a founder of the Dōda Primary School Alumni Association and played an important role in supporting the school financially and socially. He and Chūhachi, who were the same age, had become close friends when they both happened to be serving on the school board as members from their respective districts. Their friendship flourished because of many common interests, particularly in new movements and recently introduced arts, such as oil painting, Western music, and the like. He was far and away the most frequent visitor to the Nakano home, both because he was one of Chūhachi's closest friends and because he wanted to marry Kuniko.

Matsumiya Hōnen, the son of a Kyoto primary school principal, was a budding painter.[17] A frequent visitor to the Nakano home, he was accompanied occasionally by another well-established painter named Hirai Baisen.

Tanaka Hozan, a ceramist, had been Chūhachi's friend since their primary school days. He emigrated to Brazil late in the year of the diary. After Matsui, Matsumiya and Tanaka were the most frequent casual visitors.

Mashimo Hisen, new principal of the Shūdō Primary School of

17. His given name was Minoru, but at the time the diary was written he used the art-name Hōnen. He later joined an artists' group called *Seiryūsha* (Green Dragon Society) and changed his art-name to Sakyō.

which Makiko's husband was an alumnus and member of the school board, also became a member of Chūhachi's circle. He was the author of the song "Senyū" (War buddies), which was better known by its first line *Koko-wa o-kuni-o nanbyaku-ri* ("Hundreds of leagues from home") and popular during and after the Russo-Japanese War.

In addition to these individual friends, we encounter throughout the diary members of two sets of close friends. One was a group of young men who were active in the affairs of the Dōda Primary School and who regularly assembled at Matsui Jisuke's home. The other group, who were primarily interested in art but also active in the Shūdō Primary School District, were frequent visitors at Chūhachi's. The groups included musicians such as Yakushiji Kōji, who lived in Matsui Jisuke's neighborhood. He was a violinist and concert master of the Kyoto University Symphony Orchestra, which he had organized; he supported himself as a clerk in the office of the Pharmaceutical Cooperative. Other members of Chūhachi's circle involved in Western music who are not mentioned in the diary were Watanabe Tsune, son of a tea merchant, who played the cello, and Yamaguchi Suejirō, a violinist who lived in Osaka.

A number of Chūhachi's friends were involved in the activities of a national organization called the Otogi Club: Suzuki Kichinosuke, president of the Kyoto branch, lived nearby; Chūhachi himself was vice president; and Matsui Jisuke was treasurer. The Otogi Club was founded in 1903 in Yokohama by Kurushima Takehiko and was later moved to Tokyo, where it flourished. The aim of the organization was to popularize the writing and public reciting of children's stories, a very new idea in Japan at the time. It appears that the club began with what are called *otogi-banashi*—fairy tales or folktales—and expanded the repertoire to include foreign tales as well. Some of its members also wrote and performed new stories for the young. Members of the Otogi Club traveled all over Japan, going wherever they were invited, no matter how small or remote the town. One of its most noted writers and performers was Iwaya Sazanami,[18] who was, with Kurushima Takehiko, a frequent visitor to the Nakano home when they were in Kyoto. Sazanami-sensei, as Makiko calls him, was a novelist best known for his children's stories. He had lectured in the

18. Iwaya Sazanami (1870–1933) made frequent visits to Kyoto in 1910 in order to give the public readings for which he was famous. See his autobiography, *Waga gojū nen*.

Department of Asian Languages at the University of Berlin from 1900 to 1902, and in 1909 traveled in the United States. He played a major role in popularizing the retelling of fairy tales—European, Asian, and Japanese alike—for children, and it was through his English translations of some of the Japanese tales that foreign readers first encountered stories like "The Tongue-Cut Sparrow" ("Shita-kiri suzume"), "Momotaro, the Peachling" ("Momotarō"), and "The Old Man Who Made the Flowers Bloom" ("Hana-saka jijii"). He also established two magazines for children, *Young Boys' World* (*Shōnen sekai*) and *Young Girls' World* (*Shōjo sekai*), and contributed regularly to both. His style of delivery was so popular that he was invited to travel all over Japan giving performances, and as his fame spread, he went on to give readings in Taiwan, Korea, Manchuria, and North China.

And so, at last, to Makiko's diary. She used a commercially printed "Diary Book," published by Sekizenkan in Tokyo, and wrote in *sumi* ink with a brush in a hand more accomplished than one would expect of so young a person. Sometime during the year, she switched to a pen. On the cloth cover in pen and ink is written "Diary: Makiko" and on the first page is written with a brush and *sumi* ink "Diary One, Makiko." On the inside of the cover she wrote in four versions of the calendar year: Meiji 43, Diary; The Year of Emperor Jinmu 2570; Western 1910; Chinese Xuantong 2.[19]

Each day is assigned one page. (See the entry for January 1, reproduced on p. 56.) In addition to the space for the entries of month, date, day of week, and national holidays, there are small columns for weather, temperature—cold, cool, warm, hot, and so forth—"Correspondence in," "Correspondence out," and "Notes." At the top of each page are recorded historical events that occurred on that date. On some days Makiko failed to make an entry and left the page blank; at other times she made entries for a certain date on the wrong pages. When she had a great deal to write, the entries spilled over onto the next page. For some reason her notes on the day's weather became quite sporadic from April to mid-June.

Since there is no way to give the full effect of Makiko's diary in a translation, let me add a word about her writing style. For the most

19. The reign of Jinmu, Japan's legendary first emperor, traditionally was dated from 660 B.C. Xuantong was the reign-name of the last emperor of China.

part, she used a colloquial style flavored by her Kyoto dialect. Whenever she was in a formal mood, she often introduced elements of the literary style in general use at the time. Whatever style she employed, however, the standard Japanese of Makiko's diary is softened by the unmistakable accent of Kyoto speech. It is a pity that we cannot hear her voice, for the Kyoto dialect as women speak it is considered to be Japanese at its most beautiful, feminine, and musical.

MAKIKO'S DIARY

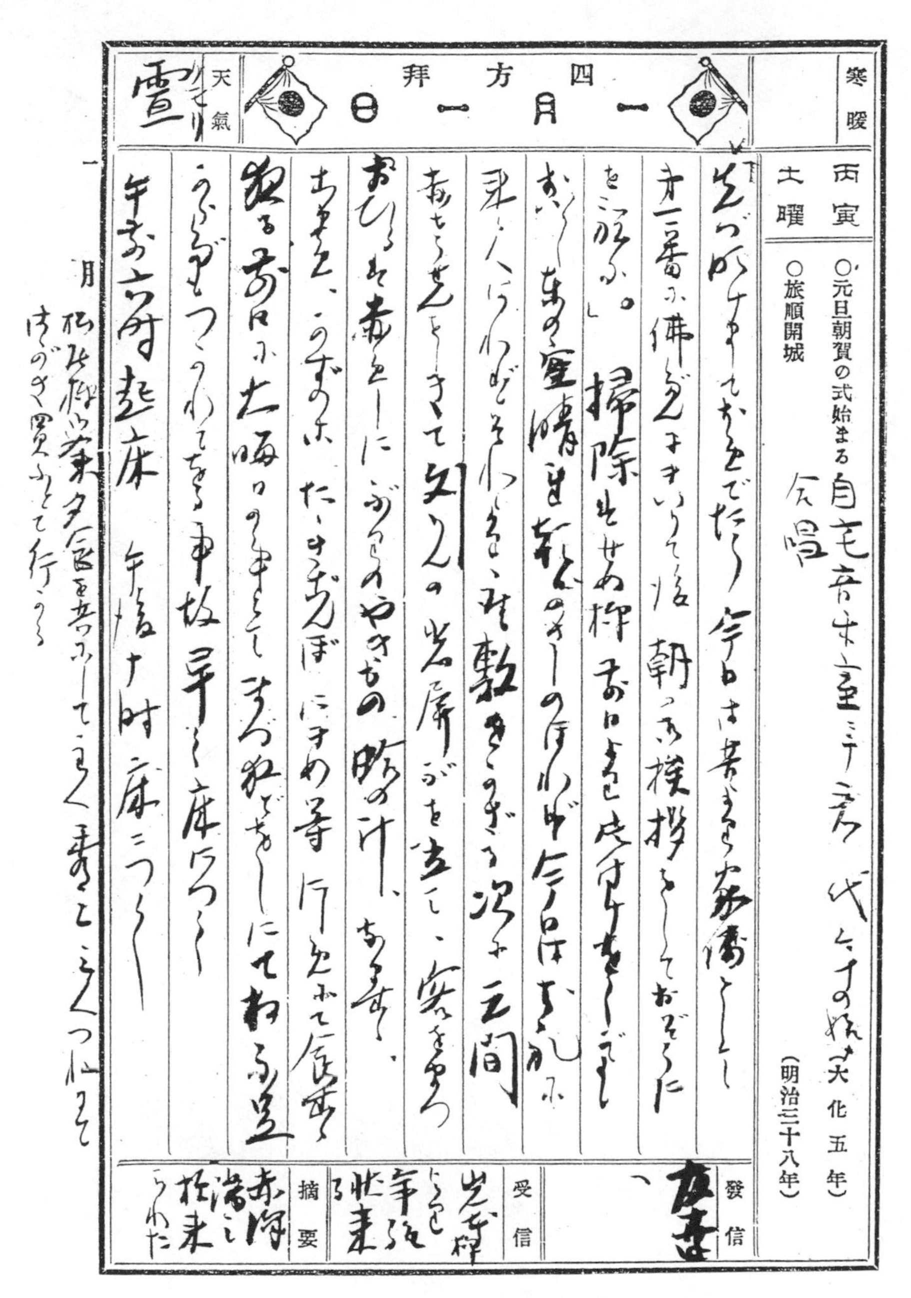

寒暖

丙寅 土曜

○元旦朝賀の式始まる

○旅順開城

（大化五年）

（明治三十八年）

四方拝

一月一日

天氣

發信

受信

摘要

Makiko's diary entry for January 1, 1910. (Nakano Takashi)

一月

JANUARY 1 *Saturday* *Cloudy*

First of all, "Happy New Year!" Observing the custom of our household, the first order of the day was to pay respects at the family's Buddhist altar. After that we exchanged New Year's greetings and had our New Year's meal of *o-zōni*.[1] Since housecleaning is not done on New Year's Day, everything was finished up yesterday.

As the eastern sky gradually cleared and the morning sun rose, callers started to arrive to exchange New Year's greetings. The parlor was decorated for the occasion. We had spread out a red carpet and displayed the folding screen of rocks painted by Bunrin[2] for our New Year's visitors.

For lunch: red-bean rice (*seki-han*), broiled yellowtail (*buri*), clam soup, grated radish and carrot salad (*namasu*), candied small dried fish (*gomame*), herring roe (*kazunoko*), cooked shredded burdock (*gobō*), black beans (*kuromame*), and vegetables cooked in seasoned broth (*nishime*).[3]

Mr. Matsui Jisuke came over and stayed for dinner. He, my husband, and Hide-san[4] went out, saying that they were going to buy New Year's greeting cards.

Went to bed early, for I felt tired and sleepy from having stayed up all night on New Year's Eve getting everything ready for the New Year.[5]

Rose at six o'clock. Went to bed at ten.

Note: We gathered in the music room upstairs and sang *Kimigayo* and *Toshi no hajime*.[6]

Correspondence out: To friends.
Correspondence in: A New Year's greeting card from Iwamoto-sama.[7]
Visitors: Mr. Akazawa Manzō.

1. In Kyoto, *o-zōni* is rice cakes in white miso soup with taro, radishes, and other vegetables. It is much heavier than the standard *o-zōni*, which uses a light broth with vegetables and fish cake (*kamaboko*). See entry for December 14.
2. The painter Shiokawa Bunrin (1801–77), a member of the Shijō school; his works are to be found in major museums in Japan and abroad.
3. All these are specially prepared New Year's dishes. Each ingredient is auspicious, signifying good health, prosperity, and other good fortune for the family throughout the coming year. Red-bean rice is served on all auspicious occasions.
4. Nakano Hidesaburō.
5. The New Year's Eve preparations are described in the final entry for this diary on December 31.
6. The first is Japan's national anthem, and the second a school song celebrating the arrival of the New Year.
7. A female friend.

JANUARY 2 *Sunday* *Windy, freezing rain*

Rose at five o'clock, following household custom. We have the first bath[1] of the year today, in the morning. As soon as he got up, one of the shop-boys came to help make a fire under the tub. After a breakfast of *o-zōni* everyone started cleaning up the place.[2]

Since today is the memorial day for Chūhachi IV, both breakfast and lunch were served without fish.[3]

Breakfast was the same as yesterday's—*o-zōni*—but made without shaved dried bonito. Lunch: grated radish and carrot salad with dried persimmon, rolls of seaweed (*kobu-maki*),[4] seaweed soup, and minced dried seaweed on rice. Dinner was a New Year's party for the staff of the store. On this occasion it is the custom of our household to serve chicken sukiyaki with *sake* and many side dishes. Sliced chicken: ordered 300 *momme* for the store employees and 200 *momme* for the family.[5]

Mr. Akazawa Manzō is visiting us today.

Visitors: Nakao Manzō, and Mr. Obata and Uncle Amano.[6]

1. *Hatsu-buro. Hatsu* means "new" or "first." The New Year brings a sense that everything is starting anew. Because it is a special day, baths are taken in the morning rather than at night, as is the usual custom.
2. In this entry Makiko is making notes of what she has learned from her mother-in-law regarding household customs of the second day of the New Year.
3. On the Buddhist monthly memorial days (*maitsuki meinichi*) it is customary

to serve vegetarian meals. Chūhachi IV died on the second of the month. As we shall see, vegetarian meals were also served on the 26th, the monthly memorial day of Chūhachi V.

4. Ordinarily the salad would contain shaved dried bonito, but the vegetarian variety uses dried persimmon. For the same reason the *kobu-maki* was made with burdock rather than octopus.

5. A measure of weight: 100 *momme* = 375 grams.

6. Mr. Obata is unidentified. Uncle Amano appears to be a distant relative of the Nakaos, for he was invited to their memorial service on February 24 and attended Makiko's brother's wedding on May 1.

JANUARY 3 *Monday Clear*

For breakfast: *o-zōni* again. For lunch: candied small dried fish, grated radish and carrot salad, codfish soup, and broiled fish.

My brother Manzō left for Dairen, Manchuria, to return to work. My husband, Hide-san, and I went to see him off at the railway station. I miss him very much. I could not help crying every time I thought about my father, so recently widowed, and my younger sister Eiko and younger brother Senzō. How can they possibly manage all by themselves? How lonely and sad.

The New Year's callers are Mr. Shimizu,[1] Mr. Kuwabara from Osaka, our former clerk who now has a successful business dealing in photographic materials, Mr. Nakano Uhachi, our old business branch-family, Mr. Kinta,[2] and Mr. Suzuki Kichinosuke, who is the president of the Kyoto branch of the Otogi Club.

Today was the day for the New Year's party for all our branch-families. The invitations were for four o'clock. The parlor had been prepared for the occasion and the dinner was catered by Harisei[3] for 90 *sen* per guest. The party began only after everyone had arrived. The group included my husband and Hide-san, the Eastside Doctor, and Mr. Moriguchi and Mr. Yamada, and Messrs. Yamamoto Matsu, Ōkita, Uejima, Hayashi, Toyoda, and others.[4] A *nakai*[5] came to help serve the meal. Everyone got drunk and had a wonderful time—there was plenty of laughter. All were most impressed by Mr. Moriguchi's "Genroku dance,"[6] Mr. Yamamoto Matsu's imitation of *Hakata Niwaka*,[7] and Mr. Uejima's songs. The party broke up after eleven o'clock.

Correspondence in: Kakemi Uta-sama.[8]

Notes: Rose a little after six o'clock. My brother's train left at 9:37 A.M. from Shichijō Station.[9] As a farewell present we gave him a bottle of gentleman's cologne.

1. Unidentified.
2. Unidentified
3. A neighborhood restaurant frequently patronized by the Nakanos. It is still in operation.
4. All were business branch-families. Hayashi was engaged in the practice of Chinese medicine.
5. Professional women who serve meals at restaurants.
6. The Genroku period, in the late seventeenth and early eighteenth centuries, has come to be viewed as the peak of development of the commoner culture of Japan's great cities. The reference is to a dance ordinarily performed by a circle of brightly clad dancers.
7. Extemporaneous farcical skits performed by masked actors, which originated in Hakata on the island of Kyushu.
8. One of Makiko's closest friends. They attended the same school and grew up in the same Nijō neighborhood, where their families had been on friendly terms for two generations. The Kakemi were a business branch-family of Keimatsu.
9. Now Kyoto Station.

JANUARY 4 *Tuesday Clear*

Got up at half-past seven. Began at once to put away screens, trays, china, lacquerware, and other things used for the party last night.

Lunch: tofu in a thick ginger sauce (*kuzu-hiki*) and vegetables cooked in seasoned broth.[1]

A little after six o'clock in the evening Mr. Matsumiya Hōnen and his brother Yūnen came to see my husband. Shortly after that Mr. Tamura Saburō[2] came over to join them. It has been a while since his last visit. They had a lively conversation about all kinds of things. My husband wanted to send a New Year's greeting card to Iwaya Sazanami-sensei and asked Matsumiya Hōnen to draw something on it. They were at it all evening and everyone had a good time.

Mother[3] made quick *chirashi-zushi*[4] for the guests and served it with clam soup. She and I joined the party, too, and polished off the sushi, which turned out to be made with 1.5 *shō* of rice! This revelation really surprised us and we all laughed.[5]

I'd better stop now. That's about all that happened today.

Correspondence in: Akioka-sama.[6]

Visitors: Mr. Kasuga[7] and Mr. Suzuki Kichinosuke.

1. Chopped radishes, carrots, burdock, taro, fried bean curd (*age*), and other vegetables cooked in a broth (*nishime*). The dish usually is left to stand and then served after the liquid has soaked into the vegetables.
2. A pharmacist and classmate of Chūhachi's at the School of Pharmacy.
3. Makiko's mother-in-law, Nakano Mine, is referred to as "Mother" throughout the diary.

4. A type of sushi that can easily be made at home by mixing vinegared rice and cooked chopped vegetables and garnishing the dish with thin strips of plain omelet and dried seaweed.

5. The amount of rice was about 2.7 liters before cooking. They laughed because they had not realized how much they had eaten.

6. A female friend.

7. Unidentified.

JANUARY 5 *Wednesday Rain*

Got up at eight—a late start this morning! It must be the unusually rainy weather. The hairdresser came early.[1]

After a while Nishimura Tokusaburō[2] arrived from Tonoshō by the nine o'clock train. He brought us a gift of tangerines and dried radish in great quantity.[3] Since he is very fond of poem-cards,[4] we all played the game with him for some time. Lunch was miso soup containing sliced dried whale blubber,[5] which the restaurant Harisei sent us today, shredded burdock, and broiled salmon.

My husband and Mr. Matsumiya invited Mr. Hirai Baisen to dinner at the restaurant Matsusada to celebrate the New Year and to thank him for the scroll-painting he had given them. Mr. Matsui joined them at dinner, which cost ¥1 per person. Toward evening we received a catered meal prepared by Harisei sent to us from Wakamiya Hachiman-jinja.[6]

I heard a fire bell sound around 11:30 at night and immediately thought of my father and the family.[7] I roused one of the employees and sent him to inquire at the Matsubara Police Station. Until he came back with the word that the fire was in Nishiki, I could not relax. Our guest Toku-san was the first to run to the site of the fire. My husband apparently went, too. He stayed to watch and did not come home until around half-past one. He is no different from others! (I hope he doesn't hear me saying this!) Went to bed after the clock struck two.

Correspondence in: Okamoto Kikuko, after a long silence. Ueda-sama.[8]

Correspondence out: Replied to Okamoto Kikuko at once.

1. At this time, before hair salons were common and when women all kept their hair long, it was not unusual for a hairdresser to come to a customer's home.

2. Makiko later refers to her husband's half-brother as Toku-san.

3. The first of scores of references to gift exchange, a feature of Japanese society today so pervasive that foreign residents in Japan invariably comment on it. Makiko's diary reveals the extent to which it was a preoccupation in her day as well. On almost

every page there is some reference to an item, usually food, sent or received. See especially entries for December 18–28.

4. *Uta-garuta*, a New Year's card game featuring 100 poems written by 100 poets of the Heian period (ninth to twelfth centuries). One person reads out the first part of a poem and the players attempt to be the first to pick up the card containing the second part.

5. *Mochi kujira*; the texture is soft and chewy.

6. The Nakanos were parishioners of this neighborhood Shintō shrine. Because Chūhachi was unable to attend the meeting at the shrine, his portion of the dinner has been sent to their home.

7. The spread of fire was a particular concern, for in the cities of Makiko's time, most buildings were of wood.

8. Both are female friends.

JANUARY 6 *Thursday* *Clear*

Got up at half-past six. I was chagrined, because Hide-san asked me last night if I could help him get ready early this morning to go to his college crew's workout. I hurried to the kitchen, but alas, Mother was already up and washing her face. She promptly started a fire for me. I, who was supposed to be responsible this morning, was still not fully awake yet—I felt so ashamed and useless! Last night I really intended to get up early without help and be efficient, but . . .

Today is the sixth day of the New Year. For lunch we had special holiday dishes of red-bean rice, broiled sardines, and soup made of *iwaina*.[1]

Tomorrow is the seventh day of the New Year's holiday and it is the custom to have breakfast of rice gruel with seven kinds of leafy green vegetables. It requires three bundles of *iwaina* and five of *nanakusa*.[2] In the evening we chopped the vegetables while singing "Tōdo no tori wa"[3] and salted them down for tomorrow.

Toku-san went to the zoo with Sei-san[4] in the afternoon. He and my husband later were invited to attend a performance of the Soganoya comedy troupe by the Eastside Doctor and Fusako-sama.

They came back around 11:30 with Hide-san, who apparently had met up with them in Shijō.[5] They brought lots of sushi for us, which we all enjoyed. They seem to have enjoyed the show very much and told us the story of one of the comedies entitled *Shinkei-shitsu* (Nervousness). How we laughed!

Correspondence out: Wrote to my sister Eiko because I was so concerned about the family.

1. Young leaves of radishes. *Iwaina* is used because the first part of the plant's name, *iwai*, means "celebration."
2. Seven kinds of greens.
3. A rhythmical children's song.
4. Nakano Seiichi.
5. Shijō Avenue remains one of the major shopping streets in Kyoto. The word Shijō is also used to mean something like "in the Shijō district."

January 7 *Friday* *Clear*

Got up at 6:50. We had our *nanakusa* rice gruel with rice cakes for breakfast, and I ate ten of them. Everyone ate well. We served twenty people[1] and in all 235 rice cakes were consumed!

Lunch: codfish soup, broiled mackerel, cooked small dried fish, radish salad.

Today is my mother's 49th memorial day,[2] and I went to both Higashi and Nishi Ōtani mausoleums[3] with Kuni-san, Shina-san, and Chūji-san.[4] We walked all the way and came back through Teramachi and Sanjō.[5] My feet are aching and I hurt my ankle slightly. It got dark on the way home, and the street lights came on.

I was sorry to find out that I had missed Mrs. Hayashi Teru[6] and Mr. Inui Hayahiko,[7] who had come calling. I realized that I should not leave the house on a holiday any more.

We played poem-cards and listened to the phonograph[8] in the evening. Since it was a holiday, a mob of people came from the store to listen to the music. Mrs. Shirakawa Omiki, who used to be a receptionist in the Eastside Doctor's office and is now a widow who lives in Uji,[9] came over to visit for a while.

My husband was not home tonight. He went to the neighborhood association's[10] New Year's party at Harisei, and came home around 10:30. He said that they served lots of good food and *sake*, and added that his turn to be the neighborhood association representative has come around this year.

1. This is more than the usual number and included some guests.
2. Makiko's mother died on November 21, 1909. A ritual is performed every seven days up to the 49th day after death, at which time the soul of the deceased is believed to be sufficiently purified of the pollution of death that its memorial tablet can be placed in the domestic Buddhist altar with the tablets of the household's ancestral spirits. This is a crucial rite in Japanese Buddhist practice.
3. Her mother's ashes had been divided between the mausoleums of the Higashi (Eastern) and Nishi (Western) Ōtani sects of Jōdo Shinshū Buddhism. Both are located east of the Kamo River, not far from the Nakao and Nakano houses.

4. Nakano Kuniko, Shinako, and Chūjirō.
5. Like Shijō and Gojō, Sanjō is both an avenue and a district.
6. The wife of the head of one of the business branch-families.
7. A distant relative.
8. This was on loan from Matsui Jisuke.
9. An area southeast of Kyoto, noted for the quality of the tea grown there.
10. The neighborhood associations (*chōnai*) had considerable responsibility in the management of local affairs.

JANUARY 8 *Saturday Clear in the morning, started to rain in late afternoon.*

Got up at 6:45. There is to be a military parade today.

Toku-san left for home, so we gave him some fine sugar to take back to Tonoshō. Since he wanted to see the parade before going to the railway station, my husband decided to go with him. They left before nine o'clock, and he came home past noon.

This is the day to cut the *kagami-mochi*[1] and use it to make *mizuna no o-zōni*.[2] We used a total of 190 rice cakes. The one offered at the family's Buddhist altar was cooked separately without shaved dried bonito,[3] and will be eaten later.

Mr. Suzuki Kichinosuke came over after the parade and had lunch here—broiled sea bream,[4] egg soup, and *sake*-lees pickles.[5] He said that he had to go to City Hall, and my husband left with him because he had an invitation to a New Year's party organized by the Association for Herbal Medicine set for four o'clock at Minokichi.[6]

A man from the Yamashina branch of Higashi Hongan-ji brought an empty food box to the house that we are to take to the main temple. As one of the officers of the association of parishioners, we have to see that it is delivered.[7]

Our monthly sukiyaki dinner on the first Saturday of the month had been postponed because of the New Year's celebrations, so we served it today.[8]

Omiki-san,[9] who has been visiting the Eastside family, left this morning to return home. We presented her a gift of refined sugar. She has been helpful in advising me in our search for a housekeeper for my family in Nijō.

Visitor: Mr. Tanii Kōtarō,[10] who is returning to Tokyo today.

1. Large, round, two-tiered ceremonial cakes made of pounded glutinous rice. They are cut up into chunks and eaten after being displayed during the New Year's festivities. See entries for December 13, 14, 22, and 27.

2. *Mizuna* is a leafy green winter vegetable, here served in a rice-cake soup.
3. Food offered at the altar should be vegetarian.
4. *Tai*, a fish served on festive and auspicious occasions.
5. *Narazuke*. In brewing *sake*, rice is fermented and strained through cloth. The residue, the *sake* lees referred to, is used widely in making soup and pickling vegetables.
6. A famous Kyoto restaurant that is still in operation.
7. The meaning of this paragraph is unclear, but it appears that the main temple of Higashi Hongan-ji had sent food to the one in Yamashina, which was returning it through the Nakanos. Yamashina lies over the hills to the east of the southern part of Kyoto. Higashi Hongan-ji is the huge temple complex to the west of the area where the store was located.
8. The eating of beef in any form was a recent practice, widely adopted only after the Meiji Restoration in 1868. It had been Chūhachi VII's idea that the family and store employees should have beef regularly. In the Meiji period such breaks with tradition were considered particularly indicative of the modern attitude sloganized as "Civilization and Enlightenment." Furthermore, Chūhachi's training would have made him aware of the nutritional value of meat. Subsequent entries do not entirely bear out the claim that the customary day for the monthly sukiyaki dinner was the first Saturday of the month, however.
9. Mrs. Shirakawa Omiki.
10. The son of Tanii Onui, Senjirō's adoptive mother.

January 9 *Sunday* *Clear*

For some reason I have been worrying about the family in Nijō since this morning, so after lunch I asked Mother and my husband if I could go and see them.

On the way I stopped at the Kōshimas to see how little Fumi-chan is doing. She has been ill, but apparently began feeling much better yesterday. Actually she looked well. I didn't stay long and hurried to Nijō, for the days are short.

My father was not home, but while I was talking to my sister Eiko, Mr. Nishimura Ryūji[1] arrived. It seems that he is going to stay with them for a few days, and it is obvious that they cannot manage with only the one maid. My father asked me to stay and help them out, but first I had to go back home to ask for permission to stay in Nijō for a few days.

1. A brother of Nishimura Toraichi, a distant relative of Makiko's mother's family who had worked at the Nakao pharmacy while pursuing his studies at the School of Pharmacy and eventually became one of their business branch-families. He owned and operated his own store.

JANUARY 10 *Monday* *Clear (In Nijō)*

Went across the street to the Keimatsu house to see the new baby boy, who was born on the second of this month. I took a bolt of silk as a gift to mark the auspicious occasion.

Toward the evening I began to wonder about the family back home in Gojō.

JANUARY 11 *Tuesday* *Rain (In Nijō)*

It has been wet, soggy, and dark since this morning, and I have been feeling somewhat lonely.

In the afternoon Elder Sister Kōshima and her daughter Fumi-chan came to visit us. She had gone to see Dr. Adachi, a gynecologist, since she has been feeling rather poorly, and it turns out that she is pregnant. What good news! I was so envious and wondered why I cannot get pregnant.[1]

Tora-san[2] came over in the evening.

I was planning to go back home this evening, but since my father had not yet returned from a meeting, I could not leave. I had to telephone Gojō and ask if I could extend my stay here. It was very painful, for I could not help wondering what is going on there and how they are managing at home without me.

1. Makiko's first child, a son, was born in 1913.
2. Nishimura Toraichi. See entry for January 9.

JANUARY 12 *Wednesday* *Clear (Stayed all day in Nijō and came home at night.)*

It was an unusually beautiful morning with a clear sky, so I decided to starch the kimono that already had been washed. Early in the morning our house guest, Mr. Nishimura Ryūji, went to the university hospital and returned just before noon. As he had suspected, the diagnosis is rheumatism, which is not good news. He said that he plans to leave tomorrow morning.

I was quite concerned about home and felt restless all morning, so as soon as Eiko came home from school I left. On the way home by *rikisha*, I realized that my thoughts were still focused on my family in Nijō. I thought about my poor sister Eiko, who although only a schoolgirl, must bear the heavy responsibilities of a housewife, managing the household since our mother passed away. Tears flowed down my cheeks as I thought, "There is nothing so hard as losing your parent when you are young."

When the *rikisha* finally arrived home, I was greatly relieved, but as soon as I entered the house I felt that something was different. It was because an electric light had been installed in the kitchen, and the family quarters were illuminated by a gas lamp. It was so bright that I felt as though I had walked into the wrong house!

Visitors: A gentleman named Ōtsuki Manjirō, who used to be an apprentice clerk in the store, came to visit while I was away.

JANUARY 13 *Thursday Rain*

It was a dark and gloomy day. The hairdresser was supposed to come, so I did not even comb my hair and spent the morning idly. Lunch was cooked leeks, as well as soybeans with kelp, which were already cooked.

I met the gentleman named Ōtsuki Manjirō for the first time, when he stopped by the house on his way to the five o'clock dinner at Harisei.[1] He is a dignified man but rather short. He is leaving in the morning by the ten o'clock boat for Port Arthur, Manchuria.

My husband came back from the restaurant after ten o'clock. He said that tonight's dinner, which was ordered in advance, cost approximately ¥1.20 or ¥1.30 per person. We talked for a while but went to bed early.

1. Chūhachi was entertaining the visitor at this neighborhood restaurant. Ōtsuki's father, Riemon, had helped save the Nakano's family business when it faced a financial crisis. Evidently Makiko was curious to see a man she had heard so much about.

JANUARY 14 *Friday Cloudy*

The sky looked unsettled but I washed *tabi*[1] in the morning anyway. Soon after I finished it was already lunchtime. Today's lunch was broiled salmon, cooked radish with flaked fish (*soboro*), and miso soup.

Then I tidied up the parlor to get ready for the guests who are supposed to call this afternoon. We all waited for them to arrive, but nobody showed up for quite a while. Then Mr. Matsumiya Hōnen arrived, followed by Mr. Matsui and Mr. Yakushiji. After some talk they decided to go out to investigate the Keihan Railway construction site.[2]

While they were out we tidied up again and prepared their dinner. As usual, Mother cooked.[3] She made carp miso soup and a Western-style omelet. She put some cooked fish left from last night's dinner in the omelet and served a side dish of fish cake (*kamaboko*), which had been delivered earlier today by Jū-san, the fishmonger.

After dinner the conversation got lively, as it always does, and went on some time, but then they decided to go out again. This time they went to see a ceramics show and sale at some temple. They came back around ten o'clock, bringing the portrait bust of Sazanami-sensei[4] and a little ceramic rabbit and tortoise.[5] There must be a reason for bringing these things home, but they haven't told me what it is. All the guests left about one o'clock in the morning, obviously having had a good time. They are all easygoing and pleasant people.

Note: Tomorrow is another New Year's celebration day. Brought out the trays and lacquerware for the occasion. Soaked ten cups of rice and five cups of red beans (*azuki*). Soaked about 220 pieces of rice cake in water tonight. All is for the red-bean gruel (*azuki-gayu*) for tomorrow.

1. Split-toed socks worn with Japanese dress.
2. A private railway line connecting Kyoto and Osaka that runs along the Kamo River, crossing it at Gojō Avenue.
3. The custom when they served dinner to guests.
4. This reference is not entirely clear, but it appears that Mr. Tanaka, a ceramist, is working on a bust of Iwaya Sazanami. See entries for January 29 and February 6.
5. Probably a display piece, depicting the fabled tortoise and hare.

JANUARY 15 *Saturday Clear*

Today is *ko-shōgatsu*,[1] so got up at six. After paying respects at the family Buddhist altar, we all had gruel with rice cakes together. No one came for New Year's greetings today. I spent all morning doing nothing but miscellaneous chores. Lunch was a vegetarian meal, served with cooked shredded burdock and tofu soup.

In the afternoon Mr. Nabeshima came to see my husband to ask him to give a talk at the Army Reservists' New Year's party that is to

A greengrocer; the large cone-shaped vegetables at front right are bamboo shoots; to the left two stalks of burdock stand in tub of shaved burdock. (Winkel, *Souvenir from Japan*)

The Nishiki market. (*Kyotō fu shi, I*)

The family photograph taken on January 16, 1910, at Narui Photo Studio: (*seated, left and right*): Mine and Makiko; (*standing, from left*): Hidesaburō, Chūjirō, Chūhachi, Seiichi, and Shinako. (Nakano Takashi)

Hidesaburō in his college uniform, ca. 1910. (Nakano Takashi)

The Nakano family grave in Higashi Ōtani. (Kazuko Smith, 1992)

be held today.[2] My husband refused politely over and over again, but after repeated pleas he finally agreed to put in an appearance.

This is the third Saturday of the month, when we customarily serve beef sukiyaki for dinner. After dinner two friends of Kuniko, Morino-sama and Okiyo-sama came over. We all played cards, but my husband had to leave for the Army Reservists' party. He took the phonograph and records, which we had borrowed from Mr. Matsui on New Year's Day. Everyone left at 10:40.

When my husband got home, he told me that the party was not well attended. He said that the school principal's talk was long and boring (this is just between us), so to entertain people they played some phonograph records and Mr. Nabeshima played the violin, but evidently he was awful! My husband thinks he deserves to be a student of Mr. Hōjō.[3]

Today is the day to settle accounts that were left unpaid on the last day of the previous month,[4] but because it is a holiday, everything has been postponed until tomorrow. Went to bed around one o'clock.

Note: The ceremonial trays were used only for breakfast. Lunch was served in the usual manner.

1. Little New Year's traditionally was celebrated on the fifteenth of the first lunar month, but after New Year's Day was changed to January 1 by the new calendar, *koshōgatsu* was necessarily moved to January 15. The custom has almost disappeared since the end of World War II.

2. Chūhachi had not seen military service; he was invited primarily because he was an active member of the community. Mr. Nabeshima is unidentified.

3. Mr. Hōjō is not identified, but the tone clearly is sarcastic.

4. The usual days to settle accounts were the fifth and last days of the month. However, New Year's observances had thrown the schedule off. December 31 is still the most important day of the year to clear bills and debts.

JANUARY 16 *Sunday* *Freezing rain*

Since it rained, Hide-san's college crew training session in Ōtsu was canceled, and this gave us a good opportunity to go have family group photographs taken. We decided on the Narui Photo Studio and went there after lunch.[1]

Today is the day the geisha are out in the streets visiting their clients' houses to pay their respects, and the streets of Shijō and Hanamikōji were filled with people trying to get a look at them all dressed up in their beautiful kimono.[2] I saw two geisha while our *rikisha* ran through Shijō Avenue. Much to my surprise, in the crowd I saw the face of Adachi Ryūko, whom I haven't seen for a couple of years. Our eyes met momentarily, but since I was in the *rikisha* that was all. She looked very different from the way I remember her.

Shortly after we arrived at the studio, the men joined us. Posing for photographs made me nervous. I felt my body stiffen, but at the moment the photographer said, "Now, please, hold still," it was all over. He took five different pictures, and the cost was ¥1.60.

On the way home we stopped at Higashi Ōtani and paid our respects to our ancestors[3] at the family grave. We also went to the mausoleum there, where my mother's ashes are deposited, and I felt that she must be very pleased to see us all together.

We bought some sweet steamed buns to take home. It was very cold—my fingers were chilled to the point that I could not feel anything! The electric light came on shortly after we got home.[4] It was dinnertime again.

Our accounting went smoothly without incident. The staff of the store and their families went to the theater today.[5]

I had planned to try to find out something about my friend, Adachi-san, whom I saw today, as soon as I came home, but I was unable to do so.

Note: For lunch we had thick soup made with a base of *sake* lees.[6]

1. The studio was located not far away in the grounds of Yasaka-jinja, a large Shintō shrine at the eastern end of Shijō Avenue in the Gion district.
2. It was rare to see geisha dressed up and out during the day.
3. The ancestors of the Nakano household.
4. The electric lighting system, which was centrally controlled, was shut down during daylight hours.
5. The cost was borne by the store as a holiday treat.
6. This soup is very popular during the winter months, as the touch of alcohol provided by the *sake* lees warms the body. See entry for January 8.

January 17 *Monday Clear*

Unlike yesterday the sky is clear, and it is a beautiful day, but chilly because it is still the middle of winter. Lunch was broiled salmon and seaweed soup.

Mother said she had a headache and was resting in the warm *kotatsu*[1] when Mrs. Hiraoka Okoma from across the street came to visit about three o'clock in the afternoon. It has been a while since she last came to see us, so there was a lot to talk about. It was fascinating to listen to her because she has a wide range of social contacts and is a skilled conversationalist. I stayed the whole time listening to her even though I didn't have to. When the lights came on, we were surprised to find that time had gone by so fast, and our visitor rushed back home when she realized how late it was.

It was already dinnertime. Mother prepared fresh sea cucumbers (*namako*) to be served with a vinegar sauce and grated radish. She said that they could be served with ginger sauce, too. I tried one but did not like it.

After dinner my husband wanted to conduct an experiment to find out if sea cucumber dissolves upon coming into contact with straw, as he had heard somewhere. We immediately chopped up some straw, placed it on the sea cucumber, and watched. The straw made indentations but did not dissolve the creature.

After the experiment was over, a Buddhist priest came to see my husband. I was told that he is planning to open a pharmacy and needed my husband's advice.

Correspondence out: To Tanii Yae to let her know that we received the money. To Mrs. Shirakawa Omiki, asking if there has been any progress in the search for a housekeeper for Nijō.

1. A square or rectangular opening, in which charcoal is placed, is cut into the floor. A wooden table or frame is put over the opening and the whole thing covered by a quilt. In the modern version, the charcoal has been replaced by an electrical heating element.

JANUARY 18 *Tuesday*

Today is the memorial day for Mother's half-sister and we are supposed to serve vegetarian meals, but apparently we are not taking it seriously.[1] Served cooked radish for lunch.

The weather turned very peculiar this morning, and sure enough, a little before noon the first snow of the year began to fall. I watched for about three minutes, but then the sun came out and started melting the snow as it fell. It snowed lightly from time to time all afternoon.

We had sent a wedding gift to the Nagasawas, who are in the umbrella business, as representative of the neighborhood association on behalf of its 24 member-households. Today Mr. Nagasawa sent us a special gift of sweet cakes, with a thank-you note and return gifts totaling ¥25 in cash, which we deposited to the association's account.

Mr. Matsumiya dropped in to say that he had gone to the Kiyomizu temple[2] to sketch some snow scenes. Quickly I cut the big sweet cake that we had just received into fourths and served a piece to him with tea. He didn't stay long as he was on his way to the Third Primary School in the Rokuhara district.

Today we had baths. I took mine before dinner. After dinner we played a card game.[3] The Eastside Doctor came over to join in and it got wilder. I did not fully understand the rules, but it was fun watching everyone get so excited. The game ended when the Doctor went home just after ten o'clock.

Correspondence in: From Mrs. Shirakawa Omiki. Good news regarding the search for a housekeeper for Nijō.

1. Perhaps because she was not Mine's real half-sister, but a close relative who had been accorded the status of a sister. She may have been the daughter of Chūhachi V's sister.

2. This spectacularly situated Buddhist temple, built into a hillside on high stilts, has for centuries been a favorite of visitors to Kyoto. It is reached by a very steep path leading up from Gojō Avenue, where the Nakano store was located. The way to the temple is lined with souvenir shops, ceramics shops, and eating places.

3. Not poem-cards, but Western-style playing cards called *toranpu* from the English "trump."

JANUARY 19 *Wednesday Clear*

A beautiful day since early this morning. Before I realized it, it was already noon. Today's lunch was a rich soup made with a base of *sake* lees.

My husband attended the Pharmacists' Association[1] party at the Nakamura-rō[2] and came home around ten o'clock. He said that it was not well attended.

After dinner one of the kitchen maids left, saying that she was going home just briefly, but did not return. I wanted to know why she hadn't come back, and telephoned to inquire, only to find out that she had quarreled with a member of the staff working in the store. She is rather talkative and something of a troublemaker, so that no one seems to miss her. However, being shorthanded did cause some problems. So at once I sent an inquiry to the agency about hiring a new maid, but was told that there is no one suitable for us at the moment. Everyone helped out in the kitchen, and we managed somehow. What a nuisance that girl is!

1. *Yakuzaishi-kai*. Makiko mentions several other associations and groups having to do with the pharmaceutical business and refers to this one again on June 17 and 26.

2. An inn and restaurant, located not far from the Nakano store near the entrance of the Yasaka-jinja at the end of Shijō Avenue in the Gion district. It is still in operation.

JANUARY 20 *Thursday Cloudy*

The maid did not come back last night. I was hoping that she might return this morning, but so far she has not done so.

In the afternoon the radishes we had ordered for pickling were delivered. We are going to make seven kegs of pickles this year, and the cost per keg is ¥1.35. We started to work immediately by washing the kegs, cutting off the radish leaves at the neck, and putting salt between the layers of radish. Each keg takes two *shō* of salt. I mostly watched while Mother and my husband worked hard, for which I was thankful, but felt guilty nonetheless.

My husband went to see Mr. Murai's villa[1] with some other, mostly older, people from the neighborhood. Mr. Murai is the president of a tobacco company, apparently. While my husband was out, my father came to pay his first visit since New Year's Day. He seems to be having a hard time trying to cope with everything all by himself. I am praying that he will be able to find a good housekeeper.

My husband hasn't returned yet. I am certain that he has dropped by Mr. Matsui's house and is talking with him right now. They are such good friends!

1. An imposing Victorian mansion built by the wealthy owner of the Murai Tobacco Company just south of Maruyama Park. Today called Chōrakkan, it has been converted to a small hotel for women. On the first floor is a popular coffee shop.

JANUARY 21 *Friday Rain*

A rainy, dark, and gloomy day. This is my mother's monthly memorial day. I cannot forget it even for a moment. Today my heart is filled with her memories, and I cannot stop my streaming tears as the rain falls steadily outside.

Lunch was radish cooked with dried small fish.

The faithless kitchen maid still has not returned. We have been looking for a replacement for her by many different means, but have been unable to find anyone. Even though her absence creates a lot of problems around the house, I decided that I am not going to be defeated by this. We can manage without a maid for a month or two. Nevertheless, everyone is busier than before, and I have to work harder along with the other maids. I haven't been able to do my sewing at all. "Wretched woman! Disloyal servant! What has happened to her?" I cannot help thinking about her although I know that it won't do any good.

I wrote a short letter to Eiko, for I heard that she has a cold.

Correspondence out: To Eiko.

JANUARY 22 *Saturday Cloudy*

It is another dull, gloomy day. Not much happened.

Lunch was boiled leeks.

The hairdresser came unusually early in the morning today. I felt uneasy because she changed my hairstyle and kept raising my hand to touch the big mound of hair sitting right on top of my head.

My husband went to a meeting of the *Tokusei-kai* in the afternoon, and to a *Keishin-kai* New Year's party from four o'clock, both in connection with the Fushimi Inari shrine.[1]

We made *o-zenzai*[2] for dinner because the rice cakes are starting to get moldy because of the warm New Year's weather, and we have to use them quickly.

My husband came home shortly after ten o'clock. He said that the party got noisy and wild, which usually is the case when there are many *sake* drinkers.

1. *Tokusei-kai* is an organization of parishioners of the shrine; *Keishin-kai* is a group of representatives of parish groups drawn from a much wider area of the city. Inari is the rice deity, whose messenger is the white fox. The deity, associated with general prosperity, is much favored by merchants; many places of business today have a small Inari shrine.

2. Rice cakes in sweet red-bean sauce; usually this dish is eaten as a snack.

JANUARY 23 *Sunday Clear*

Unlike yesterday, today is beautiful and sunny. Mrs. Shirakawa Omiki has arranged for a housekeeper for Nijō, and I was expecting

The gates at the Fushimi Inari shrine. (Asian Collection, Herbert F. Johnson Museum of Art, Cornell University)

Fushimi Inari shrine, 1897; the symbol of the shrine, a fox, is set in the cage on the left. (Yokohama Archives of History)

Print of Fushimi Inari shrine, ca. 1900; the inset shows a streetcar with a young man running ahead to warn pedestrians to make way. (Yokohama Archives of History)

Festival at Kitano Tenman-gū, 1902. (Kyoto Prefectural Archives)

The five-tiered pagoda at Tō-ji, ca. 1910. (*Shashin shūsei*)

the woman to come to the house. I waited all morning and afternoon for her, and about three o'clock, just as I was wondering if she would really come today, she appeared all by herself, bearing a letter of introduction. She looked like a good person, so I got ready quickly and took her over to Nijō right away. She said that she is willing to work for a trial period of a few days, so I left her there and came back home about 6:30.[1]

Our missing maid still hasn't returned, but a little after nine in the evening the woman from the agency came to see us. She said that if we haven't found anyone to replace her yet, our maid wants to return to work, but since she has delayed so long, it is getting harder and harder for her to ask to be taken back. We said that unless the maid changes her attitude, it would be impossible to keep her on and that if she wants to quit, she should come and pick up her things. The woman from the agency replied that she will tell her what we said and make her come tomorrow morning.

Note: Prepared a special dish of thick soup made with a base of *sake* lees.

1. The woman's name was Oasa, and Makiko had cause to regret her hasty decision. See entries for September 11, 12, and 17.

JANUARY 24 *Monday Clear*

It has been warm and pleasant since this morning, which made me feel restless, and I thought how wonderful it would be to take a walk on such a beautiful day! I assumed that our maid surely would come back today, but she didn't.

For lunch we had cooked small fresh-water clams without shells and seaweed soup.

Yesterday Hide-san told us that a comet can be seen in the sky, so we all got excited and climbed up on the rooftop to try to find it. We saw something immense, but not clearly. Apparently it's not Halley's Comet.[1] I realized that we were the only family in the neighborhood observing the sky, getting all excited, and making a racket. Aren't we a noisy bunch!

This evening Mother, Kuni-san, Shina-san, Chūji-san, and I went to the Mieidō,[2] where the night stalls were set up in the temple compound.

Correspondence out: Mrs. Shirakawa Omiki, a thank-you letter for helping find a housekeeper for Nijō and asking further help in finding a maid for us.

Note: We had sushi today.

1. Halley's Comet did make a pass of the solar system in 1910, an event that was widely covered in the world's press.

2. A unidentified Buddhist temple.

JANUARY 25 *Tuesday Cloudy*

It is the first Tenjin festival of the year at Kitano Tenman-gū,[1] and it must have been packed with people.

We received a gift of three large turnips from the maid's family in Yamanashi[2] today and promptly made them into a salad with some left-over pickled plums and shredded seaweed.

It was an uneventful day. The weather was fine this morning, but it started to rain about noon, which means that both the fairs at Tō-ji[3] and Kitano Tenman-gū were rained out. They do everything together, don't they?[4]

1. A famous Shintō shrine in the Kitano district, dedicated to Tenjin, the apotheosis of the Heian courtier Sugawara no Michizane. It holds an open-air market on the 25th of every month, but the biggest and liveliest are the first and last of the year.

2. The maid is Kishi, who later is replaced by another maid from the same place. See entry for April 1.

3. Tō-ji is a massive temple complex of the Shingon sect of Buddhism located about one and a half miles southwest of the Nakano store. Its justly famous monthly outdoor market is held on the 21st (which had been a rainy day). See entry for December 21.

4. Makiko writes this in such a way as to appear to be referring to the two deities of the temple and shrine, Odaishi-san (Kōbō Daishi) and Tenjin-san (Sugawara no Michizane), respectively, as though they are two men who get along well together.

JANUARY 26 *Wednesday Clear*

Still no letter from Mrs. Shirakawa Omiki about a maid for us. We had vegetarian dishes today because it is the monthly memorial day for grandfather Chūhachi V.[1]

In the evening my father came to see us, bringing some whole steamed sweet potatoes for a snack. Then Mr. Tanaka Hozan arrived, followed by Mr. Matsui. Obviously Mr. Matsui had already had some *sake*; his face was as red as a demon's. He brought the newly mounted hanging scroll and framed painting that he had done for us. They were so beautifully done that both look much better. As a matter of fact, the Hokuto[2] painting looks much more valuable now. My father went back home around nine o'clock.

After he left, the party got livelier because my husband and Mr. Matsui are such good friends. Suddenly they got into an argument about Mr. Matsui's distaste for Western-style clothing. My husband criticized him, saying, "Why don't you like to wear Western-style clothing?" They went on arguing about who is right and who is wrong, and in the end Mr. Matsui lost. In the meantime Mr. Tanaka, who was also wearing kimono, looked very uneasy, as though he were the guilty one; I felt so sorry for him. We were rather frightened, for they were at each other's throats. Our visitors left around 1:00 A.M. Mr. Matsui really is a good-natured man, I thought, because he did not look angry even after being so badly battered.

Note: Today's menu was trout fry and seaweed soup.

1. Also noted in the entries for February 26 and September 25.
2. An unidentified painter.

JANUARY 27 *Thursday* *Clear*

There is a big assembly for readers of *Young Boys' World* and *Young Girls' World*[1] at the City Assembly Hall today. Fortunately, it is a beautiful day.

My husband was looking forward to attending the meeting as an officer of the Otogi Club, but he is not well and his temperature was slightly over 100° this morning.[2] He was trying very hard to get well when someone called out at the front door. It was none other than our favorite visitor Kurushima-sensei[3] who came with a gentleman named Numata,[4] saying that they had gone to pay a visit to Kiyomizu temple just up the hill and had dropped in to see us. They did not stay long. He is a wonderful man, so modest. No wonder everyone likes him.

My husband's condition did not improve in the afternoon so Kuniko-san, Shinako-san, and the other children in our family left before six o'clock to attend the assembly without him. Mother and I stayed home. When my husband's temperature rose to 103° around nine o'clock and he looked very uncomfortable, I knew that he could not have gone. I was upset, but didn't know what to do, so tried putting an ice-pack on his head.

Everybody who had gone to the meeting came home about ten,

saying that it was well attended and that they had a good time. I was not interested in their report at all, however. Mother thought that we should try a hot pack and put a steamed towel on my husband's chest, which he liked. Mother tried other ways to make him comfortable as well. His temperature went down to 100° around 2:00 A.M., so I dozed a little beside him. Every time I woke up I checked his temperature, but it stayed around 100° all night.

Note: We had soup with a base of *sake* lees.

1. Two popular children's magazines founded by Iwaya Sazanami; see Makiko's Social World.

2. Makiko uses the Fahrenheit scale here, as she does throughout when reporting the weather. In her account of a later illness, however, she uses the Celsius scale (see entries for July 25 and August 2 and 3). This must have been about the time the switch to the Celsius scale began, for certainly it was in general use by 1930. Although the Japanese adopted the metric system in 1924, the conversion from indigenous systems of weights and measures was not completed until some time in the 1960's and 1970's.

3. Kurushima Takehiko.

4. Unidentified; he also appears in the entries for October 22 and 23, where Makiko refers to him as Numata-sensei.

JANUARY 28 *Friday Clear*

I have been worried about my husband's sudden illness since yesterday. His temperature this morning was still over 100°, and he is on a liquid diet. I prayed that his temperature will go down today. Fortunately, it went down to 99° around noon, and he looked more comfortable. The Eastside Doctor came to see him in the afternoon and said he will be all right.

As soon as the doctor left, Mr. Tanaka, the ceramist, came to see my husband, who is still in bed. He told him about the meeting yesterday, chatted a while, and left about the time the electric light came on. My husband is gradually feeling better—his temperature was down to normal, but like an old man he complained of a backache, which must have been caused by the fever. He wanted to go out to visit Sazanami-sensei, who is still in Kyoto, tonight. Mother was very concerned, as was I, about his going out in this condition, so he finally gave up. I was so relieved.

Note: We had vegetarian dishes today, with *mizuna* and fried bean curd (*age*).

January 29 *Saturday*

I was expecting that my husband would be well by this morning, but his fever rose again about 11:30 last night, and stayed at about 100° until this morning. We decided to ask Dr. Kitawaki[1] to make a house call since my husband has never been like this before.

Mr. Suzuki came to see him in the morning, and they talked about a lot of things. My husband had no appetite and would take only some milk and an egg. About one o'clock in the afternoon the doctor came and told us that it is only a cold, but since he has a fever he should take it easy. Since his temperature is still hovering around 100° or over, I was very worried that it might develop into typhoid or something like that.

Mr. Tanaka came over again in the afternoon. He didn't seem ready to leave even when dinnertime arrived, and in the meantime Mr. Matsui also came to talk to my husband about the portrait bust of Sazanami-sensei.[2] We served them a dinner of broiled flounder and beans, along with trout fry and *mizuna*. Mr. Matsui left shortly after dinner, saying that he had errands to do. Mr. Tanaka left with Hide-san. They went to their primary school alumni association meeting tonight.

My husband is still not feeling well. About three o'clock this morning he was nauseated and had a chill, and his temperature was still around 100°. I was feeling very concerned and tried to make him feel better and he fell asleep for a while. When I woke up it was 7:00 A.M. and everyone had already started house cleaning—I jumped out of bed.

Note: Today we had trout fry and *mizuna* with miso soup.[3]

1. An internist who formerly had a practice in the building across the street where the Eastside Doctor now had his office.

2. See entries for January 14 and February 6.

3. Note that in addition to the dishes that the family members had eaten the guests were served fancier flounder and beans.

January 30 *Sunday* *Rain*

Today is the Festival for the Kōmei emperor, and Okuni-san was going to Sennyū-ji to visit his tomb,[1] but canceled her plans because of the rain.

My husband was still feeling poorly, with a temperature around 100°. Around 11:30 A.M. when Mother was over at the Eastside family, helping them make radish pickles, and I was writing a letter to Nijō regarding the details of the hiring of a housekeeper for them, I heard my husband yelling from the toilet. I dropped everything and rushed to him. It turned out that he had passed a very long tapeworm, which had been the cause of his discomfort all this time.[2] All of a sudden he felt fine and his temperature dropped to near normal, but no sooner were we feeling relieved than the fever came back and his temperature rose a little again. Apparently, because he was feeling too weak to eat, the worm was starved and therefore expelled.

Obviously feeling much better, he was able to eat some sea bream *sashimi*,[3] soup stock made of sea bream bone, and steamed pudding of milk and egg for supper. His temperature was 99.5° around 11:00 P.M.

Correspondence out: To Eiko and Mrs. Shirakawa Omiki.
Correspondence in: From my brother in Dairen, Manchuria.
Note: Cooked tofu with flounder.

1. The festival, long since dropped from the calendar, was called *Kōmei tennō sai* and honored the emperor whose death in 1867 was followed by the accession of the Meiji emperor in 1868. The temple is situated on a hillside about a mile and a half south of the Nakano store. Twenty-five tombs of emperors, empresses, princes, and princesses are located at Sennyū-ji. Since the death of the Meiji emperor, however, members of the imperial family have been entombed elsewhere.
2. Intestinal parasites, once very common in Japan, are now quite rare. Chūhachi had another tapeworm episode on July 25–26.
3. Sliced raw fish, considered a nourishing delicacy.

JANUARY 31 *Monday*

It was a beautiful morning with a clear sky, but bitter cold. For the first time this winter, the wet towels hung out to dry overnight froze stiff, and the water in the wash basin turned icy in no time at all. My hands and feet felt numb while the cold wind whistled outside. It was an unusually cold day.

On this chilly day, my husband still had a low fever in the morning. His temperature dropped early in the afternoon, and just as I was feeling really happy, it went up again. But he seemed to feel well and was beginning to get bored. For lunch he ate rice gruel and a chilled mixture of milk and egg;[1] for supper, thinly sliced *sashimi* of sea bream and its soup stock with rice gruel. I was so relieved to see that it all seemed to have gone down safely without any trouble. After 11:00 P.M., when I took his temperature, it was slightly higher again, but he was able to sleep.

Since it was so cold today, I decided to make some ice. When I put some hot water in a metal pan and went to set it outside, I thought for a moment that my hands had turned to ice instead.

Note: Lunch: soup made with *sake* lees. Dinner: plain tofu soup. Evening snack: noodles.

1. Western style; the recipe is given in a separate note.

February 1 *Tuesday*

This is the first day of February. The people from our business branch-families came to pay their customary calls. The first to arrive was Mr. Yamamoto Matsu, and Mr. Ōkita Toyosaburō followed. The wife of the Eastside Doctor came over to join us.[1]

I am so happy that my husband seems much better today. Around eleven this morning, Mr. Matsumiya came by, saying that since he is out today to do some outdoor sketching, he dropped by to see him. How kind of him! He had lunch with us and left.

Today is the day to make the midwinter *o-kaki*.[2] After dinner we started by pounding steamed rice with mortar and mallet in a cleared area of the kitchen. This year we are going to make seven big square sheets for *o-kaki* and small round rice cakes. All together we used two *to* of rice, which includes a share for the Eastside family. A young man who used to work for Komatsuya[3] came to help us. He is very proud of his skill at swinging the mallet in perfect rhythm, especially in the presence of a lot of young women cheering him on, and we all had a good laugh and good time, so it went very fast. It was only 9:30 in the evening when we finished. While those who had worked were away at the public bath-house, we quickly made an evening snack of delicious *o-zenzai*[4] with the freshly made rice cakes.

Because it was a cold night with the wind howling outside, I decided it would be a good chance to make frozen tofu.[5] I took the tofu I bought for this purpose out onto the big roof, poured hot water over it, and left it there overnight. It was bitter cold. I thought my ears were going to freeze! I can hardly wait to see the result tomorrow.

Our family photographs, which we had taken on January 16, are ready.

Correspondence out: To Mrs. Shirakawa Omiki.
Note: Today's festive menu: miso soup, salad of grated radish and carrots, and broiled mackerel.[6]

1. Because the Eastside family is a Nakano branch-family it ought to have been represented by its head, Chūichirō. His wife Fusa has come in his stead.
2. Rice crackers. It is the midwinter cold season called *kan*.
3. A confectionery shop that also sells rice cakes.
4. See entry for January 22.
5. *Kōya-dōfu* or *shimi-dōfu*. Freezing coarsens the tofu, which then takes on a distinctive flavor when cooked in a mixture of soy sauce and sugar.
6. The family custom was to serve this same menu on the first day of each month.

FEBRUARY 2 *Wednesday*

As soon as I woke up this morning I thought about the tofu I left outside last night and hurried up to the roof in spite of the cold. It was frozen solid. In fact it was so thoroughly frozen and stuck to the board that pouring hot water over it did not help much to loosen it. I was finally able to dislodge it by pounding on it with a hammer for some time. I cooked it with *katsuo-dashi*[1] right away and served it to my husband for breakfast.

Contrary to my expectation of praise and appreciation, I got nothing but criticism. First of all, he didn't like the seasoning, and said that the frozen tofu had a strong odor that reminded him of dried tofu, and on and on. I was very disappointed, but recognized that I was at fault. I bought more tofu this morning and will try again tonight, in hopes that this time he will approve my efforts.

In the evening Mr. Suzuki Kichinosuke came over to talk about the forthcoming visit by Iwaya Sazanami-sensei of the Otogi Club on the fifth of this month. I know that they all have been waiting eagerly for this visit and realized that even I feel the same way.[2]

1. Broth seasoned with shaved dried bonito.
2. Obviously affected by their conversation, Makiko writes this and the next day's entries in the style used in children's storytelling.

FEBRUARY 3 *Thursday*

When I woke up this morning, the first thing I remembered was the tofu I left out last night. Without even putting away the bedding, I rushed to pay a visit to the tofu on the roof to see how it had turned out. It was beautiful! I soaked it in hot water first, then cooked it in soy sauce, *sake*, and sugar. It was perfect, and he liked it! My experiment was a success.

My husband had no fever today and seemed to feel much better. I hope and pray for his complete recovery, for which I cannot wait a day longer. My only regret is that I was so helpless that Mother had to do everything.

Today we had broiled salted salmon with seaweed soup. This evening we cut the fish heads into small pieces and pickled them in vinegar.[1] The Eastside family came over to help and took home their share.

Mr. Miyoshi[2] and Mr. Matsui dropped in on their way home from a meeting or a party at Yoshinoya[3] in Kiyomizu and stayed until past midnight. Mr. Yakushiji, who hasn't been seen here for a while, also came to see my husband, who has been staying home lately because of his illness. He brought a pound cake[4] for the patient.

1. This variety of pickled salmon, a popular winter food, is mixed with shredded radish and carrot to make a salad.

2. Unidentified.

3. A restaurant located just up the street in the Kiyomizu district where the famous Buddhist temple is located. See entry for January 18.

4. *Kasutera*, from *pão de Castella*, is a confection introduced into Japan by the Portuguese in the sixteenth century.

FEBRUARY 4 *Friday Clear*

Today being *Setsubun*,[1] everybody automatically adds a year to their age.

My husband has been feeling better gradually, and today he had a bath, which we prepared especially for this festive day.

Lunch for *Setsubun* was broiled sardines, radish salad with small dried fish, and miso soup. I roasted three-and-a-half pans of beans after lunch.

In the evening when the time to add a year of age arrived, the Eastside family came over to join us. We offered beans to our ancestors in the Buddhist altar first, then each ate as many beans as our age plus one. Thus we all gained a year according to the custom.

In the meantime in the kitchen the evening snacks of sushi and soup were being prepared for the occasion. Strips of dried gourd (*kanpyō*), *shiitake* mushrooms, *yuba*,[2] tiny dried fish, and eggs are cooked and added to the sushi rice. The soup, made with *mizuna* greens and chicken in a clear broth, is called "crane's soup." The amount of chicken was 200 *momme*.

More important to the staff than tonight's *Setsubun* observances seemed to be the *sake* we served them after the close of business for the day. Women always seem to be busy preparing meals whatever the occasion. Tomorrow we will spread out the square rice cakes on straw mats to dry, just as we did when we played poem-cards at New Year's.[3]

Mr. Amagasu[4] came to see my husband about something. He brought some eggs.

1. This festival occurs out of order in the annual round now that New Year's Day is observed on the Western calendar's January 1. Reckoned by the ancient solar calendar, *Setsubun* is the last day of the year and thus the eve of *Risshun*, the first day of spring and the first day of the new year as well. It is the occasion for exorcism and purification, marking the end of the old and beginning of the new. It is the custom to eat a number of roasted beans corresponding to one's age, plus one. Today the intent of this practice is said to be not to add a year to one's age, but to secure safe passage through the year that is just beginning. See entry for November 30.

2. Sheets of dried soybean milk much favored in Kyoto cuisine.

3. The thin rice cakes are about the same size as the playing cards, which are spread out face up on the tatami mats before the game begins.

4. Unidentified; he appears only once more, on March 28.

FEBRUARY 5 *Saturday Clear*

This is my happy day! My husband is completely recovered, so we could put away his bedding.

Since it is very cold, we decided to make a hot soup with a base of *sake* lees. In the afternoon a new kitchen maid arrived, sent by Otafukuya, the employment agency.

My father came to thank us for finding them such a good housekeeper, and we discussed my brother's coming back from Manchuria in March to get married. He asked me to sew a new kimono for him. There is a meeting of the Otogi Club tonight that we are going to attend, and I was feeling somewhat pressed for time, but he seemed to be enjoying himself and not a bit in a hurry to go home. He left at last, only because it was getting dark.

Since we had received some rice cakes from Yamanashi, we enjoyed them before taking off for the meeting. The women fixed their hair in a hurry while the men went on ahead. We[1] went with Morinosama[2] later, and when we arrived at the meeting hall, it was already filled. We listened to Sazanami-sensei tell one of his stories, which was entitled "An American Dog." It was very interesting. The meeting lasted until eight o'clock and when we got home it was 9:30. My husband and Hide-san came home after 11:30. He told us that the ticket sale for today's meeting brought in ¥70.

1. The women.
2. A friend of Kuniko's. See entry for January 15.

FEBRUARY 6 *Sunday Clear*

I truly had a good time last night, and I have the impression that Sazanami-sensei was very happy, too. In the afternoon my husband went with Mr. Suzuki to see him at the inn where he is staying. He didn't return until well after midnight. My husband said that since he had to attend a meeting of the Nijō Pharmacists' Cooperative,[1] he had dinner at Mr. Matsui's house, which is on the way. But there was more to the story, for he said that he was able to come home so early only because Mr. Tanaka had come to see him at the club while the meeting was still going on. Mr. Tanaka is indeed an interesting man, who apparently made a special trip to Nijō just for that. My husband brought back the portrait bust of Sazanami-sensei with him.[2] It is the clay model, not yet cast in plaster of Paris. I can see some resemblance, but it certainly does not look like what it cost—the price of the clay alone was ¥5!

1. *Nijō yakugyō kumiai*.
2. Apparently Mr. Tanaka delivered the bust of Sazanami-sensei to her husband at the club. Why this meant that her husband could come home early is unclear. Concerning the bust, see entries for January 14 and 29.

FEBRUARY 7 *Monday Clear*

I remembered that this is the memorial day of my grandmother in Nijō. Once again memories of her bring tears to my eyes.

The kimono merchant came yesterday to show me samples of material to be made up for my brother Manzō.[1] I thought it would be better if my father would also take a look at them, so I asked him to meet me at Nijō today. I went there early in the afternoon to confer with him and my father, but, alas, I had forgotten to telephone ahead and my father had already gone out. According to Oasa-han[2] he left with a visitor named Mr. Ikebe, who arrived this morning from Tokyo. Apparently he is a friend of my brother Manzō, and is on his way to Dairen, Manchuria. What a big mistake I made!

Since father hadn't telephoned me to say he would be going out with this gentleman, I assumed that he wouldn't be gone for long. I had already waited for three or four hours when the kimono dealer arrived. Since he could not stay, I had to ask him to leave the material with me. I waited till 9:00 P.M., but could wait no longer. I felt so guilty and foolish when I got home and realized that I accomplished nothing at all today. All at once I felt very tired.

Mr. Matsumiya arrived in the evening, smiling mysteriously. No wonder he was smiling! I soon discovered that he had found some oil paints, which they have been talking about for some time now, and brought them with him. I knew how anxious they all are to try oil painting, and sure enough, no sooner had they reached for the brushes than they were slapping paint all over the canvas.

1. Manzō's wedding day had been set for May 1. Had she lived, their mother would have selected the kimono material.

2. The recently hired housekeeper at Nijō.

FEBRUARY 8 *Tuesday Rain*

My husband had to go to a meeting of the *Tokusei-kai*[1] in the afternoon, but as soon as he returned in the late afternoon, he spread out his oil-painting materials and started right in. I was curious to see what he would paint, and the first one was a head of a dog, this being the Year of the Dog.[2] I was quite impressed by it, for it is very well done. However, it seems to me that oil painting is more difficult than watercolor. That may be only because I am trying to find a good excuse for him, but, after all, he has never even held long brushes like these and tried to paint with them before.

After dinner he started in again, spreading out canvas and paints—this time trying a larger and more ambitious painting of two children reading books. I can't say that it is better than Mr. Matsumiya's works,[3] but it's pretty good. I am so impressed with his ability to handle practically anything!

1. See entry for January 22.

2. One of the twelve animals of the Chinese zodiac, which the Japanese adopted very early in their history.

3. Matsumiya painted in the Japanese style, using *sumi* ink and watercolor.

FEBRUARY 9 *Wednesday Clear*

Mr. Suzuki came to see my husband about an incident at Shūdō Primary School where they are members of the school board. Apparently there is a dispute among the board members concerning some teachers who have been going to the red-light district. I was appalled and wondered how the principal could have let this happen! But I really must not say anything, for it might cause trouble—never, never!

Just as we were talking about him and Okuni-san, Mr. Matsui sent us lots of *sake* lees by one of his shop-boys. They are delicious![1]

At night my husband goes upstairs and turns into a painter nowadays. Today's subject was apples. He worked very hard and finished the painting after ten o'clock. He is getting better and better at it—the second one was better than the first, and the third better than the second. The apples look splendid, with a vase on the side, and the glow on the mahogany table looks so real. If he can paint so easily, why shouldn't I be able to? He makes me overconfident.

1. The Matsuis operated a *sake* brewery. Okuni-san was Makiko's husband's 18-year-old sister, whom Mr. Matsui wanted to marry.

FEBRUARY 10 *Thursday*

It has been a cold, blustery day with occasional snow flurries. Today is the *Hatsu-uma* festival,[1] and lots of people were out. It must have been a busy day at the Inari shrine in Fushimi with the street that leads to the shrine crowded with people, but I wonder what it was like to be out in this weather.

We had red-bean rice, tofu soup, chunks of tofu cooked in sauce thickened with arrowroot (*kuzu*), a green vegetable mixed in sauce made from a combination of tofu, white miso, and roasted white sesame seed.

Sent a box of three dried bonito,[2] which cost 85 *sen* each, to mark my husband's recovery to both Moriguchi and Yamada in return for their gifts of 50 eggs while he was ill. Also sent dried bonito to Mr. Yakushiji in return for the box of pound cake and 30 bananas that he had sent.

1. A major festival at the Fushimi Inari shrine, which is said to date from the eighth century.

2. *Katsuobushi* remains a popular all-purpose gift, as bonito flakes are used in all kinds of cooking, most notably as the base for soup stock.

FEBRUARY 11 *Friday Clear*

Today is the national holiday of *Kigensetsu*[1] when ceremonies are held at the schools. We also held a ceremony at home at 10:00 A.M.

My husband went to an art show at the Kūya temple in Teramachi with Mr. Suzuki, Shina-san, and Chūji-san. It is by a group of artists, including his friends Mr. Matsumiya Hōnen and Mr. Hirai Baisen.

Okuni-san came back home with two friends. One of them, Yasuda-sama, is unusually tall. I served them rice cake in sweet red-bean sauce for a snack. They left after four o'clock.

Since the store received a gift of cash from one of our customers, the employees decided to use it to have a sukiyaki dinner. We liked the idea of having beef tonight, so we prepared the sukiyaki and waited for my husband's return. However, he didn't come home for dinner, but instead ate at Mr. Matsui's place again, and got back around one o'clock in the morning. How kind of them to feed him so often![2]

He announced that he is inviting five guests to dinner tomorrow to celebrate his recovery. He said that he would like to serve them a soft-diet dinner. Since I had no idea what to serve, I had to consult with Mother about it.

Fusako-sama of the Eastside family went to visit her natal family in Takatsuki, Osaka, taking her two boys with her.

Correspondence in: Sister Tanii wrote to ask us to buy a set of dolls from the Ōki Doll Store for her daughter's first Girls' Day Festival.[3]

Note: Made a half-cask of turnip pickles, using 1.5 *shō* of salt. They ought to be ready to eat around May.

1. National Founding Day, the day selected by the Meiji government to mark the mythical founding of the Japanese state in 660 B.C.

2. The mildly sarcastic tone cannot be missed.

3. Although Makiko seems to be somewhat irritated by the request, it is hardly surprising that the Taniis made it. Kyoto has long been famous for the elegance of its dolls, the likes of which surely were not readily available in Kyushu, where the Taniis were living at the time.

FEBRUARY 12 *Saturday Clear*

My husband invited his friends for dinner tonight to celebrate his complete recovery. In the morning we conferred with him about the menu, which took a while, for we planned and replanned it many times. At last we came up with a good one: (1) soup and bread, (2) egg custard with sauce, (3) stew, (4) *sashimi*, and (5) chicken and tofu cooked together.

Mother and I went shopping in the morning, and I learned a lot from her about buying the ingredients. We started to cook in the afternoon, but unfortunately Mother did most of it, since I don't have much knowledge or experience in preparing these dishes. I wish I could have done more, and as usual, I felt grateful to her. Kept a separate note on how to prepare them.

In the late afternoon Mr. Matsui and Mr. Matsumiya came with Mr. Yakushiji. My husband joined them, and they all took off immediately to do some landscape painting in oils. While they were out, I was able to set up the parlor for the party, but felt increasingly uneasy as time for this unusual dinner approached. In the meantime, Mother was working busily in the kitchen.

Fusako-sama of the Eastside family returned home from Takatsuki and brought us some confections, red-bean glutinous rice (*o-kowa*),[1] and a chicken. We decided to cook the chicken while it's fresh, and added it to tonight's menu.

The four men came back, and Mr. Tanaka and Mr. Suzuki arrived for the party. It began with a speech by my husband, who told the guests that tonight's dinner would be made up entirely of items suitable for a soft diet, since this is a celebration of his recovery. He then introduced the menu and explained how the dishes were going to be served. The guests liked the idea and responded with great enthusiasm. They seemed to enjoy the meal very much.

After dinner there was a lively conversation that touched on all kinds of topics, and then, as I expected, the group painting began. Tonight the subject was a table lamp. Mr. Matsumiya and my husband carried on, saying such funny things that all of us laughed our heads off. All in all it was a huge success.

1. *O-kowa*, which differs from the ordinary red-bean rice called *seki-han*, is used mainly for presentation as a gift, for it keeps longer than *seki-han*. Soaking the rice in the bean juice overnight turns it pink.

February 13 *Sunday Clear*

My father called last night to ask me to come to Nijō this morning, since he has business to attend to later in the day. Mother kindly said, "Hurry up and go," so as soon as my husband got up I left without even tidying up the room. Feeling guilty for my selfishness, which causes so much trouble for my family, I asked myself why my mother had to die so young, causing me such pain. I push away the thought every time it arises, because I know I should not think about her in any way that makes me feel sad and angry. I arrived at Nijō before ten o'clock.

My father wanted to confer with me mainly about the arrangements for my brother's forthcoming wedding. We talked well into the afternoon, and just as I was feeling an urge to go home, my husband came in to say that he had to go to a meeting of the Nijō Pharmacists' Cooperative, so he stopped by. Father and I talked some more and it was four o'clock when I left. On the way home I did some shopping in Shijō. Just as I got home, large hailstones fell. My husband got back after ten o'clock.

My observation while I was at Nijō tells me that the housekeeper we hired recently seems to be working well, but that the young kitchen maid is not doing so well these days.

February 14 *Monday Clear*

Since there was not much to do around the house today, I felt I must work on my sewing. The kimono merchant came over in the afternoon about Manzō's and Eiko's kimono. I wish I didn't have to do all these things. Mother must be wondering how much more time I will need to finish them. I felt that I should apologize to her for taking so long.

Okuni-san returned home with a novel entitled *Yadorigi*,[1] which she borrowed from a friend. I look forward to reading it tonight.

Hide-san moved into a boardinghouse today. He left after dinner with all of his belongings. I told him that it must be inconvenient living in such a place, and asked him please to come back as often as he can, to which he replied, "No, I won't unless there is something specifically to attend to." I was impressed by his decisive, manly reply!

Mr. Yakushiji came to see my husband about the primary school, where I have heard there is some trouble.[2] He left about 10:00 P.M. I started to read the novel and was totally absorbed in it, when around midnight I realized that my husband had started to write a long letter to his sister Yae about the matter involving Mr. Matsui[3] and about the Girls' Day dolls. It took so long that when we went to bed it was exactly 2:30.

Correspondence out: Tanii Yae.

1. *The Parasite* by Tokutomi Roka was published in 1909. The novel is based on the autobiographical notes left by a young man, Ogasawara Zenpei, whose life was tragic. With the help of General Nogi, hero of the Russo-Japanese War, he realized his dream of becoming an army officer. The young lieutenant survived the war, but left the army after a disastrous love affair. He contracted tuberculosis, and when he learned that his condition was terminal, he put a bullet through his head at the age of 28. Tokutomi Roka had been acquainted with Ogasawara over a period of years and was so impressed by him that he agreed to write his life story, using the extensive notes that the young man had sent him. The book's title was inspired by Ogasawara's success in ingratiating himself with influential men, on whom he depended for protection and support for most of his short life. *Yadorigi* is a very long novel that was published soon after Tokutomi's best-seller, *Hototogisu* (The cuckoo). Because of his fame, *The Parasite* was widely read in Makiko's day, but today is considered a minor work.
2. See entry for February 9.
3. That is, Mr. Matsui's plan to marry Kuniko.

FEBRUARY 15 *Tuesday Clear*

Hide-san came home late this afternoon because he and my husband were going to the theater this evening, which is very unusual for Hide-san.

However, my husband had gone out in the afternoon on some business at the School of Pharmacy and had not got back yet. We thought he must have dropped by Mr. Matsui's home and probably was still there, only to find out that we were wrong. When we telephoned, they told us that my husband had gone somewhere with Mr. Yakushiji. Just as we were finishing our conversation, I heard a commotion in the front which, of course, was my husband returning. When we asked where he had been, he said that indeed he had stopped by Mr. Matsui's house, but that he had already gone out to a meeting somewhere, so he went on to Mr. Yakushiji's place, which is just on the other side of the same street, and found that Mr. Yakushiji was free. Together they went to see about buying a set of Girls' Day dolls for his sister's new baby daughter.

He had dinner in a hurry, and he and Hide-san went to the

Minami-za where they were to see a play called *Hototogisu*.[1] We all waited for their return so that we could hear about the play, which sounds very interesting. Apparently it is a tragedy and was performed in an unusual style. Both Mother and I couldn't help crying as we listened to the story, perhaps because they told it so skillfully.

1. The Minami-za, Kyoto's largest theater, is located on Shijō Avenue, only a short stroll from the Nakano store. As in Makiko's day, performances of a variety of genres are given there, but it is the only theater in Kyoto where kabuki is performed. The play *The Cuckoo* was based on Tokutomi Roka's novel; see note 1 to entry for February 14.

February 16 *Wednesday* *Clear*

There is nothing particularly interesting to write about today. My husband seems to be improving his oil-painting technique. Today he did a scene of two horses in a field. I thought that one of the handlers of the horses looked very real. I was very impressed!

February 17 *Thursday* *Rain*

We haven't had rain for a while, but it started in the late afternoon today.

We received a gift from the bride of Mr. Koyama, who is Hide-san's friend. It came in a fine lacquerware food box (*jūbako*) with a beautiful silk brocade cover bearing a design of the elderly couple of Takasago[1] woven into a red background. It must be very expensive. We promptly opened it and had some of its contents—delicious sweets made by Surugaya.[2] I telephoned Hide-san to tell him about it. We hope he will stop by tomorrow.

I think that the rain was caused by my husband getting up so unusually early this morning.[3]

1. A felicitous symbol of a long-lasting marriage.
2. A famous Kyoto confectionery on Sanjō Avenue that is still in operation.
3. There is a saying in Japan that a person's unusual behavior may bring rain. Makiko continues to exploit this conceit in subsequent entries.

February 18 *Friday* *Snow*

Mr. Matsui telephoned this morning to say that he is coming to visit us today. Indeed, he came in the afternoon, and Mr. Matsumiya

Food shops. (Asian Collection, Herbert F. Johnson Museum of Art, Cornell University)

Dried and salted fish shop. (Asian Collection, Herbert F. Johnson Museum of Art, Cornell University)

Minami-za theater, ca. 1914. (*Shashin shūsei*)

Gojō Bridge over the Kamo River, ca. 1914; the Keihan Railway terminal was located at the end of this bridge. (Kyoto Prefectural Archives)

and Mr. Hirai arrived a little later. They get along so well and seem to have a good time together just talking. Hide-san came and joined them. When dinnertime came, we served a simple meal of fish cake and mushroom soup thickened lightly with arrowroot and *kōya-dōfu*,[1] since we didn't have any good, fresh ingredients.

Mr. Matsui showed us a tea set he had purchased at Hiraoka Store[2] to take to Harada[3] in Osaka as a gift. It is a good one, and I found out that it cost ¥3.40. When he heard that the play that Hide-san and my husband saw the other day is very interesting, Mr. Matsui wanted to go see it, but changed his mind when he learned that it is closing after today's performance.

A shop-boy from Hiraoka's brought a basket of navel oranges, a gift from Mrs. Mutō,[4] who is visiting them.

My husband got up early again this morning, resulting in today's snow.

1. Frozen and dried tofu soaked in broth and cooked. See entry for February 1.
2. The ceramics store owned by a relative of the Nakanos. See Makiko's Social World, p. 47.
3. Unidentified.
4. A distant relative.

FEBRUARY 19 *Saturday Clear*

Mrs. Mutō and Mrs. Moriguchi[1] came to call.

There was a telephone call from my father about the kimono.

My husband went to Shūdō Primary School to attend a training session for those who will be teaching the ethics classes.[2] The principal was away because his wife is ill. Apparently the school is still in turmoil.

Today being the third Saturday of the month we had our monthly beef sukiyaki dinner.

Eiko came over about her kimono as my father had said she would this morning.

While I was supervising the cooking of dinner in the kitchen, my husband came home with a box containing a set of dolls, which he had bought for his sister's baby girl as requested. Naturally we had to see them right away, so opened the packages one by one and spread them out in the parlor. The room looked like a doll shop! They are adorable and look very elegant and authentic. I kept the price list that came with them.

Mother kindly suggested that I should walk back to Nijō with Eiko and Okuni-san so that the three of us could stop at the kimono shop on the way to see which of the patterns are suitable for Eiko. I really appreciated her suggestion. When I got back it was already ten o'clock.

Whenever I visit home in Nijō, whether in the daytime or at night, I cannot help but feel a strong sense of loneliness in the house. I think that the ultimate happiness is to have both parents at home and to know that family members enjoy each other.

Note: Since my husband got up early again it was supposed to rain, but it turned out to be a fine day.

1. The wife of the head store manager.
2. At this time courses in morals and ethics were just being introduced into the public school curriculum.

FEBRUARY 20 *Sunday Clear*

I was expecting a fine, clear day, but it turned out to be rather cloudy. My husband slept very late this morning, so it should have been a clear day, but it must be his rising so early recently that caused today's cloudiness.

Shortly before noon Mr. Suzuki came to see my husband regarding the school scandal again. Then Mr. Matsui Matabei[1] came, and the three talked intensely until they left just after noon. My husband showed me a vicious article in a scandal sheet that was very unfair to the school.

Mr. Murakami,[2] whom we haven't seen for a long time, came to call. Evidently he has been sick for some time and appears to have been weakened by his illness. He brought a gift of candied beans but did not stay long.

My husband went out to a meeting at Yūrin Primary School,[3] and then on to the alumni association meeting at the School of Pharmacy. Since he didn't come home for dinner, I assume that he must be eating at Mr. Matsui's house again.

1. A merchant who lived in their neighborhood, unrelated to Matsui Jisuke.
2. Head of an old business branch-family.
3. Unidentified.

February 21 *Monday Clear*

Snow flurries in the morning. I wonder how long we will have to wait before it gets warm again. I had to do the household accounts today because I couldn't do them last night, and it took me the whole morning.

It is my mother's monthly memorial day. My father called to say that he wants to send a gift to the Taniis for their daughter's first Girls' Day celebration. I arranged to have two doll-size *tansu* (chest of drawers) and a *nagamochi* (chest) from him to be added to her doll set. The Eastside family wanted to add a set of ten small hand-painted dishes, so I packed everything up and shipped it off by rail, which cost 60 *sen*. It's amazing how time flies. I can't believe that Toshiko-chan is already celebrating her first Girls' Day! I wish she were mine!

February 28 will be my mother's 100th-day memorial service,[1] but since it falls on the busy last day of the month when all of the accounting is done, my father wants to observe it on the 24th instead. He asked me to come and help him prepare for the service.

My husband suddenly had to go out after six o'clock to attend a gathering at the Nijō Club for the sake of the School of Pharmacy. I read the novel *Yadorigi* every night. It is very interesting.

1. The next major Buddhist memorial service after the 49th day ceremony, marking the further transition of the spirit of the dead from this world to the next.

February 22 *Tuesday Clear*

This morning my father telephoned to say that my mother's memorial service has been scheduled for ten o'clock on the morning of the 24th, and we are invited, of course. He asked me to notify the Eastside family as well.

I finished sewing the kimono for all the store clerks and shop-boys today. Although I had been planning to start sewing Manzō's kimono as soon as I finished these, I realized that it would not be a good idea to start the task tomorrow, since my father asked me to come and help out. He said that even if I could come only in the afternoon it would be a great help since Matsu[1] is away. If I were to tell Mother this, I know that she would urge me to go in the morning, so my plan to start sewing the kimono would not work in any event. Having thought about all this I decided on my own to go to Nijō in the morning of the 24th.

Correspondence out: Letter to the Taniis, somewhat sarcastic in tone.[2]

1. A maid who worked for her father.
2. Sarcastic probably because they had asked for help in buying an expensive set of Girls' Day dolls.

FEBRUARY 23 *Wednesday Clear*

I was determined to finish sewing a lined jacket today and had been working on it hard since this morning, when about three o'clock my sister Eiko telephoned and pleaded, "I know this will be terribly inconvenient for you, but could you come and help me?" I was afraid that this might happen, but what can I do? I told Mother and my husband and, of course, once again, they urged me to go at once. I rushed to change my kimono and called a *rikisha.*

It was the first time I have ever ridden in a *rikisha* with rubber tires. It rides so smoothly and comfortably! Every time we encountered pedestrians, the driver sounded his horn to warn them, which made them turn their heads to look up at me. Although I was very embarrassed every time this happened, I tried to keep my composure and look cool, since I was riding a rubber-tired *rikisha.* It was all very trying. I started to work right away when I arrived at Nijō.

I later learned that Mr. Kimura[1] came to see my husband about the school while I was away and that after he left, my husband started another of his projects—evidently he has finished repapering all the doors[2] in the music room. Because I wasn't there, Mother had to help him, and I heard that it was past midnight when they finished. Once again, I felt sorry that I had to take off like this, causing inconvenience for everyone.

1. A friend of Chūhachi's who lived nearby.
2. The sliding doors called *fusuma* are covered with decorative paper.

FEBRUARY 24 *Thursday Clear*

I spent all day at Nijō. First thing in the morning I started to clean the house and was surprised by all the dust. The service was scheduled for ten o'clock, so I had to rush. At 9:30 I realized that I had only 30 minutes to comb my hair and change. The Buddhist priest from our temple arrived, and my husband came, too. I had to cut short putting on my makeup, for the priest had already begun to chant the sutras.

We all sat in front of the altar and listened to the sutras. Fusako-sama of the Eastside family was there, but Elder Sister Kōshima, who is sick in bed, could not come. Uncle Amano could not make it either because of other commitments. We had also notified the neighbors. The service ended just after eleven o'clock, and we served lunch afterwards. The guests stayed until about three.

Uta-sama[1] came to see me. We talked a while and then went over to her house to see what she is preparing for her forthcoming wedding. She showed me all the kimono and a set of furniture, but said that I should come again next month because not everything is ready yet.

We had dinner at Nijō, and I returned home with my husband. We talked about Kuniko-san's coming marriage to Mr. Matsui until two in the morning without noticing the time.

1. Her friend Kakemi Uta.

FEBRUARY 25 *Friday Clear*

It is the monthly Tenjin outdoor market at Kitano Tenman-gū[1] today, and many people must have gone to the shrine.

Somehow we talk a lot about weddings and brides these days. Because I missed my bath yesterday, I went over to the Eastside family and had one there.[2] My husband, having heard that one can visit England for ¥1,000, seems to feel the urge to go there, but of course, it is impossible.

Today being accounting day,[3] we worked in the evening and, contrary to my expectation that it would take a long time, I was amazed how fast it went! It may be because I was so sleepy. My hands and legs felt like those of a stuffed doll. Since it was only eleven at night when we finished, my husband suddenly had an urge to start a project, as usual. This time he installed the hinges for the new Western-style door in the music room to replace the old one. It looks like we are gradually converting the room to the modern style.

1. See entry for January 25.
2. The Nakanos and the Eastside family prepared the bath on alternate days, so that both families could bathe every day at half the expense.
3. Although she calls February 25 the accounting day, she writes on February 28 that they settled the accounts then.

February 26 *Saturday* *Rain*

It has not rained for a while, but it did today.

Today is grandfather Chūhachi V's monthly memorial day.

Started sewing Manzō's kimono.

We received a fan and the program of the *kyōgen* performance from Shigeyama Sengorō[1] to commemorate the 25th anniversary of his grandfather's death.[2] Looking at the program I found many interesting plays listed.

Recently my husband has been painting Mother's portrait in oil. He has been working hard at it every day, adding more layers of paint, and it gradually has been taking the form of a face. He has finished it at last and it does resemble her a little.

We have been discussing Kuniko's marriage a lot lately, but the time has come to complete the arrangements for it, mainly because there has been an urgent request for our response on this matter from Mr. Suzuki.[3] After everyone had gone to bed, Mother, my husband, and I had a discussion about Kuniko's marriage.

I have developed a habit of reading novels every night.

1. A noted *kyōgen* performer whom Chūhachi V had patronized. *Kyōgen* performers have roles in some *nō* plays and provide the comic interludes between performances of the *nō* drama. The Shigeyama troupe is still performing today.
2. One of the periodic Buddhist memorial days.
3. Acting as go-between in the preliminary stage of the marriage negotiations.

February 27 *Sunday* *Clear*

Even though the end of February is approaching, it is still very cold.

Nothing in particular happened today, except that my father came to give me money to buy various things for my brother Manzō, including some kimono. The bill for the kimono alone came to ¥103.58 and five *rin*. It is dreadfully expensive to buy material for even one or two kimono these days![1]

1. This price probably includes the kimono for Eiko and Senzō as well.

February 28 *Monday* *Clear*

Today is my mother's 100th memorial day but I didn't go to Nijō because the memorial service was held last week on the 24th.

It being the end of February, a lot of bill collectors came one after another. Even though it is not my responsibility,[1] I was very pleased that both the store and household accounting went so well, leaving no loose ends. As is our custom we ate buckwheat noodles (*soba*) after we finished settling the accounts.

I cannot believe how time flies! Here we are, February is ending and we are about to greet March! Sometimes I feel like we are running all the time.

1. That is to say, she has no direct role in settling the store accounts, and her husband's mother probably still bears primary responsibility for the household accounts. It is likely that Makiko was being trained by her mother-in-law to take over that responsibility, which ordinarily would be in the hands of the wife of the household head. See entry for February 21.

MARCH 1 *Tuesday Clear*

How long will this cold weather last? Who said that March is the month when plum blossoms appear? In fact, there were occasional snow flurries in the air today. It is disgusting.

The customary visits on the first day of the month were made this morning by Mr. Yamamoto Matsu and Mr. Ōkita Toyosaburō as well as the Eastside family. Menu: broiled fresh yellowtail, miso soup, radish salad, and red-bean rice (*seki-han*).[1]

Mrs. Hiraoka Okoma came to call and told us that since tomorrow is an auspicious day, they will hold the wedding of Oharu-sama and Shūshichi,[2] and on the fifth, the wedding of Eishichi[3] and a former housemaid will take place. It sounds like this is a happy time for them. She is a wonderful conversationalist and a good listener, so we thoroughly enjoyed her visit. All our callers left before noon.

In the afternoon Mr. Suzuki came about Kuniko's and Mr. Matsui's marriage. He said that since this is an auspicious day we should make some decisions, such as accepting the betrothal gift[4] on the third of this month, and holding the wedding in April. My husband is not happy, for this is too much of a rush.

1. The standard menu served on the first of every month when the business branch-families come to pay their respects. See Introduction.

2. Shūshichi was one of their store clerks. This union will create a branch-family (*bunke*).

3. Another store clerk, who will be established as a business branch-family (*bekke*) as a result of his marriage. For a discussion of branch-families, see Makiko's Social World.

4. *Yuinō*, presented by the groom's family to the bride's.

March 2 *Wednesday*

Mr. Suzuki telephoned this morning to apologize for his hastiness yesterday and to cancel the dates he had proposed. He suggested that we deal directly with the other party because it causes misunderstanding when you talk through a go-between.[1] Since that is exactly what we want to do, we discussed the matter, and as a result came to an agreement to present the betrothal gift on March 27 and hold the wedding on October 24.

We talked until after lunch, but then my husband had to go to a funeral. He went on from there to the Shūdō Primary School on some business, but came home for dinner. After dinner he left again, this time to go to the Pharmacists' Club in Nijō, but apparently he dropped in at Mr. Matsui's house on his way. Later we received a telephone call from the club asking for my husband, so I called Mr. Matsui's house and found out that indeed he was still there. Thinking how relaxed he must be feeling, I nevertheless asked them to give him my message that the Nijō Club had called and that he was to go there at once.

1. I found this remark quite surprising. I had always thought, and most Japanese will tell you, that go-betweens are so widely employed precisely in order to avoid misunderstandings between the two parties to almost any kind of arrangement. See entry for March 23.

March 3 *Thursday* *Clear*

Today is the official Girls' Day, but in the Nakano household we celebrate it a month later on April 3, according to the old calendar.[1] So all we did was hang a scroll with a painting of the pair of dolls in the *tokonoma*.[2] I did bring out my dolls, however, because I thought it would be nice to offer them sweet mugwort[3] dumplings.

We made *takuan* pickles[4] today since it was a good day to get help from the shop-boys. Mother said that normally we would make this variety of pickle earlier in the year, when the days are really cold, but that this winter's persistent cold weather has made it possible to put it off until now. Actually I didn't help, but stayed home while Mother went over to the Eastside family's house where our shared pickle storage room is, and supervised the whole operation by herself. I felt rather bad about that. The amount of salt used for two big kegs of radishes is three *shō* each, totaling six *shō*, and one *to* of rice bran.

1. The entry for April 3 contains a full accounting of the festival as it was observed by the Nakanos. I have called it Girls' Day throughout the diary in order to avoid the awkwardness of such expressions as "the Dolls' Day dolls" and "the dolls for the Dolls' Day."

2. The alcove in the parlor in which a hanging scroll and a flower arrangement are displayed.

3. *Yomogi*, a fragrant wild grass that appears early in the spring.

4. *Takuan* pickles are made from *daikon*, a long winter radish.

MARCH 4 *Friday* *Clear*

There were no incidents today. However, two things are always on my mind these days: One is a letter that should come from the Taniis, acknowledging receipt of the box containing the dolls and other gifts. The other is a reply to my letter from my brother in Dairen, Manchuria.

The principal of Fuyū Primary School was visiting Mr. Matsui Matabei, so Mr. Kimura and my husband went to see him concerning the troubles at Shūdō Primary School.[1] He came home around midnight and told me about the meeting. Although it seems to be a very complicated story, apparently the principal will be transferred to Taipei, Taiwan, as a result of the scandals for which he has to take responsibility.

1. The Fuyū Primary School has not been identified. For the troubles at Shūdō Primary School, see entries for February 9 and 20.

MARCH 5 *Saturday* *Snow*

We woke up to a beautiful silvery world of snow this morning! I stepped outside at once to discover the snow is about an inch-and-a-half deep. After everyone had gone to school, I made snow balls and ate them. I had heard that spring snow is very light and fluffy, and so it is.

As I was thinking that it would be nice to go somewhere for snow viewing on a day like this, and not just look out into the garden all day, the extreme cold temperature made me hesitate. But then the Eastside family sent word that we should come and view snow-covered Kyoto from their third-floor room that has been shut up, but is open today especially for this purpose.[1] Mother and I went over immediately and enjoyed the magnificent view of the whole snow-covered city. It was beautiful everywhere one looked; Higashiyama[2] especially looked like a *sumi* ink painting. I must say that it was far superior to garden viewing. We also enjoyed the tea and cakes they served us.

Mr. Suzuki came to see my husband regarding the scandal at the school.

Since my husband is going to see a *kyōgen* performance by Shigeyama Sengorō tomorrow, we placed an order with the shop for several different kinds of sushi today and asked to have them put in our lacquerware lunch box with the peony design. It cost ¥1.25.

We were busy tonight doing the accounts.

Correspondence in: A letter from Taniis saying that the dolls haven't arrived yet. We made urgent inquiries about the matter at the shipping agency.

1. The Eastside family's house did not have a full third story; a small room had been added over one part of the second floor. In Japan in 1910 dwellings of more than two stories were rare.

2. The "eastern hills," still one of the most beautiful areas of the city and a favorite place for strolling in contemporary Kyoto, are filled with temples, shrines, tea shops, restaurants, and other places of interest.

March 6 *Sunday Clear*

There were snow flurries again this morning, and it is still cold.

My husband telephoned Mr. Suzuki and Mr. Matsui in the morning about today's schedule and got ready in a hurry when he found out that the *kyōgen* performances start at ten o'clock. He went there with Mr. Suzuki in a two-passenger *rikisha*. He arrived in good time before the performances started. Someone named Fujiki-sensei joined them at the theater, which was already packed. The plays were all very amusing, and apparently the costumes were elegant. The performances ended at 11:00 P.M.

The first meeting of a Western-style cooking class at Mr. Matsumiya's house[1] was held today, and my husband was going there to have a dinner made up of dishes the class had prepared, but he changed his plan and had the food sent to Mr. Matsui's place. He came home around one o'clock in the morning, having enjoyed the meal greatly. I would like to attend the class next week, but it seems that the number of places is limited. We'll see.

Correspondence in: My brother in Dairen wrote to say that he hasn't decided when to return home to get married.

Note: The *kyōgen* theater cost ¥2 per booth; we reserved two booths for five people.

1. The father of Matsumiya Hōnen and a retired school principal.

MARCH 7 *Monday Clear*

My husband had to go to a meeting of the Inari shrine parishioners scheduled for nine o'clock this morning, but because he had to wait for Mr. Moriguchi to come to work,[1] he was unable to leave the house until about two in the afternoon.

A shop-boy sent by Mr. Matsui returned our lacquerware lunch box that they took to the *kyōgen* theater yesterday.

I was expecting my husband for dinner, but received a telephone message from Mr. Matsui saying he will eat there. As I suspected, he came home very late, about half past two in the morning. It turned out that Mr. Matsui invited all the teachers from the school in order to serve his guests new *sake*,[2] so he and Mr. Matsumiya joined the party as well.

When the teachers started to play *go*,[3] their favorite game, it seems that my husband and Mr. Matsumiya went over to Mr. Yakushiji's place in back of Mr. Matsui's house to play the organ. The teachers did not leave until after ten o'clock, when he returned to Mr. Matsui's house to conduct some business with him, and thus got home late.

1. This must have been highly unusual behavior for a store manager.
2. He invited the teachers because he is a member of the school board and served *sake* brewed by his family.
3. The Japanese board-game that is often compared to chess.

MARCH 8 *Tuesday Clear*

I decided to go to Nijō today to get the material for the lining for the kimono I am making, in spite of the cold I have had for the last few days. Left home around ten, had lunch at Nijō, and visited the Kōshimas after that. I found everyone well and brought Fumiko back with me to Nijō.

On the way I thought that it was a good chance to visit another friend in the neighborhood and dropped in to see Hanako-sama. She looked awfully thin and weak. I found out that she not only has lost her baby but also is sick—I felt very sorry for her. I didn't stay long, since I had Fumiko with me.

Fumiko's mother came to get her, so we resumed our conversation. Fumiko was so happy and got so excited in the presence of all these adults that she was bouncing around, but finally fell asleep from exhaustion. I decided to go home to Gojō, but they decided to stay the night at Nijō.

MARCH 9 *Wednesday* *Clear*

It was clear again this morning, but started to cloud up in the afternoon. A messenger from Mr. Kimura came this morning, and my husband left home to talk about matters at the school again. He came home briefly just before noon, but left again to go to a meeting of Inari shrine parishioners. While he was out, Mr. Matsui telephoned to say he may come to see my husband tonight.

Mr. Matsumiya stopped by late in the afternoon on his way home from outdoor sketching in Fushimi, but didn't stay long, for he is very busy lately. Mr. Tanaka also came, but left at once.

Mr. Matsui came in the evening, just as he said he would this morning. He did not seem to have anything in particular in mind, and talked only about buying land or making money and stayed until one o'clock in the morning. As always, he is really a happy-go-lucky fellow!

MARCH 10 *Thursday* *Rain*

The weather has been really unsettled these days. It started out as a nice day this morning but began to rain in the evening.

A Buddhist priest from Hōtoku-ji[1] came around 8:00 P.M. and stayed until ten. After that a woman named Hayashi Teru[2] came to the store. She seemed very strange, complaining to the clerks and shouting at this late hour, but she left after a while, still talking up a storm. I found out that she is indeed a little mad.

1. The connection of the Nakano family to this temple is unclear. The priest, who visits again on March 23, may be the same person who came earlier to seek Chūhachi's advice about opening a pharmacy.

2. The wife of one of the old business branch-families, whom Makiko obviously had never met before. See entry for January 7.

MARCH 11 *Friday Cloudy*

My husband went to another meeting of Inari shrine parishioners in the afternoon and said that he will have dinner at Ningyō-tei restaurant tonight. While he was out, Mr. Matsui called to give me a message from Mr. Matsumiya, which is an invitation to attend the Western-style cooking class tomorrow at their house. He said that they are expecting me and added that Mr. Matsumiya had said especially, "Please do come." I replied that I was happy to accept, but on second thought felt nervous, thinking, "Will I really be able to learn? Will I be able to face all those people?" But after reporting the conversation to Mother, who urged me to attend, I finally made up my mind to go.

As I suspected, my husband had gone to Mr. Matsui's place after the dinner party. When he came home, he was bragging about a painting of a mountain he had just done in an hour or so. I shouldn't tell anyone about his boasting!

Mrs. Hayashi Teru came to see Mother again.

MARCH 12 *Saturday*[1] *Snow*

It has been a cold day, snowing off and on. This is the day I attended my first lesson in Western-style cooking. Although Mr. Matsui kindly phoned yesterday to tell me that I am invited to join the class, I could not help feeling ambivalent about it, which I thought is unlike me. However, off I went with Okuni-san to the noon lesson.

When we arrived at the house, I bravely called out, "Hello! Is anyone here?" and Mr. Matsumiya's father came to the door. We found out that five people had arrived already and were waiting for the class to begin. The teacher is Mr. Tanigawa, who is the head chef at the Miyako Hotel. He is a small bald man and looks kind and rather gentle. We began around two and finished around five o'clock. We made four dishes, and I made notes about them in a separate notebook.

Mr. Matsui and Mr. Suzuki joined us and showed us how these dishes are supposed to be served and eaten. My husband was also invited but declined, saying that he has another engagement, but I know the real reason is that he has been going out too frequently these days and felt he should not accept the invitation.

After class, everyone was given the food they had prepared to take home. It was not easy to carry because the streets were so muddy and slippery from the melting snow, and we had to be very careful not to spill anything on the way.

1. See next entry.

March 13 *Sunday*

I made a mistake and skipped the Saturday entry.

March 14 *Monday Clear*

The well at the Eastside family's is drying up, so that their maids have had to carry water from our well every day. I wonder how long this inconvenience will last!

The light wool *hakama*[1] we had ordered for my husband to wear to the Inari shrine parishioners' meeting today have not been delivered. They had promised that they would be ready in time, so I suppose they just couldn't do it.

1. Skirt-like trousers worn over kimono on formal occasions.

March 15 *Tuesday Clear*

I had a telephone message this morning from Nijō saying that I should come to look at some very reasonably priced *obi*[1] at Kakemi Uta-sama's, so I went over in the afternoon. Indeed they are quite inexpensive; those which normally are priced at ¥40 were reduced to ¥28. I promptly asked if we could have one,[2] but it was too late. Apparently they have all been sold, but the dealer promised to let me know when more come in. What a pity!

I came back home right away, since I knew that Mr. Matsui might pay us a visit tonight, but as it turned out, he couldn't make it because he had to attend some meeting.

We had sukiyaki for dinner, using the gift of beef we received today from Mr. Moriguchi to celebrate his recovery from illness.

A lot of our visitors lately are schoolteachers. A gentleman named Ōshima[3] came today and would not leave when dinnertime came, so we had to serve him.

It started to rain early in the evening.

1. Kimono sash.
2. Makiko was helping find appropriate *obi* for Kuniko's trousseau. A young

woman from a family like the Nakanos was expected to take with her substantial numbers of kimono, *obi*, and accessories when she married.

3. Unidentified.

March 16 *Wednesday Clear*

A nice day again. About four o'clock in the afternoon Mashimo-sensei[1] came to visit. It seems that he is going to be the new principal of Shūdō Primary School. I have never met him before. He seems quiet and reserved. Immediately after dinner he left with Mr. Suzuki.[2]

Soon after, Mr. Matsui and Mr. Matsumiya arrived. While they talked about art and painting, my husband drew a sketch for a portrait of his father. I knew that he was dying to paint it in color, but, alas, it was nighttime and too dark, so he had to wait until tomorrow.

They talked and talked, and once we heard someone snoring loudly in the next room. Apparently I fell asleep, too, and had a nice snooze, probably lulled by the snoring. When the clock struck one at last, Mr. Matsumiya suggested that we call it a day, and they all left.

1. Writer and poet; see Makiko's Social World.
2. Suzuki Kichinosuke was a member of the school board.

March 17 *Thursday Clear*

Tomorrow is the vernal equinox. I wonder how long this cold weather will continue!

Mr. Kimura of Sakura-machi[1] came to tell my husband that the school principal has received official notice of his transfer to Taiwan and will leave tomorrow morning by the 7:15 train. So it's been settled at last!

Just before noon the principal came to say his official good-bye. He looked grave and very unhappy to me. There was a farewell party for him at Harisei restaurant at seven o'clock tonight. I heard that it was really some party! Mr. Suzuki and the principal got into a long, violent argument, which was very amusing at times, and the affair lasted until midnight, much later than I had expected. So we won at last, and the principal lost!

Note: The portrait of his father that my husband has been working at finally got some paint applied to it today and is beginning to look like an oil painting.

1. A nearby neighborhood.

March 18 *Friday Clear*

Today is the beginning of the vernal equinox.[1] It was a beautiful day and there were lots of people out walking.

Mr. Matsui came early in the afternoon and invited my husband to take a stroll in Higashiyama since it was such fine weather. They went on to the study-meeting of the fairy-tales group[2] that started at three o'clock at Yūrin Primary School.

Although my husband got up very early this morning—at 6:30—in order to see off the former principal at the railway station, we had a beautiful day. Just after three o'clock, while my husband was out, Mashimo-sensei came to pay a visit in his capacity as the newly appointed principal.

My husband came home later with Mr. Matsui, with whom he had done some shopping. At first they did not show me what they had brought back, but I found out that they had bought some handcrafted dolls (*kimekomi ningyō*) made with cloth-covered wooden forms. There were three dolls, which made it difficult to divide up the purchase. They had quite a time figuring out how to do it and even considered bidding on them, but after more than two hours they settled on a solution. Mr. Matsui got two of the dolls and my husband got one. I was surprised by the price they paid—¥2.65 for the three. Mr. Matsui went home early, which is very unusual for him. All in all, it was great fun and we had a good laugh.

Note: My husband's father's portrait is completed, but his eyes do not look right. Alas, this means that they will have to be redone!

1. *Shunbun.* During the week-long observance of the equinox it is the custom to go to the temple and clean the family graves there. Special offerings are made to the ancestral spirits at the household's domestic altar.

2. Those who formed this group must have been inspired by the Otogi Club movement. See Makiko's Social World.

March 19 *Saturday Rain*

Unlike yesterday, today is dark and gloomy.

We called Hide-san at his boardinghouse this morning to let him know about the regular *nō* performance by the Kongō school[1] today, which my husband plans to attend. Mother decided to go with them when she discovered that one of the plays is none other than everyone's favorite, *Ataka*.[2]

They left right after dinner, since the performance starts at five o'clock. There were six of them tonight—Mr. Matsumiya, Fujiki-sensei, Mr. Matsui, and three from our household. The streets were wet and muddy, but it cleared up and the moon was gorgeous. They came home after eleven o'clock and said that they thoroughly enjoyed the plays. Hide-san is staying for the night. Tomorrow is already the day for the cooking class!

1. One of the five schools of *nō*.
2. *Ataka* recounts the flight of the twelfth century hero Yoshitsune and his faithful retainer Benkei from the capital, seeking to escape death at the hands of Yoshitsune's brother Yoritomo. Ataka is the name of a barrier station through which they must pass. It may fairly be said that *Ataka* is still "everyone's favorite" in both the original *nō* and later kabuki version, *Kanjinchō* (The subscription list). The play gains particular poignancy from the audience's knowledge that in the end Yoshitsune, Benkei, and all their men died at the hands of Yoritomo's forces. Like many of Japan's great heroes, Yoshitsune's failure does not diminish the high regard in which he is held. For further detail on these and dramas mentioned later, see Muraoka and Yoshikoshi; Nippon Gakujutsu Shinkōkai. See entry for July 28, when Makiko attends a performance by geisha of a version of *Kanjinchō*.

MARCH 20 *Sunday Clear*

It looked as though it was going to rain in the morning, but it turned out to be a nice day.

Without warning, Kurushima-sensei telephoned this morning to say that he is in Kyoto to attend a meeting of members of the Around-the-World Travel or something like that, and is staying at Sawabun,[1] and would like to come out in the afternoon after the party. Since I was going to the cooking class, I was hoping that he would come late.

The morning went fast. I took a bath and fixed my hair and face, and when I finished dressing and left home it was a little before one o'clock. The cooking teacher came after I arrived at Mr. Matsumiya's house. The menu sounded complicated, but he showed us how to prepare the dishes, and the dinner was ready around five o'clock. There were many guests today—some teachers from Dōda Primary School, Mr. Suzuki Minoru,[2] Mr. Matsui, and my husband among them. The food was carried to the table and served. I was assigned to be a "boy,"[3] but I was not competent at all in this unaccustomed role, and it was almost comical at times. The whole thing was quite difficult for me, but I survived!

Shortly after I came home around eight o'clock, Kurushima-sensei came over, but my husband had already left to attend the class reunions of both the School of Pharmacy and Shūdō Primary School tonight. Since my husband was not home, *sensei* said that he will call again tomorrow and left without coming into the house.

1. A restaurant and inn. It is still in operation.

2. Unidentified.

3. Waiters and waitresses were called "boy" without respect to gender until the 1930's.

March 21 *Monday Clear*

Today is the middle day of the vernal equinox, and my mother's monthly memorial day.

My husband was planning to pay a visit to Kurushima-sensei today, but just as he was inquiring on the phone if he was at the inn, Kurushima-sensei himself arrived. They talked a while and went out to take a walk around Kiyomizu temple. Apparently they stopped by to see Mr. Imose[1] and Mr. Tanaka, and had lunch at Hiranoya[2] in Maruyama Park. My husband had to part with him there in order to take the leading role in our neighborhood association's *segaki-e*[3] service, since he is the representative this year.

Kurushima-sensei returned to our house around two o'clock, and then Mr. Tanaka arrived. We sent a shop-boy to call my husband back so the three could talk until Kurushima-sensei had to leave for Kobe.

It was only three o'clock when he left, so I went shopping with Okuni-san as I had planned. I bought two wedding gifts for my friends in Nijō: a summer shawl for Kakemi Uta-sama, and a pair of gloves for Torii Yasuko-sama.

Note: One of the kitchen maids took the day off and went home.

1. Unidentified.

2. A restaurant noted for a Kyoto specialty called *imobō*, dried cod cooked with taro. It is another of the eating places mentioned in the diary that still carries on business in the same location.

3. A rite in which the ancestral spirits and wandering ghosts are fed during the vernal equinox. This one was held for the dead of the neighborhood.

MARCH 22 *Tuesday Rain*

It rained again. If the weather had been good, I was planning to go to Nijō today to take the kimono that I had finished, and the wedding gifts to my friends. Just as I decided to postpone my visit, Kakemi Uta-sama telephoned to tell me to come and see the *obi* that I was interested in the other day, which are available once again. The maid who took the day off hadn't returned, and I was reluctant to leave but finally decided to go.

I was glad that I went to see the *obi*, for they are all of excellent quality and design. They let me take some home to show to my family. I carried them in my arms and got home around eight o'clock. I also took the gift to Torii Yasuko-sama, whose wedding will probably take place on the 27th of this month, I was told. There are so many weddings planned this year that there will be many happy people.

The *obi* were a great hit! They are all so reasonably priced that everyone in the family thought they were a wonderful buy. However, we finally decided on a summer one, a brocade one, and two satin ones. Fusako-sama of the Eastside family also bought one. I especially fell in love with the one with the pink flowers—it is elegant, and I know that it will get everyone's attention!

MARCH 23 *Wednesday Rain*

It is still raining. I spread out the *obi* I brought home last night and looked at them again. No matter how many times you examine them, they are still incredibly fine. We gathered up those we did not select and sent them back by a shop-boy along with the payment for those we kept. I understand that the money will go directly to the weavers in Nishijin,[1] skipping the kimono dealers, which is why the prices are low.

In the evening my husband received a call from Mr. Suzuki to come to their place, since Mashimo-sensei is visiting them. While he was gone, the Buddhist priest from Hōtoku-ji came to see him.[2]

Since this is an auspicious day, Mr. Hiraoka came to talk about Okuni-san's wedding,[3] and mentioned that at last the gardener had come today. They had put him off, for Mrs. Hiraoka has been sick in bed and didn't want to be bothered by the odor of the fertilizer[4] they use.

My husband finished the portrait of his father he has been working on. It looks very good, and that makes me want to try painting myself. He has started on another one—this time a boat being built.

1. A district in Kyoto known for its fine silk brocades.
2. See entry for March 10.
3. Mr. Hiraoka was the official go-between now representing the Nakano family. Mr. Suzuki, who initiated the marriage arrangements, had withdrawn; see entry for March 2. The Matsui family was officially represented by Mr. Kataoka. It was the practice in Kyoto merchant houses of the period that there be two go-betweens, one for each party. Today, most marriages that utilize the services of a go-between have only one, who deals with both families. At the wedding ceremony itself, the actual go-between is often replaced by a formal one, usually a middle-aged or older married couple of some social standing, such as a teacher or university professor, a company president, a high-ranking bureaucrat, or a politician.
4. Probably night soil.

March 24 *Thursday Clear*

It was a beautiful day. It would have been wonderful to spend a day like this outdoors walking around just to enjoy the sunshine and feel free. Unfortunately, I didn't go anywhere, but spent the whole time just looking at the sky from time to time. Since it is the last day of the vernal equinox, I can imagine how crowded it must have been at the Hongan-ji main temple.

While my husband was out attending the neighborhood association meeting this evening, Mr. Matsumiya came with Mr. Hirai and gave us tickets for an art exhibit.[1] Although I told them that I would send someone to call my husband out of the meeting, they insisted that it wouldn't be necessary and left at once. Then my husband came home.

We received some Chinese cabbages[2] from Nijō, which were brought back from Manchuria by Dr. Keimatsu and Mr. Kakemi. We also got some lightly salted dried flounder from Nijō, which were sent by the Nakajima family in Wakasa,[3] whose daughter is to marry my brother.

Oshina-san[4] left home at four this morning in order to take the five o'clock train to Nagoya, where she will spend the night.

1. As artists, they probably had free admission tickets to pass out to friends.
2. Now very common, Chinese cabbage apparently was still a rare vegetable in Japan at this time.
3. North of Kyoto on the Japan Sea coast.
4. Nakano Shinako, who was going on a school trip.

Nakano Mine ("Mother"), ca. 1913.
(Nakano Takashi)

Makiko (*below left*) and Kuniko ("Okuni-san"), ca. 1911. (Nakano Takashi)

Shinako ("Oshina-san") in kimono and hakama, typical dress of girls in middle school, ca. 1912. (Nakano Takashi)

Shijō Avenue after a rain. (Kyoto Prefectural Archives)

Nishi Hongan-ji rest area where tea is served, 1909; see entry for March 24. (*Ketteiban Shōwa shi*)

MARCH 25 *Friday Clear*

It has been another beautiful day. Not a cloud in the sky!

A messenger arrived this morning from Mr. Tanaka bearing the bisque-fired ceramic soup bowls that we asked him to make for us. The idea is for us to paint designs on them ourselves before the final firing.

My husband was to go to a meeting of shrine parishioners in the afternoon, but he started to play with the ceramic bowls and painted two or three. Not surprisingly, he received a telephone call urging him to come to the meeting at once.

Then my father came to visit and talk about my brother's homecoming. He received a letter from Manzō yesterday, which he had given to Dr. Keimatsu and Mr. Kakemi when they visited him in Dairen. The letter says that it will be difficult to come home in April, but that the end of May will be all right. I was very disappointed because I had rushed to finish sewing his kimono in time for an April wedding. However, I understand that the change in plans is inevitable.

After my father left, my husband gave up going to the meeting, and settled in to be a ceramic artist for the night. He thought that he should share the fun with his friends, and so invited Mr. Matsumiya Hōnen, his brother Yūnen, Mr. Hirai Baisen, and Mr. Matsui. They all came about eight o'clock. They painted one bowl after another, but everyone agreed that the best ones are those done by Hōnen, which are painted with scenes from Japanese fairy tales.

Sent a sea bream and prawns to the Kakemis to show our appreciation for the *obi*.

MARCH 26 *Saturday Clear*

Nothing happened today.

MARCH 27 *Sunday Rain*

Today has been an unforgettable day. It is the day of accepting the betrothal gift from the groom's family before Okuni-san's marriage.

The go-between, Mr. Kataoka,[1] was supposed to come at eleven o'clock and we all waited, but he did not arrive until after noon, bringing the betrothal gift on a new wooden tray.[2] After the presentation ceremony was over, we served *sake* and food. As he got drunker and drunker, he began repeating himself over and over again. We listened to him politely, but it was painful and went on until four o'clock! By the time he left, I had a headache from being in a warm room too long, and from boredom. It is truly unpleasant to have to listen to a drunk.

Since this is an auspicious day, it was also the wedding day for my friend, Torii Yasuko. Okuni-san and I went to Nijō as soon as we could. The bride was very beautiful!

I had a chance to talk to Elder Sister Kōshima, who came to get Fumiko, who had been at Nijō. When I got home it was 11:00 P.M. My husband and Mother had gone to see the extension of the Keihan Railway[3] at Gojō that is soon to be opened.

Mr. Tanaka sent someone to get the painted bowls today; he probably will fire them tomorrow.

1. See entry for March 23.

2. The tray would be of unfinished wood in the Shintō style to suggest the sacred nature of the gift. The gift itself (*yuinō*) consists of money and *sake* and ceremonial foods of various kinds. The items are elaborately wrapped and decorated with auspicious and felicitous symbols.

3. See entry for January 14. Service on the railway started about three weeks later, on April 15. In 1915 the line was extended to the Sanjō Bridge.

March 28 *Monday Clear*

Although I started sewing early this morning, I spent half the day not working because the kimono merchant came to the house.

There was a welcoming party for Mashimo-sensei, the new school principal, at Harisei this evening. My husband went to the Shūdō Primary School before seven and came home after ten o'clock. Mr. Amagasu stopped by at about that time just to say that he was in the neighborhood. The place was a mess since I was sewing at night, which I haven't done for a while, and because I had things spread out all over the room, we used the room in Mother's quarters to entertain him in.

It began to rain. No wonder it has been warm and humid since yesterday.

March 29

[No entry]

March 30 *Wednesday Rain*

This is the day to send out bills to our customers. The rain made it somewhat difficult to distribute them.[1]

We brought out our Girls' Day dolls[2] and put up the decorations. The doll palace made of mulberry wood, which has been stored away for 30 years, was brought out for the first time for my dolls.[3] In the palace, they looked far more classic and elegant than ever. I fussed with them for almost half the day, looking at them closely and deciding where and how they should be placed. I discovered that the Girls' Day Doll Festival is great fun no matter how old you are.

1. Bills were delivered by shop-boys and clerks who went on foot or by bicycle.
2. See entry for March 3.
3. It was the custom for brides to bring a set of dolls when they entered their husband's house. This was apparently the first time that Makiko's dolls were displayed in this particular palace.

March 31 *Thursday Clear*

The last day of March. There is a rumor that the new Keihan Railway trains will start running tomorrow, but evidently it was just a rumor. We have been busy today with the quarterly accounting.

April 1 *Friday Clear*

Another first day of the month. It is unbelievable that a whole month has gone by already. As usual, some business branch-families came for the "first-of-the-month" greetings. They were the Eastside family and Mr. Ōkita Toyosaburō; Mr. Yamamoto Matsu, who always arrives first, did not come at all. Tada-san from across the street[1] has entered primary school, and he went to the ceremony that was held at the school today. Congratulations!

I was relieved to see that a new maid has come from Yamanashi to replace Kishi,[2] but I learned that she is coming just to meet the family today, and that she will start working on the third. Somehow, we don't have much luck finding a good kitchen maid.

Kuni-san came home with Eiko and Fumiko, having run into

them on Shijō Avenue. They were going home, so I walked with them to Shijō where we met Uncle Kōshima.[3] He bought a ring for Eiko.[4] He insisted that we all go on to Nijō together and called a *rikisha*, so reluctantly I went along. However, I was delighted to find that Uncle Onjō[5] was there, visiting from Tokyo. My father decided to take him and Uncle Kōshima to see the Miyako-odori.[6] After they left, Fumiko fell asleep, and I had to take her home to Senbon on my way back. What a complicated day!

1. Nakano Tadao, the Eastside family's six-year-old son.
2. The maid who left on January 19.
3. An otherwise unidentified senior member of the Kōshima family who appears again in the entry for July 23. Makiko calls him "*oji-san*," a kinship term literally meaning "uncle," used by speakers of both sexes to refer to older men. The same rule applies to "aunt" (*oba-san*).
4. Probably fashionable costume jewelry for schoolgirls, rather than real jewelry.
5. A relative of Makiko's mother.
6. This dance performance by geisha in a theater called Gion Kaburenjō was started in 1872, shortly after the removal of the capital to Tokyo, in an effort to attract tourists and shore up the faltering economy of Kyoto. A great success, the Miyako-odori continues to play to full houses for the entire month of April.

April 2 *Saturday* *Clear*

Today we made dumplings with mugwort to celebrate the arrival of spring. We started in the morning, with Mother supervising and doing most of the work of kneading the rice-flour and water mixture with the chopped herb. After lunch the maids and I took the dough and made half-moon shape dumplings filled with sweet red-bean paste. We made a huge quantity—we used about six *shō* of rice flour today. While we were busily making them, we had a lot of fun commenting on their shapes and sizes, which one is good and which one is bad, and so on, so that the whole operation went very quickly.

We distributed the dumplings among friends and relatives: the Hiraokas, the Matsumiyas, the Matsuis, the Eastside family, and Nijō, and kept some for ourselves. They were delicious! Mother and I kept up a stream of comments like, "They came out just right, and the taste is superb!" and "Let's go out and pick mugwort again and make some more!"

My husband finally teased us, saying that "Each comment is as different as the shape of each dumpling"—a sharp observation!

A primary school class. (Kyoto Prefectural Archives)

Primary school girls dancing in the schoolyard to organ music played by a teacher. (Kyoto Prefectural Archives)

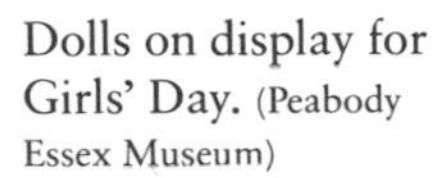

Dolls on display for Girls' Day. (Peabody Essex Museum)

Shijō Avenue; the sign at center right advertises photographs. (Collection of Ukiyo-e Books)

Shijō Bridge, ca. 1910; the Minami-za theater is on the right in the distance with a banner that reads "Kawakami Troupe." (Asian Collection, Herbert F. Johnson Museum of Art, Cornell University)

APRIL 3 *Sunday* *Clear*

Today is the Emperor Jinmu[1] festival. Every house put out the national flag to celebrate.

The official Girls' Day was March 3, but at our house we still follow the old calendar and celebrate it on April 3.

Having finished the shopping for the feast in the morning, everybody started to work in the kitchen. Some were making rolled sushi (*maki-zushi*), some were preparing the ingredients for *gomoku-zushi*,[2] and others were making rolled omelet (*tamago-yaki*), while still others were arranging the prepared food decoratively in lacquerware boxes, and so on. There were a great many things to do, but we all enjoyed working together.

The menu was tofu soup—ordinarily we would have used riverbed clams (*shijimi*), but the vendor did not come today, so we had to use tofu—a salad of shellfish (*akagai*) and scallions (*wakegi*), bulk sushi garnished with strips of vinegared mackerel (*saba ki-zushi*), rolled sushi, side dishes of trout, eggs, and *tsuto* tofu,[3] and finally, *yuba*[4] and fish cake cooked in seasoned broth. In addition to all of these, we made Western-style rolled cabbage, using the Chinese cabbage given to us, especially for Mr. Matsumiya and Mr. Matsui.[5]

When all the preparations were finished around 2:30, we sent the shop-boys to fetch our guests. After they arrived we all sat and began our feast. As we drank *shiro-zake*[6] and ate, the happy smiling faces of the big female dolls and the small male dolls and varieties of other dolls[7] were gradually starting to turn cherry-blossom color.

As we were finishing eating, the children went out one by one to play, as though cherry-blossom petals were scattering in all directions. There was a brief interlude before the drinking party for the big male dolls began. It lasted until one o'clock in the morning. These male dolls are a hardy bunch!

Note: The gardeners came today and trimmed and cleaned the place. As a result the view of the garden is quite different. I like it.

1. Japan's legendary first emperor. This festival has disappeared from the annual calendar.
2. Five kinds of vegetables, such as mushrooms, carrots, green beans, bamboo shoots, and burdock mixed in vinegared rice.
3. An unidentified variety of tofu.
4. See entry for February 4.
5. Both of whom were fond of Western cooking.

6. An undistilled *sake* served on Girls' Day.

7. The reference is to Kuniko, Shinako, and the other young women; Chūjirō and the other little boys, and her husband, Matsumiya Hōnen, Matsui Jisuke, and the other adult males, respectively.

April 4 *Monday Clear*

Another beautiful day. I spent all morning putting the dolls away—it sounds like work, but actually it was play for me.

My father sent us a crab, which came from Wakasa along with word that Mrs. Nakajima and her daughter, Oyuki-sama,[1] are arriving this evening.

My husband went to a meeting of shrine parishioners scheduled for nine o'clock this morning and said that he will stop by Mr. Matsui's place on the way home. I expected that he wouldn't be home before midnight, but he returned while we were still dining on the crab, to which we had added other ingredients to double the portions so that everyone could have a taste.

I heard that the people from Wakasa are arriving about seven or eight o'clock tonight and are not staying at Nijō, but at an inn instead. Since my mother is no longer there to look after the guests, and the wedding has not yet taken place, they probably decided it was better not to stay there.

1. Manzō's fiancée, Nakajima Yukiko.

April 5 *Tuesday Clear*

An incredibly beautiful day again!

I had been expecting a call from Nijō because I thought the people from Wakasa surely would visit them this morning, but the call never came.

Mr. Suzuki came over in the evening to tell us that he is planning to take the school children to see an educational play, *Kusunoki Masashige*,[1] performed by the troupe of Kawakami Otojirō and Sadayakko[2] on the tenth of this month, and that there will be a meeting of the Otogi Club on the seventeenth. It is going to be an interesting month with such a variety of activities.

1. The play's title is the name of another of Japan's great, doomed heroes, whose loyal support of the beleaguered Emperor Go-Daigo in the fourteenth century earned him a permanent place in song, story, and drama. Although Kusunoki realized the hopelessness of his military situation, he engaged the enemy in a climactic battle and,

while it was still in progress, withdrew to commit suicide. By 1910 he had become a fixture of primary school textbooks, where his life was said to exemplify the twin virtues of imperial loyalty and patriotism. That is why Makiko refers to it as an "educational play."

2. Kawakami Sadayakko (1872–1946) was a geisha who married the left-wing political activist, actor, and theater manager Kawakami Otojirō in 1891. Her first stage appearance, filling in for a female impersonator, was with her husband's company in Boston in 1899. An immediate sensation, she was compared favorably with Sarah Bernhardt. In Japan the troupe performed Shakespeare and European plays in translation in a kind of pseudo-kabuki style. Otojirō is usually credited with a major role in the founding of the new theatrical form called *shinpa*; Sadayakko was her country's first female stage star and co-founder with Kurushima Takehiko of the children's theater movement in Japan. See Salz, p. 71.

April 6 *Wednesday Clear*

I think that this run of good weather will make the cherry blossoms smile soon.

We got a telephone call from Nijō this morning, at last, informing us that the visitors from Wakasa will call on them today. I ran to the hairdresser in the morning, and carefully put on makeup and dressed in my good kimono, although the result is not so great, in spite of the long hours I spent, and arrived at Nijō about two o'clock in the afternoon. However, much to my surprise and dismay, the bride-to-be was not there. Only her mother and an older woman of her family came. I was quite upset at her unusual behavior! We served a snack of sushi and talked about trivial matters until they left around six o'clock.

I wonder why I cannot get along with the Wakasa people? Just facing them is disgusting now. Why on earth the bride-to-be did not show her face today is beyond my comprehension!

I came home just before 10:00 P.M. Although Mr. Tanaka was present, I was so annoyed by today's events that I told my husband that I may tell my brother in Dairen about what happened. Mother, who was also there, scolded me for saying such things.

April 7 *Thursday Clear*

We had splendid weather again, but the wind was strong. It is the memorial day for my grandmother at Nijō.

Mr. Matsumiya came over in the late afternoon to say that Mr. Matsui is at Mr. Suzuki's place. In a while Mr. Matsui came to our house, and the three of them went out for a walk around Kiyomizu. Anticipating their return for dinner, we bought a flounder. Just as I was beginning to think it would be wasted, they all returned. We served only a simple dinner of broiled flounder and egg soup.

After dinner the usual lively conversation followed. Everyone present, the family members and the guests, were all talking and laughing, so that it got very noisy. The funny thing is, apparently it's fashionable for adults to play string figures[1] these days, so all the grown-ups started to play the game, and next thing you know some kids' toys were brought out. We laughed and screamed and had a great time! The party broke up at one o'clock in the morning, and we walked with our guests to the intersection of Daikoku-machi and Gojō Avenue.

1. Similar to cat's cradle and related games found in the West.

April 8

[No entry]

April 9 *Saturday* *Rain*

This was to have been the day for the big spring cleaning had the weather been good, but since it was canceled, I decided to go to Nijō to see Oyuki-sama's trousseau, which she is taking to Manchuria. First I consulted with Elder Sister Kōshima and arranged to meet her at Nijō in the afternoon.

We were shown the items in her trousseau, one by one, and were surprised by the quantity. After that Elder Sister and I decided to take Oyuki-sama to a performance of the Kawakami Otojirō and Sadayakko troupe, as a gesture of welcome. It was the first time I have ever seen them, and I enjoyed it very much. There were two plays, *Kusunoki Masashige* and *Bondoman*,[1] but unfortunately we missed most of the first one.

I came home around 11:30. Mother was waiting up for me, looking very sleepy.

1. Based on *The Bondman: A New Saga,* by the British novelist Sir T. H. Hall Caine, published in 1890.

April 10 *Sunday* *Clear*

I had decided not to go to cooking class today, which had been postponed because Saturday was scheduled to be our spring cleaning day, which had to be postponed because of the rain. We took out the tatami mats and finished cleaning the wooden floor under them before noon, and were able to clean the upstairs and Mother's quarters thoroughly, as well as the storehouses, because the days are getting longer. When we finished everything, I myself felt clean and as if a heavy burden had been lifted from my shoulders.

My husband went to see the Kawakami troupe's performance of *Kusunoki Masashige* today, which was sponsored by the Otogi Club.

Around nine o'clock in the evening a shop-boy sent by Mr. Matsui delivered the food that was cooked today in the class I missed. Then Uncle Nishimura[1] from Tonoshō, who is visiting a sick relative in Kyoto, arrived. My husband returned and then the Eastside Doctor came over. Since Uncle Nishimura does not like Western food, the doctor, Mother, and I happily ate everything that Mr. Matsui had sent. We served *sake* to our guest while my husband kept him company.

1. The adoptive father of Nishimura Tokusaburō. See entries for January 5, 6, and 8.

April 11 *Monday Cloudy*

It was a bit cloudy this morning, but looked promising.

Our guest from Tonoshō, who apparently was concerned about his house and farm, went home as soon as we served him breakfast with *sake*. It seems that he always drinks in the morning. He told us that we should come to Tonoshō to view the cherry blossoms, which will be at their best in a few days.

My husband went to the exhibition of new merchandise in the afternoon, because he had heard that tables and chairs made of rattan are for sale. He came back about six o'clock with Mr. Matsui, whom he had met at the exhibition hall. He said that when he found that he could not buy what he wanted there, he went to the trouble of going down to the main store of the furniture dealer to order the items. They told him that the furniture should be delivered on the fifteenth.

There was a boat race at Hide-san's college today. I wonder how his team did? I hope they won.

April 12 *Tuesday Clear*

Mr. Tanaka himself brought the fired ceramic bowls that we have been eagerly waiting to see for days. They turned out to be quite wonderful! The ones that Mr. Matsumiya painted with the scenes from Japanese fairy tales are especially good. It is too bad that the bowls have no covers![1]

I was told that Minosuke's[2] mother has died. I feel very sorry for him, for there is nothing like losing one's mother. He must be grief-stricken and very lonely. I still remember that when my mother died, I would wonder why, and images of her working busily around the house would appear, making my eyes fill with tears.

1. Covered bowls are considered to be finer than plain ones.
2. A live-in store clerk.

April 13 *Wednesday Clear*

It was a beautiful day. They say that the cherry blossoms at Maruyama Park are at their peak today and tomorrow.

Otake-don[1] returned from Kyushu this morning, where she has been helping out at the Taniis'. She said that everyone in the family is well, and that Toshiko-chan[2] is a quiet child who smiles a lot. I can hardly wait to see her!

Mother, Kuni-san, Otake, and Okiku[3] went out to see the cherry blossoms in the evening, since this is the peak period.[4]

Hide-san, looking very thin and tanned, came home from Ōtsu[5] about 9:30, bringing three very tall friends. Unfortunately, they lost the boat race even though they had trained very hard all week without even eating properly. It's too bad, but at least he is well and safe. Whenever we talk about boat racing, I remember Mr. Nishi's story, which frightens me.[6] Although it was very late, he and his friends had not eaten, so we prepared dinner right away and served them.

1. A housemaid.
2. The infant daughter to whom the Girls' Day dolls and furniture were sent.
3. Another maid.
4. Viewing cherry blossoms by moonlight is considered a particularly elegant activity.
5. A city on the shore of Lake Biwa.
6. There is no other mention or explanation of Mr. Nishi's story.

April 14 *Thursday Clear*

Since it was a warm spring day, I felt restless, and that prompted me to go up on the roof with the binoculars to find out if I could see some cherry blossoms. Looking out over the city, I saw clouds of light pink blossoms in full bloom everywhere! I peered through the binoculars. Zoom! Suddenly I was looking at the famous big gardens, which appeared as though they were right there in front of me! I could see Gojō-an and Nishi Ōtani temple,[1] the famous weeping cherry trees at a temple whose name I forget, and so on. I was so excited by the view and so immersed in beauty that I forgot all about the things I had to do. When I realized that it was getting late, I ran down the stairs and went through the house, quickly cleaning up here and there, and prepared dinner.

I had planned to go cherry-blossom viewing with Shinako-san and Chūji-san after dinner, taking the maid who has not yet seen the cherry blossoms in Kyoto. However, since Hide-san was home from college, neither Shina-san nor I felt like leaving the house. We canceled our plans, but the maid went out with some other maids from the Eastside family.

In the evening Mr. Matsumiya came over, and shortly afterward Mr. Suzuki arrived. Today the conversation included Hide-san as well, but Mr. Suzuki left early, just a little after ten o'clock. I thought it was because Mr. Matsui wasn't here tonight. Nevertheless, we carried on, trying to compose a melody to the lyrics of the Otogi Club's birthday song and had a good time.

Otake-don[2] left by the 4:45 P.M. train to visit her family.

1. Gojō-an has not been identified. For Nishi Ōtani, see entry for January 7.

2. It would appear that because she had been sent all the way to Kyushu to help out at the Taniis', surely a somewhat unusual assignment, the maid was given leave to visit her family.

April 15 *Friday Clear*

A letter arrived from Kurushima-sensei this morning notifying us that he will be arriving in Kyoto early this evening, the event that we had been waiting for.

In the afternoon Elder Sister Kōshima stopped by on her way back from visiting a temple and said she is going to Maruyama Park to see the cherry blossoms. She had Fumiko with her, so I decided to go with them. The park was crowded, and the cherry blossoms were in full bloom. Some people were having big parties right in the middle of the dusty area, and others were sitting on the grass and eating their lunch. Others were heading for the restaurants and tea shops in great numbers. They say that Kyoto and Osaka people spend all their money on food,[1] which certainly seems to be true, for I have to confess that we, too, joined the crowd today and went into a tea shop for a tray of dumplings, which, I think, is the lightest sin of all.

From the park we walked through the grounds of the Gion-jinja,[2] then down Shijō Avenue to Kyōgoku,[3] and the street lights came on. I hurried home and found that our guest Kurushima-sensei had already arrived! He always seems to arrive whenever I am gone.

In the evening Kurushima-sensei, together with Sazanami-sensei and several others, went to see the Miyako-odori and came home late, past eleven. He went to bed right away, saying that there were so many people and the light was so bright that he felt dizzy.

1. This famous saying is quoted accurately in the Introduction. Makiko quotes it incorrectly here.
2. A Shintō shrine located at the eastern end of Shijō Avenue, better known by its formal name Yasaka-jinja. It is much patronized by geisha of the nearby Gion district. See entries for January 16 and 19.
3. An entertainment district known for its theaters, restaurants, and shops.

April 16 *Saturday Clear*

Today was another beautiful day. Kurushima-sensei is a lucky man! He accompanied Sazanami-sensei, who was going to pay his respects to his ancestors at the Nishi Ōtani mausoleum, and they walked all around the Higashiyama area, visiting the mausoleum, Kiyomizu temple, Uta-no Nakayama, Shirutani, Hiyoshi-jinja, and the Kyoto Imperial Museum on the way.

After leaving the museum, they came back here, and Mr. Matsui, Mr. Suzuki, and Mr. Tanaka came to see them. During their conversation someone suggested that it was a good occasion to ask both of the *sensei* to do calligraphy for them. Sazanami-sensei was so fast! I was amazed by the speed of his brush. He not only writes fast but did a painting as well. Kurushima-sensei also did calligraphy. Sazanami-sensei went back to his inn, saying that he would stop at Jidaiya, an antique shop, on his way.

The new school principal, Mashimo-sensei, came to visit after that. Since the Eastside family made special dishes for Girls' Day

Cherry blossoms at Maruyama Park. (Kyoto Prefectural Archives)

Gion-jinja (Yasaka-jinja). (Collection of Ukiyo-e Books)

Nishi Ōtani temple; see entry for April 16. (Collection of Ukiyo-e Books)

Kurodani cemetery; a Buddhist priest stands on the bridge. (Collection of Ukiyo-e Books)

today[1] and shared them with us, we showed the beautifully packed food to both gentlemen. The group left about 6:30 for the Chimoto restaurant,[2] where a dinner has been arranged for the two visitors. Kurushima-sensei and my husband returned home after eleven and went straight to bed.

1. They had deliberately postponed the observance from April 3 so that both families could enjoy the festive food twice.
2. Chimoto, which is still in operation, is located on the bank of the Kamo River directly across from the Minami-za just off Shijō Avenue in the Ponto-chō district.

April 17 *Sunday Clear*

Both Kurushima-sensei and Sazanami-sensei had to take the 7:30 train this morning to Arashiyama[1] to attend a meeting of the readers of *Young Girls' World*, to which they were invited. They apparently did not want to go, but felt obliged, and are going straight from there to the meeting of the Otogi Club at noon, which was held at the newly built Youth Center building in Tera-machi off Sanjō Avenue.

I attended the cooking class at Mr. Matsumiya's house, but Okuni-san decided to skip it and went instead to the Otogi Club meeting with the children. There were only three of us at the class, but we had seven guests, so we were very busy. I was really thinking about getting back home early but had to help—unwillingly. It was already eight o'clock when I rushed home, only to find that Kurushima-sensei was already there! He teased me about it. He took a stroll with Hide-san to view the cherry blossoms in Maruyama Park at night. When they got back, it was a little early for him to leave for the station, so we gathered around and persuaded him to tell some stories, which were very interesting. I only wished that he had been standing, using hand gestures, and speaking loudly, as he does when he performs on stage.

When the time did come for him to leave, my husband and Mr. Matsui accompanied him to the railway station. He left by the 10:45 P.M. train. I wonder why Mr. Suzuki did not show up?

1. A scenic area some distance to the northwest of Kyoto.

April 18 *Monday Clear*

Although it was a nice day again, I was dragging myself around and felt tired. That sounds as if I have been working very hard, but

Mother's the one who actually did everything. I spent the day doing nothing in particular.

It is election day for the Kyoto City Council, and there was a big to-do. Notification of it came by telegram this morning, and a *rikisha* was sent to our house to pick up my husband. He went to cast his vote in the afternoon.[1]

He is having stomach trouble again and has not been feeling well lately, which makes us worry about a recurrence of tapeworms. He decided to start taking herbal medicine again today.

Our housemaid, Okiku, has been homesick for her family since shortly after she came to work for us, but we have been putting her off until today. She finally went home to Yamanashi, a village north of here. She looked very happy when she left this morning, and I understand that she will stay with her family tonight.

1. At this time, only property-owning males could vote. Women were not enfranchised until 1946.

April 19 *Tuesday Clear*

There is nothing special about today—everything was routine, except that we are short a housemaid.

Since the store urgently requested us[1] to help them make medicine bags, I did the folding and creasing of the material, and Mother ran them up on the sewing machine. We all worked hard.

1. The women of the family.

April 20 *Wednesday Clear*

It was a beautiful day again. The morning started with a telephone call from my father, who told me that the family visiting from Wakasa had come back to Kyoto from their brief visit to Osaka, and now are planning to make an excursion to Arashiyama, and asking if I could join them on the trip. I said "yes" and went over to Nijō at once, only to find out that they were not there yet. They arrived after we sent a shop-boy to pick them up.

Five of us, three Wakasa family members,[1] my father, and I, started out from our house in Nijō, and stopped at the Kitano Tenman-gū, Hirano-jinja, Kinkaku-ji, Tō-ji-in, Ninna-ji, and Arashiyama—all places I haven't visited for a long time.[2]

We had been riding in *rikisha* all day long. When we left Arashiyama, it was already getting dark, and the arc lights on the bridge across the Hozu River were on. Although it was too late for the cherry blossoms, the reflection of the lights on the river was so beautiful that I felt like I wanted to stay there forever.

On our way back, rushing home in our *rikisha*, we overtook a train, which sometimes got ahead of us and sometimes fell behind. We raced all the way along the Sanjō Highway.

When I got home about eight o'clock, I found that Uncle Nishimura was visiting us from the country. My husband was out at a neighborhood association meeting, and our guest went to bed early, before he got back.

1. The bride-to-be, her mother, and the older woman referred to in the entry for April 6.

2. Kitano Tenman-gū and Hirano-jinja are major Shintō shrines. For Kitano Tenman-gū, see entries for the 25th of January, February, June, and September. Hirano-jinja is especially noted for its cherry blossoms and flowers. Kinkaku-ji is the famous Golden Pavilion, built in 1397 by the third Ashikaga shōgun. Tō-ji-in is the funerary temple of the Ashikaga shōguns. Ninna-ji is an enormous temple complex founded in 886, partially burned in the late fifteenth century, and restored in the 1630's. All are in northwestern Kyoto and still number among the most popular tourist destinations in the city.

April 21 *Thursday Clear*

It was Tō-ji's Odaishi-san festival[1] today, and one of the big events was a procession of *tayū* from Shimabara,[2] so I was expecting to hear that there was a big turnout. However, it rained off and on, and that kept the people away.

Uncle Nishimura, who is staying with us, had *sake* with lunch, went out to the open-air market at Tō-ji, and then left for home. It seemed that the purpose of his visit was to issue an invitation for us to visit his house in the country. So Mother, Shinako, Chūji, and the Eastside family's Yuri-san[3] have decided to go to Tonoshō on the evening of the 23rd.

In the evening Mr. Matsui came over, and Hide-san came from his boardinghouse. They went out somewhere together.

My friend Kakemi Uta-sama, who recently got married, had planned to pay visits to several houses today in her beautiful wedding kimono, but unfortunately it rained. I was hoping to be able to see her, but the combination of having guests at our house and the bad weather made it impossible for me to go out. I wonder how it went.

1. Kōbō Daishi (Odaishi-san) is the posthumous name of the monk Kūkai (774–835 A.D.), founder of the Shingon sect of Buddhism. April 21 is his death date, marked annually by the sect's major festival. See entry for January 25.

2. The *tayū* were courtesans of the highest rank. Shimabara was once a famous pleasure quarter of Kyoto.

3. Nakano Yuriko, the eight-year-old daughter of the Eastside family.

April 22 *Friday Clear*

Today was nicer than yesterday. Nothing special happened. The only visitor was Mrs. Mutō, who stayed just for a little while.

April 23 *Saturday Clear*

As we planned the other day, Mother and the others have gone to visit the Nishimura family in Tonoshō. They took the 3:45 P.M. train.

My husband and Okuni-san left home early in the afternoon to attend a concert at Kyoto First Girls' School, performed by students from a music school in Tokyo.

After everybody had gone, the house seemed deserted with just Sei-san and me left. Even the store seemed very quiet because so many people were taking part in the procession that brought Inari from its shrine in Fushimi to its lodging place in Tō-ji tonight.[1]

Eventually the three men returned, and Okuni-san came home, but my husband went straight from the concert to a meeting of the Kyoto German Academic Society at the School of Pharmacy tonight.

1. See entry for January 22. According to Professor Nakano, because participation by the citizenry was virtually mandatory, all the neighborhood associations and school districts of Kyoto were involved in organizing the day-long procession in which the deity's heavy portable shrine was carried through the streets. Each household was required to send male representatives. This year the Nakano family sent the two store managers and a head clerk, representing the absent household head. Today the portable shrine is taken by truck to Tō-ji on April 22.

April 24, 25, 26

[No entries]

April 27 *Wednesday*

Together with Mrs. Nakajima from Wakasa, I went to Kyoto Station in the late afternoon to meet my brother Manzō, who is back from Dairen for a short visit and to get married. He came back with

Kitano Tenman-gū with statue of a bull; see entry for April 20.
(Asian Collection, Herbert F. Johnson Museum of Art, Cornell University)

Kinkaku-ji, the Golden Pavilion, built in 1397. (Asian Collection, Herbert F. Johnson Museum of Art, Cornell University)

Arashiyama in northwestern Kyoto; timber rafts float on the Katsura River. (Asian Collection, Herbert F. Johnson Museum of Art, Cornell University)

Bridges at Arashiyama. (Asian Collection, Herbert F. Johnson Museum of Art, Cornell University)

Wedding portrait of Nakao Manzō and Yukiko; see entry for May 1. (Nakano Takashi)

Dr. Keimatsu, who is the director of the research institute where my brother works. I hear that so many people turned out to greet them at the station because Dr. Keimatsu is going on a trip to the West soon.

Tsune-san and Ishimatsu-san,[1] who had gone to Kobe harbor to meet their ship, were with them on the same train. I was very happy to see them, for both seem to be in fine spirits. We got home first, bringing their luggage. My husband came home with Mr. Tanaka shortly after that.

I heard that Dr. Keimatsu is going to see the Miyako-odori tonight.

1. Clerks from the Nakao store, sent to help with the baggage.

April 28

[No entry]

April 29 *Friday*

They were saying that since this is a very auspicious day, the wedding should take place today. However, it is so close to the end of the month when everybody is so busy, that it is now set for May 1.

Goodness gracious! Now I suddenly realized that my kimono and other accessories to wear to the wedding are not ready. I have been thinking about what to wear, but had thought that there would be plenty of time.

In a panic, I sent an urgent request to a seamstress and ran to Nijō for help. What a struggle! I wish that the wedding was over. I can't take this much longer!

April 30 *Saturday*

No time for writing.

May 1 *Sunday*

This is the wedding day. Luckily the weather was splendid. The invitations had been sent out for 3:00 P.M. We were the first to arrive at the Heian-jingū[1] where the ceremony was to be performed. The guests began to arrive slowly, but the bride did not arrive until 4:30, and things finally got under way. It rained during the ceremony but fortunately stopped just as it was ending. It did rain a little again, though, while they were taking the wedding photographs.

From the shrine, we all went to the Nakamura-rō restaurant for the banquet. Uncle Amano impressed everyone with his exceptional talents as an entertainer. It was quite an affair.

1. In 1910 this great Shintō shrine was only fifteen years old, having been built in 1895 to commemorate the 1,100th anniversary of the founding of Kyoto. It is about a mile and a half north of the Nakano store. Shintō weddings were also quite new; see Introduction.

May 2, 3, 4

[No entries]

May 5 *Thursday*

Went to Nijō for the Buddhist memorial service for my grandmother and my mother. It was the third anniversary for grandmother, and the first for mother, although it is much too early to hold hers.[1] It is sad to think that we have lost two of our dear family members in just three years. Sister Tanii attended the service, which must have meant a lot to mother and grandmother. Aunt Nakamura Oyasu, who lives in Osaka, and her married daughter, Nishimura Sumiko, both of whom are members of families on my mother's side, also came.

The service began at 10:00 A.M., and lunch was served after it was over. Everyone else left around three o'clock, but I stayed on. Sumiko-sama took the five o'clock train home.

In the evening, my brother, his new bride, and I went over to Azumaya.[2] We had soup, fried prawns, chicken chops, pancakes, and black tea. I had already eaten dinner at home so it really filled me up. I did not tell my husband—it's a little secret just between us.

1. Her mother's would have been observed on the 21st. It is not uncommon to hold joint services for more than one ancestor, both for convenience and as a means of reducing the expense.

2. Azumaya seems to have been a restaurant where Western-style food was served.

May 6

[No entry]

May 7 *Saturday*

Today is the memorial day for my husband's grandmother, whom I never met. May her soul rest in peace. "Hail, Amida Buddha."[1]

The Buddhist memorial service for her is to be held here at home tomorrow.[2] In preparation, I have polished the brass altar vases, bowls, bells, candle holders, and so on, arranged the decorations for the altar, and got out the utensils needed for serving the guests. I ordered the flowers for the altar a day ahead.[3]

1. *Namu amida butsu*, the most common of the mantras, is recited to give comfort to the mourner and soothe the spirit of the dead. Amida is the bodhisattva of infinite mercy.
2. Sundays seem to have been the preferred day rather than the actual anniversary date, because it was more convenient for everyone; see Introduction.
3. Then, as now, it was the duty of the wife of the household head to see to the preparation of the altar personally.

May 8 *Sunday*

We held the memorial service for the ancestors today. In the morning I cleared the parlor and placed the offerings on the altar. The service was set for one o'clock, and the invitations were sent accordingly. In the past, when we invited a large number of people, we held separate services, one for family members and relatives and the other for the business branch-families, but this time we combined them. All of the guests, without exception, paid their respects at the altar. Today's memorial service was for six ancestors altogether. One was to observe the hundredth anniversary of death, two for the fiftieth, two for the seventh, and one for the thirteenth.[1]

The Buddhist priest from our temple who performed the ceremony usually wears Western-style clothing when he goes out, but he looked quite different today in his dignified ceremonial brocade robe, worn over a white kimono, sitting on a thick, soft silken cushion reserved just for him.

Since we could not possibly serve meals to everyone, we arranged to have the dinner at the Nakamura-rō following the service. All the guests left before ten o'clock. It was a good dinner, and we enjoyed it; it cost ¥1.50 per person. Total number of guests: 26.

1. Depending on the sect of Buddhism, these observances are held on successive anniversaries of death. A common pattern is 1, 3, 5, 7, 13, 17, 23, 25, 27, 50, and 100.

May 9 *Monday*

We presented a bolt of one or two *tan*[1] of white cotton cloth to each of our intimate acquaintances and tradesmen[2] to mark the holding of the memorial service for the ancestors. We also sent a box of dried food to the Nishimura family in Tonoshō, who had been unable to attend.

1. One *tan* is the unit of cloth required to make one kimono.
2. The term she uses, *de-iri-mono*, indicates that these were people with whom the household maintained a standing relationship. They were regularly called upon whenever extra help was needed at weddings, funerals, packing, and so on. Many middle- to upper-class households maintained such *de-iri-mono* relationships until the 1940's.

May 10

[No entry]

May 11 *Wednesday*

It is the memorial day for Father.[1] We had planned to go to the family grave at Higashi Ōtani to pay our respects, but because it rained, we canceled the visit.

1. Chūhachi VI.

May 12 *Thursday*

Since tomorrow is the eve of the festival to celebrate the return of Inari to its home shrine,[1] we had to do all the preparation of the food for the festivities. This year, we ordered 44 rolls of pressed mackerel sushi from Harisei. Ordered only 33 fresh fish for the festive meal from the fishmonger this year.

For red-bean glutinous rice: cook red beans, put them in a basket, and set aside. Soak washed rice in the cooked bean juice overnight. Leave some of the juice to be sprinkled on the rice before steaming it.[2]

1. See entry for April 23.
2. This recipe is for *o-kowa*; see entry for February 12.

May 13 *Friday*

Today is the festival eve. Began cooking early in the morning starting by steaming the rice.

We delivered our red-bean rice with a roll of mackerel sushi to the Yamamotos and Yamadas,[1] the Shibatas,[2] and the Nakaos.

At home we prepared a simple meal of processed bonito[3] and miso soup. Mr. Moriguchi had someone bring a phonograph from Mr. Matsui's house for entertainment. Tomikichi[4] was in charge of the machine, and they played records constantly from half past five until eleven o'clock, which I think is a bit too much.

1. Both business branch-families. Yamada Suekichi was one of the store managers.
2. Unidentified.
3. *Namabushi*, which is steam-cooked, has a firmer texture than fresh bonito, but is not as hard as *katsuobushi*, the dried form.
4. One of the young store clerks.

May 14 *Saturday Fair*

The festival day that everyone has been eagerly awaiting has come at last. The boys in the store started up the phonograph again in the morning, obviously not having had enough last night.

At lunchtime the red carpet was spread in the parlor, and we all sat at individual red lacquerware trays and ate our festive meal,[1] which included broiled sea bream and spring-vegetable miso soup. The Eastside Doctor and the two head managers joined us for lunch, and we served an extra dish of cooked sea-bream roe and spring vegetables. Sister Tanii, who is visiting us, was at the lunch this year, too. Mr. Matsumiya, Mr. Matsui, and Hide-san's four friends also came. I was excited and happy with all these people present.

In the afternoon Oyuki-sama,[2] Eiko, and Okuni,[3] came from Nijō, followed by Mrs. Yamada Osei,[4] whom we hadn't seen for a while. I took them out to see the Inari festival procession, but it was too late. Instead we went to watch the festival procession of the Hiyoshi-jinja.[5]

After we came home, we feasted on mackerel sushi (*saba-zushi*), sea-bream *sashimi*,[6] sea-bream soup, broiled fish, red-bean glutinous rice, and so on. We served the same meal to the store employees in between seeing to our guests. For entertainment the phonograph was started up again. Everyone left about seven o'clock.

Mother was really busy all day. She never stopped a moment. I feel that I did not do enough.

Note: The maids had no chance to enjoy the day and got no rest until well after eleven o'clock.

1. While Makiko probably had her own tray, it is unlikely that she had much time to eat, for it would have been her responsibility to serve the others.

2. Her new sister-in-law, Yukiko.

3. A maid, who accompanied Yukiko from Wakasa.

4. Tanii Senjirō's half-sister, the wife of Yamada Genzaburō, manager of Kyūkyodō, a famous stationery store.

5. In Makiko's time the festival days of the two Shintō shrines coincided, but today Hiyoshi-jinja's *Sannō-matsuri* is held on April 14 by the new calendar. Inari is taken back to Fushimi by truck on May 3.

6. A great delicacy using a festive fish, indicating that this was a very special meal indeed.

May 15 *Sunday*

It is the fifteenth day of the month and also the *Aoi-matsuri*.[1] The streets must have been bustling. I had planned to go to a bazaar at the First Girls' School with the others, but did not feel like it and so stayed home.

In the afternoon Mr. Yamada Genzaburō came to visit, followed by Mrs. Tanii Onui.[2]

Sister Tanii, who has been visiting us, has decided to go home tomorrow. Mrs. Nakajima from Wakasa, who has been staying in Nijō, is leaving by an early morning train as well, so I went to Nijō before dinnertime to say good-bye. Fortunately she was there, and so was my Elder Sister Kōshima. It's funny, but the same thing happened once before when I went to visit Mrs. Nakajima at Nijō. It's almost as though it had been arranged in advance. Although I was not planning to stay long today, I actually stayed quite late, until after eight o'clock, as I always seem to do.

1. Said to be one of Kyoto's oldest major festivals, *Aoi-matsuri* originated in the sixth century and was revived in its present form in 1884. A procession of people dressed in the costume of the Heian period, Kyoto's heyday as the capital, moves from the Nijō palace to the Kamo River, stops at Shimogamo-jinja, and ends at Kamigamo-jinja.

2. Tanii Senjirō's adoptive mother.

Makiko (*left*) with her brother, Manzō, and sister-in-law Yukiko, ca. 1911; a maid kneels at left. (Nakano Takashi)

A domestic altar of the Buddhist sect Jodō Shinshū; see entry for May 8. (Robert J. Smith, 1951)

Nakano Chūhachi VI; see entry for May 11. (Nakano Takashi)

The gates at Shimogamo-jinja. (Asian Collection, Herbert F. Johnson Museum of Art, Cornell University)

Spectators watch the Aoi-matsuri procession passing over a bridge, ca. 1920. (Kyoto Prefectural Archives)

May 16 *Monday*

Today is the festival day at the Ebisu-jinja,[1] but unfortunately it rained.

Sister Tanii and her baby daughter Toshiko left today by the 3:50 P.M. train. I miss them very much. Just before their departure time there was a sudden downpour, but luckily it tapered off for a while, so they were able to leave on time. She is brave to travel alone without any help, but, of course, she travels a lot and is quite used to it. Ironically, after they left it stopped raining and the skies cleared! I miss the baby particularly—the house got very quiet without her.

1. A shrine to Ebisu, a Shintō deity, believed to bring good fortune and prosperity, and therefore closely associated with mercantile activities. It is located between Shijō and Gojō Avenues, due north of the Nakano store. See entry for October 20.

May 17 *Tuesday*

Today is the festival eve of the local shrine in Nijō. I thought that this would be a good day to go there to make the rounds with Oyuki-sama to thank the people who had attended the wedding.[1] I got permission from my husband and Mother to go to Nijō today and tomorrow.

My brother came over in the afternoon, since he was going to Mr. Tanaka's house with my husband to do some painting on ceramics. He was carrying a lot of books that all contained drawings of one kind or another to serve as models and for inspiration. I wonder what kind of paintings he will come up with.

I hurriedly changed and went to Nijō. As soon as I arrived there, I changed again, this time to formal kimono for the occasion, and just after five o'clock I set out with Oyuki-sama. We got back to Nijō about nine o'clock and found my brother sitting in the house with his hat still on. Apparently he had just got home after having had dinner at Gojō. Oyuki-sama and I changed and set out to the local shrine for the evening festivities, taking Oasa-han[2] with us. My brother went out with Tsune-san[3] to play billiards. He didn't come home until one o'clock in the morning. Oyuki-sama and I waited up for him all that time.[4]

1. Here again Makiko is filling a role that would have been her mother's, had she lived.

2. The housekeeper at Nijō.
3. A clerk at the Nakao store.
4. Note that the new groom and his bride operate in almost completely separate worlds, especially when out in public.

May 18 *Wednesday*

No wonder that when I woke up this morning I felt that something was different. I stayed in Nijō last night! Since this is the festival day, I went to see Fumiko in the morning to take her back with me, dropped in to see Akioka-sama,[1] and promised her that I'd come back in the afternoon, which I did. We talked about a lot of things and had a good time. I returned home to Gojō around 10:00 P.M.

Although it was a festival day, and even though my brother and his wife are staying there, the house in Nijō felt empty and lonely without mother. I know I shouldn't be this way, but I cannot hold back my tears when I think about her.

1. Makiko's friend in Nijō; see entry for January 4.

May 19, 20

[No entries]

May 21 *Saturday*

Today was the weekly cooking class. The lesson was a rehearsal for the stand-up party to be given next Saturday. We learned to cook something very complicated and were told to come at eight in the morning next Friday, when the lesson for desserts will be given.

May 22 *Sunday*

It was a beautiful morning. Received a telephone call from Nijō asking me and my husband to join them for an excursion to Ishiyama[1] for the day. My husband had a previous engagement at the School of Pharmacy, but I was free and took Sei-san and Chūji-san with me. From Nijō my father, Eiko, my brother, and Yukiko-san came along with us.

We tried some fishing, but I didn't catch a thing. We spotted Hide-san practicing rowing on the Seta River[2] and invited him to join us for lunch at the Yanagiya restaurant in Ishiyama. All in all we had a good time.

1. A town on Lake Biwa where there is a famous temple, Ishiyama-dera.
2. Which flows into Lake Biwa.

May 23

[No entry]

May 24 *Tuesday*

My brother and his wife are leaving for Manchuria on the 26th, so I went over to Nijō to talk about their farewell gifts. I was hoping that they would suggest something specific, but since they did not, I decided on stockings and handkerchiefs. I realize that they are not especially imaginative choices, but they are useful and they will need plenty of them.

May 25 *Wednesday*

I did not go to Nijō today, thinking that there won't be anything for me to do at this point.

May 26 *Thursday*

My brother's visit has been a long one, but the time has come to say good-bye. They left tonight by the 8:13 P.M. train for Kobe. They will stay there tonight and board the ship for Dairen tomorrow. I already knew all about their plans, yet when the time came I was sad, and realized that I will miss him very much. I went as far as Shichijō Station to see them off. There were lots of people at the station. My brother repeatedly said that he was surprised at the size of the send-off party and obviously was somewhat embarrassed.

Sister Tanii had written to suggest that they stop by to see them when their ship calls at Moji, since they live not far away. However, my brother had decided to go back without stopping anywhere on this trip and declined the invitation. His decision to turn down such a kind offer was regrettable, and somehow I felt caught between my two families.

As a matter of fact, it is a sad night for me, not just because my brother has left, but also I could not go with them to Dairen. I begged my husband to let me go, but he said that there is no reason why I should go at this time.[1] I was very sad, for I know this is the only chance I will ever have to travel with my brother and his wife by ship. I was terribly disappointed.

1. That Makiko would make such an unusual and patently unreasonable request shows how close she was to her brother and how upset by the finality of his departure for Manchuria with his new wife.

May 27 *Friday*

As was arranged the other day, I went to the cooking class at eight o'clock. The teacher arrived shortly after that and gave us lessons in how to make all kinds of dishes. Our assignment was determined by lot, and I drew the pound cake.[1] It took us all morning to finish cooking, and in the afternoon we helped set up a mock Western-style room by moving the furniture and changing things around. It was four o'clock when we finished. I got pretty tired, but have to go again tomorrow.

1. *Kasutera* (see entry for February 3). It would have been very unusual to find an oven in a private home at this period. Since there were no stoves of the kind familiar to Westerners, the cooking class probably used a simple box-type oven heated by charcoal.

May 28 *Saturday*

Today is *Chikyū-setsu*,[1] a national holiday.

On this day at Mr. Matsumiya's house they customarily display all kinds of things their pupils have learned to make, such as flower arrangements, sewing, and Japanese and Western-style cooking, as well as demonstrating the tea ceremony. Even though it was raining, Okuni-san and I went to see the display. The parlor that we redecorated yesterday to make it into a Western-style room looked very nice. In fact, it looked so formal that it didn't seem like Mr. Matsumiya's house at all. A lot of other people came to see the exhibit in spite of the rain. They served us a box lunch and later a dinner in "stand-up" style.

Came home around ten o'clock at night feeling tired.

1. The birthday of the Meiji Empress.

MAY 29 *Sunday*

Went over to Mr. Matsumiya's house again early in the morning to help clean up the place and stayed until noon. In the afternoon there was to be a party and entertainment for those who had helped. I did not go, but Okuni-san, Chūji-san, Sei-san, and the Eastside family's Yuri-san did. They said that dessert was served and that box lunches had been prepared for Okuni-san and me. They got back after five o'clock.

MAY 30 *Monday*

Kurushima-sensei arrived this morning. He came to Kyoto to give a public storytelling performance sponsored by *Kedee*-san.[1] However, when he arrived at the place where he was to speak in the early evening, only a few people were there, and he says that he did not feel like giving a talk at all, which is unprecedented.

What I just wrote is not what happened at all. Apparently I misunderstood.

1. Makiko writes the name *Kedee* in the *katakana* syllabary, which was never used for Japanese surnames at that time. The sponsor may have been Otis Cary, a well-known American missionary in Kyoto. See Introduction.

MAY 31 *Tuesday*

Kurushima-sensei arrived this morning from Tokyo in order to give two talks today, one in the afternoon and another in the evening. *Kedee*-san is the sponsor. My husband and his friends had made a prior commitment to attend a rehearsal of children's plays performed by the writers and could not go with him.

Kurushima-sensei returned home from his engagement later in the afternoon saying that hardly anyone came to hear his talk. There were some children on one side of the hall and some old ladies on the other, so he told only three short stories. After dinner he went back to the meeting place, but returned here right away. This time, he said, finding only one or two people there, he had canceled the whole thing. Moreover, my husband was not back yet from the plays he had gone to see, so Kurushima-sensei, feeling lost, returned to Tokyo immediately.

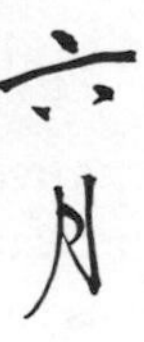

June 1 *Wednesday*

I wonder why I am so lazy these days? In the evening when the lights are turned on, I get sleepy. All I do is practice dozing and don't want to do anything at all, including writing.

June 2 *Thursday*

The children's plays sponsored by the Otogi Club and performed by their writers are starting today and will run for the next two days. The program sounds very interesting.

June 3 *Friday*

Went to Nijō because the other day my father asked me to come and check their summer clothing. Spent all morning sorting out items that are no longer of any use and sold the lot to a second-hand clothing dealer for only ¥25.

It was my younger brother Senzō's birthday, so I was treated to a surprise beef dinner (sukiyaki) for the special occasion before I came back to Gojō.

June 4 *Saturday* *Clear [June 5, 6]*[1]

Today's cooking class at the Matsumiyas' began at nine in the morning, and as I feared, took longer than I had hoped—it ended after noon. Rushed back home, since my husband was planning to leave on a camping trip with some friends. They first assembled here and took off at 2:30. Their plan is to take the Keihan Railway to Fushimi and then start hiking, but since the weather was not quite what it should have been, I am concerned about their trip. We had beef sukiyaki tonight, since it is the first Saturday of the month.

Well, there was an incident tonight. I had saved some of the dishes I learned to cook in this morning's class for Hide-san, thinking that he might come home tonight. Since he did not, I served them to Mr. Moriguchi instead. He got very angry, sat cross-legged, slipped his kimono off one shoulder,[2] and began telling me why he was so upset. He started by calling me "*o-maki-san*,"[3] and I answered innocently, "Yes?" He spoke in a slow, deliberate manner, emphasizing each sentence, saying, "I appreciate your thoughtfulness in offering me a taste of your Western-style cooking, but I am not going to touch it. If you ever again have a notion to serve me this stuff, please kindly observe this fortyish male happily eating his *chazuke*."[4] He went on and on, repeating himself, making it clear how very angry he was.

I was astonished and appalled by his behavior, and had no idea why he was so angry, speaking to me like that in front of the maids and shop-boys. I became as upset and angry as he was, but said that I was sorry, trying to put an end to this incident. Later that night, the more I thought about it the more upset I got and felt sick to my stomach. After I went to bed, I cried from humiliation at what he had said and how insulting he had been, and could not fall asleep for a long time.

Even this morning I was still upset, and was waiting for him to come to work, just wanting to see how he would appear. He came in through the store and the kitchen, and into our quarters and said, "I am sorry about last night." I was not in a forgiving mood, however, thinking how he disguises his true self and behaves so nicely when he visits my father's store and other pharmacists in Nijō, and how I would tell my father what he really is like, and so on.[5]

I was upset all day long. It began to rain this morning and I was worried about what's happening with my husband and his camping trip, hoping that he would come home soon, and so on and so forth. Last night's incident increased my anxiety and impatience.

The campers came home about seven o'clock, soaking wet and hungry. They took a hot bath, and ate a big meal of thick soup with vegetables and meat (*satsuma-jiru*) and fish cake, and went home. My husband brought home a big "catch," a large *haniwa*[6] that he found during the trip. He was very proud of his discovery and told us how hard it is to find such a fine piece. Listening to him, I felt rather tired and thought to myself that I have been dragging myself around all day.

I was tempted many times to tell my husband about the incident with Mr. Moriguchi, but I didn't, for I thought he might not want to hear such a bothersome story.[7] I did not tell anybody about how I felt and cried a lot, feeling depressed whenever I recalled what had happened. I don't know if I will be able to carry on in this state.

1. The entire three pages for June 4, 5, and 6 in the diary are filled with the entry starting on June 4.
2. A rude gesture indicating that a person is about to start a fight.
3. Far too familiar a term for Mr. Moriguchi to use to the wife of his employer, no matter how high his position among the business branch-families.
4. A humble dish of cold rice warmed up by pouring hot tea over it.
5. Makiko's family had known Mr. Moriguchi from his days as a young store clerk, when he would come around to Nijō on business.
6. Prehistoric grave figures of fired clay in the shape of humans, animals, and dwellings.
7. Even though Moriguchi had crossed the boundary separating the domestic domain from the business, Makiko knew that it would be extremely awkward for her husband to have to make peace between his head manager and his wife. It is not difficult to guess what lay behind this extraordinary event. Moriguchi, who had been head store manager for some years, was far more experienced in the business than young Chūhachi VII had been when he succeeded to the headship of the household at the age of 20. However deep his dissatisfaction with the situation, he would not dare confront Chūhachi directly. Having had too much to drink, however, Moriguchi let his frustrations boil up in Chūhachi's absence, striking out at Makiko, who was even younger and less experienced in her role than was her husband.

JUNE 7 *Tuesday [June 8]*[1]

For the past few days I have been preoccupied with the incident, to the extent that I even started thinking about going back home to Nijō permanently. My father, who has been struggling without my mother, would be better off having me at home and would not need a housekeeper if he had me. But then I would think that it's foolish to worry so much about what Mr. Moriguchi said when he was drunk, and besides, I am not at fault.

If I were to leave here and go back to Nijō, I would cause trouble for everyone here. People would think that I had a fight with the employees of the store, or speculate that I did not get along with my mother-in-law, which is absolutely untrue. We get along very well, and I would never do that to her. Either way, it would not solve the problem.

In extreme moments I even imagine that it would be simple and convenient if I were to die suddenly like my mother. Why can't I die? The thought rushes through my mind, and I end up sobbing. In my sleep I dreamed about my mother and grandmother, and during waking hours, I reminisced about the days when they were alive and how much I miss them and thought about the trouble I am in now and so on. It has been terribly hard—I just cannot shake it off.[2]

1. The entry for June 7 extends to the page for June 8 as well.
2. Despite her longing for her mother and grandmother, Makiko seems to have come to terms with her anger on her own, for in later entries there is no trace of animosity toward Moriguchi.

June 9

[No entry]

June 10 *Friday*

Mrs. Matsumiya came to visit unexpectedly this morning. She brought us a gift of 50 eggs and a box of 25 moon cakes, for which we are grateful.[1] She seemed to be in a great hurry and said that she is on her way to Osaka. She did not even come into the house.

1. No reason for presenting these gifts is given. Perhaps they were meant to express appreciation for the help received for the affairs held on May 27, 28, and 29.

June 11 *Saturday* *Clear*

Another Saturday has come around. I will never forget what happened a week ago—actually I have not forgotten it for even a day. I will never forget it all my life!

I hurried back from cooking class and went to see Uncle Amano. I was happy to find him looking much better than I had expected. From there I went on to Nijō, and Eiko and I went to Shijō to buy some light wool kimono material. I hurried home after parting from Eiko in Shijō and found that Brother Tanii was visiting us. Evidently he is on the go again—tomorrow he will return to his home in Kyushu and will travel to Tokyo on the fifteenth. He will be back in Kyoto around the twentieth. His mother, Mrs. Tanii Onui, came over tonight to see him.

June 12 *Sunday* *Clear*

Mr. Nishimura Tokusaburō from Tonoshō paid us a surprise visit in his uniform this afternoon. It was his first brief leave since being drafted into the army, and since his unit was to assemble in Kyōgoku at three o'clock, he said that he had just made a quick dash over to see us. Fortunately Brother Tanii had not yet left to catch his train and was able to see him as well.

After Brother Tanii left for the railway station, we fixed a simple snack of rice balls and broiled fish for Tokusaburō and talked with him for a while before he had to go back. We should be thankful to the soldiers—their lives are not easy.

Mr. Matsumiya took the trouble to come over in the evening just to thank us for the shirt we laundered after the camping trip and delivered to him.

JUNE 13 *Monday Rain*

No incident.

This morning my husband said that someone asked him why my father has not paid a courtesy call on the go-between for my brother's wedding. I wrote to my father at once.[1] While I was writing letters, I also wrote to the Kōshimas asking about the family and to Oyuki-sama, now that she has safely arrived in Dairen, asking how she is.

1. Makiko wrote so quickly because of her father's apparent breach of etiquette. The go-between must have been someone her husband introduced to her father, who since his wife's death has been unable to cope with even routine matters, as we have seen.

JUNE 14 *Tuesday Rain*

No incident.

Received a letter from Mrs. Nakajima in Wakasa, so I replied promptly.

JUNE 15 *Wednesday Rain*

No news to write. It rained again and is oppressive.

Sent the receipt for the ceramic wares that we shipped to my brother in Dairen. Apparently he will need it when the shipment arrives.

JUNE 16 *Thursday Rain*

Rained again today. Although it is the rainy season, it does get boring when it rains constantly without a break!

Sent money (¥3) to Mrs. Shirakawa Omiki to express our appreciation for all her help.

Mr. Tanaka came over in the evening and told us about his plan to go to Manchuria, which really surprised us.[1] He stayed and talked until midnight, telling us many things including some confidential stories that had never been told before.

1. Tanaka Hozan had evidently determined to leave Japan. His plans changed at some point; see entries for September 14, October 27, and December 2, 3, and 4.

JUNE 17 *Friday Rain*

We were hoping that the rain would stop today (but it is still raining) so that we could put the Boys' Day dolls[1] back in storage. Despite the damp weather we decided to do it anyway, and four of us worked together and finished up the job. Also thoroughly cleaned the shelves and area where all the tea bowls and implements are kept next to the tea room in Mother's quarters,[2] since I was scolded yesterday for having neglected it so long.

There is a *nō* performance at the Inari shrine, but my husband said that he won't be able to go, since he has to take care of some business at the school. Mr. Matsui went alone and stopped by on his way back home, chatted with us for a while, waiting in vain for my husband to come home, and finally left. As it turned out, my husband had to attend a general assembly of the Pharmacists' Association tonight and was there all evening.

1. Boys' Day is May 5 according to the new Western calendar, but the Nakanos were still following the lunar calendar, as they did for the observance of Girls' Day. Because June 5 was the day after Makiko's crisis with Mr. Moriguchi, she made no record of the family's celebration of Boys' Day.
2. *Inkyo*, the living quarters of retired parent(s); see Introduction.

JUNE 18 *Saturday*

It was a clear day for a change. I am lucky, for whenever I go out the weather is fine. Went to the cooking class, which began at nine o'clock. Apparently today's menu is a very special one that would have to be ordered in advance and would cost about ¥2 at a restaurant. Kobayashi-sama,[1] who has not been attending the class lately, came today.

1. Unidentified.

JUNE 19 *Sunday Clear*

Fortunately, the weather was good again today. Tonight my husband went to meeting at the School of Pharmacy that started at 7:30. There was a *kyōgen* performance by the Shigeyama Sengorō troupe, which is part of the series of regular study meetings, but no one from our family attended. Probably Mr. Matsui made it.

JUNE 20 *Monday Rain*

It has been hot and humid since this morning. We spent all morning changing the furnishings[1] in the house to adjust to the summer season.

My husband left early this morning to serve as observer at the election regarding the pricing of land[2] or something like that. He came home around 7:30 in the evening, which is very early for him—inevitably it rained.[3]

1. Because the city is situated in a basin, Kyoto summers are notoriously hot and humid. To reduce the oppressive heat, sliding doors (*shōji* and *fusuma*) are replaced by bamboo screens; floors are covered with woven grass mats; and floor cushions (*zabuton*) are replaced by thin summer ones covered in linen or woven banana-leaf fiber. To heighten the sense of coolness, summer paintings, flower vases, and fans are used.
2. See entry for October 26.
3. Another play on the notion that unusual behavior causes it to rain.

JUNE 21 *Tuesday Rain*

It is still raining. Nothing much happened; it was just oppressive.

My husband went to a meeting of the shrine parishioners association in the afternoon and had dinner at Uotora[1] afterwards.

It is my mother's monthly memorial day, but I haven't been to the temple for a while. I am afraid that all the ancestors of the Nakao family must be feeling neglected and are wondering what has happened.

1. A fish restaurant.

June 22 *Wednesday Rain*

Rainy day again. Nothing much happened. We have been waiting for Brother Tanii's visit every day, but so far there is no sign of him.

A Ryukyuan traveling salesman came and showed us bolts of kimono material.[1] They are good quality and the prices are reasonable, so we bought some. We paid ¥6.50 for one, ¥4.80 for another, ¥4.10 each for two more, and he gave us a 50 *sen* discount on every one. He told us that he is staying at the Yamashiroya in Nijō, and his name is Gusuku Gozei. What an interesting name![2]

1. The material probably was *bashōfu*, hand-woven banana-leaf fiber, which makes a cool and elegant summer kimono.

2. Main-island Japanese often comment on Okinawan (Ryukyuan) names, which are quite distinctive.

June 23 *Thursday Clear*

It was cloudy this morning but became a nice clear day from noontime on. I had a telephone call from Nijō this morning asking me to come and look at a vanity and sewing box that had been delivered on approval, so I went out in the afternoon to have a look. They are not of really high quality, and the price is a little more than ¥12 for the two of them, so I asked the shop-boy to take them back. I stayed a while longer and, since I had some extra time, decided to go over to see Elder Sister Kōshima, who looked very tired. We talked a while and I left.

When I got back to Nijō and looked at the clock it was already 9:30. I ought to have gone home, but when I saw Eiko and Senzō and they asked me when I'll be back next time, I could not bring myself to leave. I became tearful and thought that ever since our mother died they have been depending on me—young and inadequate as I am—and long for my visits. I shouldn't have cried in front of them, but I was so sad and felt very sorry for them.

Mr. Amenomori,[1] who has returned to Kyoto, paid a visit to Nijō today. He lost his wife recently and is left with three young children, the oldest only five, to take care of. My heart was filled with sympathy for him.

Evidently Mr. Matsumiya came to visit while I was away in Nijō.

1. Head of one of the pharmacist households in Nijō.

JUNE 24 *Friday* *Rain*

It rained again today. There has been nothing of significance to record.

Got up in the morning, had breakfast, worked, had lunch, worked some more, had dinner, nodded off, and am about to go to bed.

JUNE 25 *Saturday* *Clear*

Although today is Tenjin-san's open-air market day,[1] it did not rain for a change.

The two gardeners came this morning and separated the palm bamboo and trimmed the overgrown sycamore trees so that the place looks much neater. We try hard to clean the garden ourselves, but it never looks this good. They really are professionals!

A messenger, bearing a thank-you gift from Nijō that was supposed to be delivered to the Eastside family, came to our house instead. It turned out to be a mistake, as I suspected right away.

The maid, who had promised to be back by yesterday or today, sent a postcard saying that she will return on the 27th. I was not happy about the delay. Obviously she has no common sense.

We have been waiting for days for Brother Tanii to arrive, but he did not come today either.

1. See entries for January 25 and the 25th of later months, where Makiko comments on the likelihood of rain on Tenjin-san's market day.

JUNE 26 *Sunday* *Rain*

I was expecting good weather today, but it rained again.

My husband went to a memorial service[1] sponsored by the Fine Arts Association beginning at nine o'clock this morning and to a meeting of the Pharmacists' Association in the afternoon. He said that he'd have lunch at Mr. Matsui's house—I wonder if he is inviting himself? He did not come home for dinner and got back after ten o'clock.

1. *Segaki-e.* The service may have been for one or more of the founders of the association, which would not have been unusual. See entry for March 21.

JUNE 27 *Monday Rain*

The gardeners came back this afternoon to plant three pine trees around the area near Mother's room and cleared away the tree branches and leaves as they always do. It looks better now that the pines fill in the empty space.

JUNE 28 *Tuesday*

It was a gloomy day with light rain off and on all day.

I haven't heard from Okyō-sama[1] for a long time but received a postcard and a photograph of her family today. It is a good picture with Ryū-chan[2] in it. Since she said that she has eye trouble, I replied at once and enclosed a photograph of our family.

Mashimo-sensei, the school principal, came to see my husband in the afternoon. Mr. Matsumiya arrived later, and they all had dinner together. Mashimo-sensei left about eight o'clock. Mr. Matsumiya left around ten o'clock or so, which is early for him. I think he left so early because Mr. Matsui was not here tonight!

1. Her friend.
2. A male child.

JUNE 29 *Wednesday Clear*

It was a beautiful, pleasant day for a change.

We have been wondering for some time about Brother Tanii's visit, and he finally arrived without warning this morning about 7:30. Apparently his business kept him in Tokyo longer than he had expected. He brought lots of presents—something for everyone. Mine was summer cotton kimono material.[1]

Right away he announced that he will be leaving this afternoon and went out to visit the Yamada Genzaburō family[2] and my family in Nijō immediately. When he got back in the afternoon, the Eastside Doctor came over to see him after he had finished seeing patients. We served them sushi that we had ordered from the Komachi sushi restaurant, together with *hamo*[3] soup we made. He took the 3:58 P.M. train from Shichijō Station.

My father came here in the evening to pay what he owed for expenses incurred during my brother's wedding. We went "modern" this time, and entertained them[4] with München beer and bananas.

1. To make a garment called *yukata*.
2. Yamada Genzaburō's wife, Osei, was Tanii Senjirō's half-sister.
3. Sea eel, or pike conger, particularly associated with Kyoto cuisine.
4. Her father, the Eastside Doctor, and her husband.

JUNE 30 *Thursday*

Being the last day of the month, it has been very busy.

Mr. Matsui came over but didn't stay long. He came to get payment for the camera we bought, for which he had served as go-between. He said that since the camera was slightly used we got it for ¥23 instead of ¥25. My husband has been using it even before it was paid for, and today he photographed our garden and the western hills of Kyoto.

JULY 1 *Friday Clear*

Today being the first day of the month, our business branch-families, Mr. Yamamoto Matsu and Mr. Ōkita Toyosaburō, came in the morning for greetings. Fusako-sama of the Eastside family also came over.

Just because yesterday was accounting day, I felt as though I was busy the entire day, but today I feel relaxed. Now I know how working people must feel before and after the day accounts are settled.

Towards evening Mashimo-sensei and Mr. Suzuki came to visit. Mr. Tanaka Hozan also was here, but he was the only one who stayed for dinner.

JULY 2 *Saturday Clear*

It's the day for our cooking lesson again. It began at nine o'clock. These days the teacher is always there before we arrive. Three more people joined the class today. When I got home, it was already two o'clock in the afternoon.

My husband went to a meeting at the School of Pharmacy in the morning and then went on to see Mr. Matsumiya after that. Of course, he just had to have the dinner we cooked in the class. Later he stopped by Mr. Matsui's house and didn't get back home until after midnight!

JULY 3 *Sunday*

Today being a Sunday, all the family members were home, making things lively around the house. Around noon a man from the Yamamoto Photo Studio came to borrow our newly purchased camera. We took advantage of his visit and had him take our pictures. He said that the prints will be ready tonight.

JULY 4 *Monday*

The photographs were ready this morning.

My husband has been busy lately working toward the publication of a magazine for the Otogi Club. Just before noon Mr. Matsui came over and had lunch with us. He stayed on, and he and my husband worked at gluing together pieces of broken *haniwa*[1] pottery all afternoon. They left together in late afternoon. Mr. Matsui had to go to some meeting, and my husband had a meeting at the School of Pharmacy.

1. See entry for June 4.

JULY 5 *Tuesday Clear*

Nothing happened today.

Today is my 21st birthday.[1] One gradually grows older without ever realizing it.

Received lots of *wakame*[2] from the Taniis. Gave some to the Eastside family and cooked some today. It was very tender and tasty.

1. Makiko was born in 1890, which would make this her twentieth birthday by Western reckoning. At the time she kept her diary, however, one was considered one year old at birth. The system has been abandoned only in recent years. Although birthdays of adults were not generally celebrated at this time, in the entry for June 3, Makiko mentions that they had a sukiyaki dinner at Nijō to celebrate her brother Senzō's birthday. In the entry for September 22, she remarks that on the birthday of her husband's younger sister Shinako, they had sukiyaki only because they were unable to find good fish for the meal. Both Senzō and Shinako were teenagers, which suggests that families had begun to mark their children's birthdays. No others are mentioned in the diary.

2. A kind of seaweed widely used in miso soup and salads or cooked with vegetables.

July 6 *Wednesday Rain*

It rained again. Tanii Kōtarō came to see us. It's been a while since his last visit here. He said that he has resigned his job in Tokyo and is on his way to take up a new position in a factory in Dairi.[1] He arrived in Kyoto yesterday and will have to leave again on the eighth or ninth. My husband took him to the Gojō Club restaurant for dinner and went on to see Mashimo-sensei after they parted.

1. Apparently Kōtarō had taken a job in the same plant where his half-brother Senjirō was employed.

July 7 *Thursday Rain*

It has been a very warm day. My husband left early in the morning for the school where they have been working on the publication of the Otogi Club magazine. I started to work early while it was still cool, putting cotton batting in a futon cover.[1]

After lunch we asked the shop-boys who were on their lunch break—I felt rather guilty about it—to take some pictures of the family in the garden. The women family members—Mother, Kuniko, and I—had a separate picture taken, posed leaning on the chairs with the table in front. I wonder how they will turn out—I cannot wait! I hope they will be developed soon.

Around three o'clock two teachers from Shūdō Primary School came over to talk about the publication of the Otogi Club magazine, which was supposed to be out by the tenth. Since it is taking longer than Mr. Suzuki planned, it will have to be postponed to the twelfth. Besides, it turns out that it would not be possible to print it before then.

1. Futon are large cloth covers filled with puffed cotton batting. The heavier ones are used to sleep on, like a mattress, and the lighter ones as covers, like a comforter. One of Makiko's responsibilities was to maintain in good condition all the futon for the family members, the live-in employees, and guests.

July 8 *Friday Clear*

It has become unbearably hot all at once. The temperature soared to 86° today.

Hide-san came home in the evening from the boat tour of Lake Biwa that started on the fourth. He was heavily tanned and had big blisters on the palms of his hands. He got home safely, but said that it was so windy that the boat was almost swamped by waves at times. He said that it was fun, but I would be afraid. Although he must have been tired he stayed up until 1:30 in the morning developing photographs. But alas, there wasn't even one good one—how disappointing!

JULY 9 *Saturday Clear*

It is just as hot as it was yesterday, or even hotter!

I went to the Saturday cooking class with Kuni-san, as usual.

Since I had received a letter from my sister Eiko, asking me please to come and get the mosquito nets out, I stopped by Nijō on my way home. Our lesson today was how to make ice cream, so I tried it right away while I waited for Eiko to come home. It turned out very well. Eiko was so late that I had to have dinner there. It is a very hot and humid night. It got up to 93° today.

JULY 10 *Sunday Clear*

I was going to finish putting cotton batting in the futon and complete work on the kimono coat this morning. I started early, but the heat was so unbearable that I thought my body was going to melt. As I was fighting the heat, which was slowing down my work, the back covers of the Otogi Club magazine that my husband has been working on were delivered to the house, so I stopped my work and switched to putting the seal of the editor, Nakano Chūhachi,[1] on every copy and ended up spending a whole half-day doing nothing else.

During the day it was as hot as yesterday, but toward evening it seemed to cool down a little. The thermometer registered 91°.

1. This is the only time Makiko uses her husband's given name.

JULY 11 *Monday Clear*

The unbearable heat seemed to ease slightly this morning. All the public schools closed at noon today.

The Otogi Club magazine, which was finished today, is very handsome and modern.

My husband went to a meeting at one o'clock at Seirin-ji[1] where they discussed matters concerning the plans to found a new Pharmaceutical Association.[2] He did not come home for dinner, but ate at Mr. Matsui's house as usual.

The temperature was 86°.

1. A Buddhist temple.

2. This association, to be called *Yakuji kyōkai*, never came into being. His participation in the planning for it nonetheless is evidence of Chūhachi's commitment to modernizing the pharmaceutical business in Kyoto.

JULY 12 *Tuesday* *Clear*

It was warmer than yesterday, and the rainy season seems to be ending. The restaurants along the Kamo River have opened up their balconies for the summer season.

Received a parcel containing a big box of rice crackers (*arare*) from the Mutōs. With it was a note saying that the gift carries delayed apologies for not sending an offering for the memorial service that they had been unable to attend.

JULY 13 *Wednesday*

It was another hot day.

Received a letter from Yukiko in Dairen and replied tonight. Also sent a thank-you note to the Mutōs on behalf of my husband, acknowledging receipt of the gift.

JULY 14, 15, 16

[No entries][1]

1. It is likely that Makiko made no entries in her diary for these three days because they are the dates of the *Gion-matsuri*, Kyoto's great midsummer festival, a month-long series of observances centering on Yasaka-jinja. The rites, designed to placate the souls of the dead, originated in 869 in an effort to arrest the spread of an epidemic. They were suspended for a time in the fifteenth century, but the festival was revived and assumed its present form in the Tokugawa period. At first glance the date seems odd, for today the major event, a spectacular procession of enormous floats, is held on July 17. On July 24, however, there is a second, smaller procession with fewer floats. See entry for that date.

JULY 17 *Sunday*

It's too bad it rained on Sunday. There was heavy thunder, too, but luckily it didn't develop into a real storm. After the thunder stopped, the skies started to clear gradually. It was strange that it didn't rain much toward the end of the rainy season, and then, just as we thought that it was about to end, apparently it really did.

After the rain stopped, Eiko came over. She had just finished her examinations at school and was feeling free and relaxed.[1] I made her a snack of sweet red-bean sauce over shaved ice.

1. Eiko stayed until July 19.

JULY 18 *Monday*

It has been a nice day. Just as I was getting ready to take my bath in early evening, my father stopped by. He was on his way to the railway station to pay his respects to Professor Nagai, who is on the faculty of the School of Pharmacy at Tokyo Imperial University, when his train stops in Kyoto on his way to Osaka. My husband went along with him.

I heard that Mr. Matsui Matabei passed away at last, and there will be a private funeral tomorrow. I feel sorry for the family. There is nothing as fragile as human life.

JULY 19 *Tuesday*

Mr. Moriguchi went to Nijō this morning on business, and came back with a message from my father asking me to buy a nice *obi* for Eiko while she is staying with us. My hair was not done yet, but I wanted to go out as soon as I could, so I just twisted and piled it up on the top of my head and left with Eiko. At Yoshikawa Kimono Store a clerk showed us nothing interesting so we had to go to Shijō later in the day to look further. We finally bought one at Daimaruichi, even though it was not what I had in mind. Because the price was low, however, we decided that it was the best we could do.

I parted from Eiko at the streetcar stop at Shijō and came home. My husband was not back yet. He was gone to a meeting at the School of Pharmacy again.

JULY 20 *Wednesday*

It was a hot day. Despite the heat my husband ran around all over town from morning to dusk visiting people and talking about the plan to develop the School of Pharmacy. He came home briefly for supper but took off right away to attend Mr. Matsui Matabei's private funeral[1] with Mr. Tanaka. After my husband got back, Mr. Tanaka came over again and stayed talking until late.

While my husband was attending the funeral, Mr. Matsumiya dropped in. He was obviously in a good mood, saying that he cannot help smiling and laughing and that he had been treated to a lot of beer today when he visited one of the music teachers at the Third Higher School. He did not stay long, since he had to go to a meeting at a friend's house where artists are to show some of their work.

1. Since it is being held in the evening, this may have been a wake (*tsuya*), but Makiko does not use the term.

JULY 21 *Thursday Clear*

Since it was the day of Mr. Matsui Matabei's public funeral, we were asked to help out by accommodating their guests in the front part of our store. Early in the morning we were busy cleaning and tidying up the place, placing ashtrays, and making barley tea[1] instead of hot regular tea to serve the eleven or so guests. Everyone praised my arrangement, saying how nice and cool it looked. I was embarrassed, since it was just an idea I had on the spur of the moment.[2] The funeral was scheduled to begin at nine o'clock, but it was nearly ten when the procession left their home.

No sooner was I beginning to enjoy a feeling of relief than lunchtime arrived. In the afternoon Mashimo-sensei, the Eastside Doctor, and Mr. Matsui came to visit. It was unbearably hot.

Since today is the beginning of the "Dog Days," we ate the traditional sweet red-bean dumplings. Somehow, it seems that Mr. Matsui has been eating his dumplings for the "Dog Days" at our house every year.[3]

They all went to hear a lecture about the expedition to the South Pole tonight, having first had dinner at the Gojō Club.[4]

1. *Mugi-cha*, still a popular summertime drink, can be served hot or cold.

2. Makiko obviously initiated the idea and supervised this operation, whereas on most occasions she followed her mother-in-law's instructions.

3. The "Dog Days" are called *doyō*. During this period, the hottest of the year, it is thought important to eat particularly nourishing food. The dumplings contain a very sweet bean jam called *anko*. A favorite dish for the "Dog Days" that Makiko does not mention is broiled eel.

4. In the early years of the twentieth century, several nations mounted scientific expeditions to Antarctica, but none reached the South Pole until Roald Amundsen in

(*Above, left*) Family members in the garden behind Mine's quarters; see entry for July 7: (*front, from left*) Chūjirō, Mine, Seiichi; (*standing, from left*) Kuniko, Shinako, Makiko. (*Above, right*) Nakao Eiko in kimono and hakama, ca. 1910. (Nakano Takashi)

The family at a restaurant on the Kamo River, ca. 1915: (*front, from left*) Kuniko, Eiko(?), Mine holding Makiko's son Yasuo, Makiko, Nakao Yukiko; (*rear, from left*) Matsui Jisuke, Shinako, Chūhachi, Nakao Manzō. (Nakano Takashi)

Gion-matsuri procession on Shijō Avenue, ca. 1910. (Kyoto Prefectural Archives)

General Nakamura Satoru, ca. 1910; see entry for July 22. (Nakano Takashi)

December 1911. The lecture may well have been about the plans for what proved to be Japan's first successful Antarctic expedition, led by First Lieutenant Shirase Nobu, which reached latitude 80° 5′ in January 1912.

July 22 *Friday*

My father telephoned this morning to say that Uncle Nakamura[1] will be passing through Kyoto Station tomorrow at five o'clock in the morning. He also wanted me to come to Nijō to supervise preparations for the festival.[2] I promised him I'll come tomorrow afternoon.

1. General Nakamura Satoru; see Makiko's Social World.
2. The best-known feature of the *Gion-matsuri* is the great procession of floats on July 17. There are two kinds of floats—huge, multi-storied ones called *hoko* and smaller ones called *yama*. Here Makiko refers to a second procession, less well-known, featuring only the smaller ones. For *Gion-matsuri*, see note to entry for July 14–16.

July 23 *Saturday*

Last night, before going to bed, I prayed that I would be able to get up this morning without any help, but Mother had to wake me up. I sprang to my feet when she said that it was already past four o'clock. My husband got ready first and was hurrying me to get dressed. I finally got ready and we rushed to make it to the station in time.

My father, Uncle Kōshima, and Mr. Nishimura Toraichi were already there. Obviously Uncle Kōshima had not had time to change, for he was wearing a wrinkled cotton kimono. The train arrived shortly after we all assembled, but it stopped for only five minutes and there was hardly any time to say anything. We had barely exchanged greetings with Uncle Nakamura when the train started to move away.

I had planned to go to Nijō after lunch, but there was a sudden downpour with thunder and lightning, and I was not able to go until late afternoon.

July 24 *Sunday*

Yesterday's showers turned to rain in the evening, interfering with some of the activities of the festival eve. However, the weather cleared up in the morning, and it turned out to be an especially nice day.

I went shopping for food very early in the morning and opened up the fish shop. The merchant grumbled as he opened the door, obviously still sleepy, but I didn't care, for I was desperate to buy fish for today's festive dishes.

After consulting with my father about what to prepare, I started to cook. In a while Chūji-san and Sei-san[1] came over. I sent red-bean glutinous rice, which was supposed to be delivered yesterday, to Gojō this morning. I also sent an invitation to the children at the Eastside family, and they came over later. With all the children in our house it resembled a kindergarten, which made my father very happy.

We watched the festival procession, ate all the delicious food, and had a good time. I asked Eiko to take the children home around eight o'clock. Then I took my bath and got back to Gojō at eleven.

1. Her husband's younger brothers have come from Gojō to watch the festival procession in Nijō.

JULY 25 *Monday*

Yesterday, while I was away from home, Professor Nagai came from Tokyo to visit again, and my husband accompanied him all day. They had dinner at Nakamura-rō restaurant.

This morning about four o'clock my husband suddenly had an attack of chills, and his temperature soared to 39°.[1] His temperature did not go down at all during the morning. I was upset at how uncomfortable he looked, so we called in Dr. Kitawaki. The doctor came in the afternoon. His diagnosis was that it's an intestinal disorder again, and he ordered a strict liquid diet. My husband's temperature dropped a little tonight, and he was able to rest a bit. I was shocked by how high his temperature got!

1. Makiko uses the Celsius scale here for the first time. Chūhachi's temperature was over 102°F. See entry for January 27.

JULY 26 *Tuesday*

My husband still has a slight fever this morning. He said that he was nauseated, so I massaged his stomach lightly and he felt better. Then he went to the toilet and passed a tapeworm again! It must have been the result of the medicine he took. His temperature went down and he felt much better, but he says that he feels weak because he hasn't eaten solid food for a while.

Mr. Matsui telephoned to ask how he is, and we told him about the tapeworm. He laughed and said, "Oh, so he delivered a baby again!"

JULY 27 *Wednesday Rain*

My husband apparently feels fine today, but is still taking it easy. However, since the *Kineya nagauta*[1] group is performing at the Minami-za theater and we heard that today's program is exceptionally good, he decided to go. Mr. Matsui stopped by around three o'clock on his way to the theater and was surprised to find him still in bed. My husband bathed and changed at once. The Eastside Doctor and Mother decided to go with them, and Hide-san went too, because they are performing a new composition called *Shin Urashima* tonight.[2] Evidently Mr. Matsumiya also joined them later.

I really wanted to go, too, but it was the cooking-class day, and even though the menu was a stew, which I don't care for, I felt I had to attend. They got back around eleven o'clock, saying that a piece called *Yoshiwara Suzume*[3] was also very well performed.

1. A type of vocal music, accompanied by the *shamisen*, a three-stringed instrument.

2. "New Urashima," based on a Japanese folk tale that resembles the Rip Van Winkle story.

3. "Sparrows of the Yoshiwara" is a delightful genre dance number typical of kabuki's romanticized version of the famous entertainment quarter of Tokyo in the period before the Meiji Restoration. Once a scene in a play, the dance, which has become a fixture in the repertoire of kabuki, has no story to tell nor any connection with the original play. To the accompaniment of the *nagauta* piece referred to, a song-bird seller and his wife make their way through the Yoshiwara.

JULY 28 *Thursday*

Okuni-san and I decided to go to the theater, so we dressed up for the occasion and set off in early evening. The place was filled with geisha all in beautiful kimono, for whom most of the seats had been reserved tonight. We particularly enjoyed the two pieces performed by Chiyo and Eiko.[1] The popular *Kanjinchō*[2] was not as interesting as we expected, but we did enjoy the part that we had learned to recite ourselves.

We got home around eleven o'clock. My husband had gone to an executive board meeting of the School of Pharmacy and was not back yet. I went to bed and slept for a while, and when I woke up I found him standing by my bedside. I jumped up, startled. It was exactly one o'clock.

1. Both are female names, which suggests that the performers were geisha.
2. The story is that told in the *nō* drama *Ataka*. See entry for March 19.

JULY 29 *Friday*

The *nagauta* group's performance is ending today, alas . . . My husband was gone all day on business concerning the Kyoto German Academic Society, and he then went on to the baseball game at the Second Middle School.

JULY 30 *Saturday*

My husband is busy conferring about preparations for the forthcoming camping trip.

JULY 31 *Sunday*

Mr. Matsui came over and talked with my husband about the miscellaneous items they will need for their camping trip. It has been arranged that the tent will be shipped to the campsite directly from Mr. Matsui's house tonight.

Received a letter from Dairi informing us that Brother Tanii is coming to visit us with his son Take-chan either tomorrow or the day after.

Went to bed at two o'clock in the morning because it is the last day of the month, and we were very busy settling the accounts.

AUGUST 1 *Monday*

As of today all schools start summer vacation.

Today is *hassaku*, and according to the old custom, it is a day to make the rounds to pay respects. As usual on the first day of the month the business branch-families called. It took all morning to receive all the visitors.

Mr. Kataoka, who is the go-between,[1] paid a courtesy call and presented us with a box of bean candy (*yōkan*).

After lunch all the campers left by the 1:40 P.M. train. They are four grown-ups, namely Mr. Shikada,[2] Mr. Matsui, my husband, and Hide-san.

After they left, Brother Tanii arrived with his son Take-chan from Kyushu. He announced that they will be staying longer this time. Take-chan went to bed early with a slight fever. He may have caught a cold because they made the trip by boat.

1. For Okuni's marriage to Matsui Jisuke; see entry for March 27.
2. Unidentified.

AUGUST 2 *Tuesday*

Brother Tanii went to Osaka this morning and on to Tokyo in the afternoon. He said that he plans to return to Kyoto tomorrow by the overnight train.

Take-chan's cold got worse. He had a headache and chest pain and was feeling miserable. His temperature reached 39.5° C., so we asked Dr. Kitawaki to make a house call. He said that Take-chan has a throat infection and a stomach problem. We were relieved to hear that it's not some epidemic disease.

AUGUST 3 *Wednesday*

My husband came back today to attend to some kind of business related to the School of Pharmacy this afternoon, and returned to the campsite by the 8:45 P.M. train, taking Mr. Matsumiya's younger brother Osamu with him.

Take-chan's temperature has dropped slightly to 38.6° C.

AUGUST 4 *Thursday*

We were expecting to see Brother Tanii back from Tokyo this morning, but he sent a telegram saying that he will be delayed for a few days because some unexpected business has come up.

AUGUST 5 *Friday*

My husband came back home again from the campsite.

Since my father had asked me to come and look at the live-in store clerks' and shop-boys' kimono that he supplies, I went to Nijō this morning, but first stopped by the Nishi Ōtani mausoleum where my mother's ashes are deposited.[1]

While we were all having lunch, we received an urgent telephone call from the Kōshimas in Senbon. I hurried over at once, to find that Elder Sister was in the middle of giving birth to a healthy baby boy, who arrived about two o'clock. I called Eiko to come and help them, for I had to go back to Nijō to check on the servants' kimono, which is what I really had come for.

I took Elder Sister's little girl, Fumiko, with me when I left,[2] but we had to go to Kyōgoku[3] first because Fumiko cried. As a matter of fact, she cried so much even when we returned to Nijō that finally I had to take her back to Senbon. Not only couldn't I accomplish my task of looking at the servants' kimono for my father, but spent all that time not really doing anything!

When I got back my husband was not home yet, but he came in a little later.

1. She probably went there to pray to her mother's spirit, for she was about to act as her surrogate.

2. To help the Kōshima family out by getting their little girl out of the house.

3. The shopping and entertainment district of Kyōgoku is almost always crowded and offers innumerable attractions certain to distract a child.

AUGUST 6 *Saturday*

Take-chan is much better today and has no fever. It looks like he will recover by the time his father returns.

This morning my husband went to take care of business for the school again. He said that he'd be home for lunch, but wasn't, nor was he back even when dinnertime came. However, he finally came home around eight o'clock, had a quick dinner, and left by the 10:40 P.M. train to return to the campsite, taking his friends a watermelon.

AUGUST 7 *Sunday*

Take-chan seems to have recovered completely, but he stayed in bed today. Perhaps the high fever weakened him.

Kurushima-sensei visited us this morning, had lunch, and went on to take a cruise of the Inland Sea with Hide-san. I heard that Sazanami-sensei joined them and that the Ashiya[1] group of the Otogi Club assembled at Osaka station to welcome them and then boarded the train to accompany them on to Kobe.[2]

Brother Tanii came back around seven in the evening. Mr. Noguchi[3] also arrived at the same time but returned to Osaka right away. Apparently Brother Tanii has been transferred to a plant in Taiwan. The news is not officially announced yet, but Mrs. Tanii Onui[4] and the Eastside Doctor have been told. We had sushi in the evening (his treat), listened to his *utai*,[5] of which he is so very proud, and went to bed.

1. A town between Osaka and Kobe.

2. This sort of gesture, an expression of respect extended to visiting dignitaries, was common at this period, but is seldom practiced today.

3. It is not clear whether Noguchi was a relative or an associate of the Taniis'. He appears later in the diary, always in the company of one or another member of the family. See entries for October 9 and November 23.

4. His adoptive mother.

5. The vocal accompaniment to *nō* plays.

AUGUST 8 *Monday*

This morning Brother Tanii went back to Dairi, but he will have to return to Tokyo in a few days.

The well-tanned campers returned today. My husband and Mr. Matsui parted from the others at Shichijō Station and came home around eight o'clock. Mr. Matsui looked horrible with his skin burned and peeling. We served them dinner, which included a chicken dish, and he went home right away. My husband was so exhausted that he fell asleep right in front of his guest.

AUGUST 9 *Tuesday*

Today our store was preparing for a special sale, and everybody was very busy.

AUGUST 10 *Wednesday*

It has been raining practically every day.

AUGUST 11 *Thursday*

It was clear this morning but began to rain again in the evening.

We cooked *sōmen*[1] early in the afternoon and served it as a snack to everyone, including the staff in the store, to compensate for their hard work on this busy sale day.

After the noodles are cooked, drain in a bamboo basket and cool by pouring plenty of cold water over them. Put the cold noodles in a wooden vat and rinse and rub by hand, changing the water many times until it is clear. Then they are ready to eat.

1. A thin noodle usually served cold in the summertime.

AUGUST 12 *Friday*

Eiko came to visit. She brought two watermelons as a gift. Somehow we seem to have received a lot of watermelons this summer! We lowered hers into the well to chill overnight, so that we can all enjoy them tomorrow. For a snack for Eiko I served the *sōmen* and steamed new sweet potatoes. The Eastside family sent over a roll of plain omelet just before dinnertime, saying that it was meant especially for Eiko.

AUGUST 13 *Saturday*

We cut the chilled watermelons today, and everyone in the family and the staff of the store enjoyed them.

AUGUST 14 *Sunday* *Clear*

It is our annual custom to have *noppee* soup for lunch on this day. It is supposed to keep us healthy during the hot season because it is full of good, nutritious ingredients such as taro, dried gourd, and burdock. Cooked more *sōmen* early in the afternoon and served it around 3:30.

AUGUST 15 *Monday* *Clear*

I made a mistake when I wrote that *noppee* soup is served on the fourteenth; I should have written the fifteenth. The slip occurred because I neglected my diary for a few days and, relying on my memory, made the entry later.

In a detail of the Otogi Club photo, seated at center behind the children are (*from left*) Matsui Jisuke (in straw hat), Iwaya Sazanami, and Kurushima Takehiko. (Nakano Takashi)

A gathering of the Otogi Club in Tokyo, ca. 1915. (Nakano Takashi)

Shin Kyōgoku Street (called Kyōgoku in the diary), ca. 1910. (Peabody Essex Museum)

A theater in Kyōgoku; the flags are those of the *Asahi* (Rising sun) newspaper. (Yokohama Archives of History)

August 16–31

[No entries]

September 1 *Thursday Clear*

I cannot claim that my diary took a summer vacation, but must admit that I have neglected it because the intense heat has made me feel so lazy. However, I intend to take it up again. Having said that, the unbearable summer heat still persists and it reached 90° today.

This being the first day of the month, several people came as usual to extend their customary greetings. Mr. Yamamoto Matsu came very early, followed by Mr. Ōkita Toyosaburō. They both left almost immediately.

Fusako-sama of the Eastside family went into labor around five o'clock yesterday afternoon, so Mother went over to assist at the delivery. We all waited for some time asking, "Not yet?" over and over again. Finally the baby arrived around midnight. It's a boy.[1] Both mother and baby are doing very well. It is a big baby—no wonder he stayed in his mother's womb eleven months! As I think how happy the Eastside family must be, I cannot help but feel envious. The people who stayed to help must be exhausted. The midwife stayed up all night, and Mother came home about half-past two in the morning.

There was a celebration of the consolidation of Japan and Korea today.[2]

1. Their fourth son, Nobuo.

2. This rare comment on an international event refers to the formal annexation of Korea into the Japanese Empire.

September 2 *Friday Clear*

My father stopped by while I was idling from the persistent heat, unable to do anything at all. He was on his way to Osaka, but he wanted to see my husband on some business first. He brought some candy called *karaita*[1] which I haven't had for a long time.

I telephoned the Kōshimas in Senbon to notify them of the happy news about the Eastside family's new baby, and they said that they'll come to see mother and baby soon. Their own baby boy has been left with a wet-nurse, since the mother hasn't been well and doesn't have enough milk, but now that the wet-nurse herself has fallen ill they'll have to bring the baby back home. They really are in trouble and are considering asking Oasa-han to come and help them.

1. An old-fashioned confection made of sugar and ginger.

SEPTEMBER 3 *Saturday*

It has been an unpleasant, especially hot day with high humidity. Hide-san had put out the scrolls and framed pictures to air the other day, so Oshina-san and I have put them back in the storehouse.[1]

I went to see the baby at the Eastside family. Both mother and baby seemed to be doing very well. The baby was crying hard—probably hungry for milk—but babies are adorable whatever they do.

We had the customary sukiyaki dinner tonight because it is the first Saturday of the month. After dinner we[2] sang the old-fashioned "Railroad" song, doing the stations from Tokyo to Kobe[3] without stopping once. The whole room shook with the sound of the chorus and the music, which Okuni-san played on the organ. It was great fun! In fact, I thought even the cotton-batting shop across the street, which is always noisy, must have been astonished by the loud sounds coming from our house today.

Mr. Tanaka Hozan came over but didn't stay because he had to go meet someone at the railway station.

We sent carp *sashimi* and candied carp to Fusako-sama to give her strength and to wish her good health.[4]

1. It is the custom to take advantage of the dry weather of early autumn to air out anything that might have grown moldy during the humid summer months, a practice called *mushiboshi*.

2. The members of the family and all the employees.

3. The song describes the train ride, the landscape of mountains and rivers, the history of the towns and cities where it stops and of the countryside between them—all as though seen from the window of the train.

4. Carp is believed to be especially nourishing and so is a particularly appropriate gift for a woman who has recently given birth. Carp also have heavy symbolic value, based on the vigor with which they swim upstream and leap waterfalls.

SEPTEMBER 4 *Sunday Clear*

In contrast to the flood they are experiencing in Tokyo, we are having fair weather day after day. The temperature was 84° this morning!

Mr. Kataoka came to visit regarding arrangements for the wedding. The Matsuis want to hold it as soon as possible, and now they are proposing the date of October 2. It is impossible from our point of view, of course, and we said so. What insensitive people they are! Besides, the Taniis will be moving to Kyoto soon[1] and we'll have more than we can handle.

My sister Eiko came with a gift for the Eastside family's new baby but went back to Nijō right away. Toward evening Elder Sister Kōshima came to see the new baby also. She came without Fumiko and said that she had planned to leave her house around three o'clock, but it was so hot that she had waited a while. She hurried over to the Eastside family's with the gift she brought. When she came back to our house it was supper time, and Mother arranged to serve her something special.[2] Later, we went for a stroll around Maruyama Park. Neither my husband nor Hide-san was home when I got back around 10:30.

I skipped the cooking lesson today because it was just too hot.

1. Brother Tanii was planning to leave his family behind in Kyoto when he took up his assignment in Taiwan. See entry for August 7.

2. Even unannounced drop-in visitors were served dishes that family members ate only on very special occasions, if at all. This is still a standard way to make guests feel welcome.

SEPTEMBER 5 *Monday Clear*

I am repeating myself, but I cannot help mentioning the heat again. Today was another hot day. I was exhausted and had a slight headache from the intense heat.

My husband left home early in the afternoon to attend to some business having to do with the School of Pharmacy. He is very busy with school affairs lately. There was a violent shower in the late afternoon, but the sun came out again and glittered relentlessly. He did not come home for dinner.

After dinner the children did gymnastics again, performing somersaults, headstands, and other exercises. It was noisy, but everyone had a good time. They ended up by competing at who has the best posture while standing at "Attention!" Chūji-san's was so peculiar that Hide-san imitated him, and we all laughed our heads off!

Mr. Moriguchi went to Maizuru by the Keikaku Railway[1] the day before yesterday and returned this morning. He brought us some sets of picture postcards.

1. The Keikaku Railway is a private line running between Kyoto and Maizuru, a port city to the north on the Japan Sea coast. Chūhachi VI had contributed toward the establishment of this rail line when he was involved in public affairs.

SEPTEMBER 6 *Tuesday* *Clear but rain later*

When I opened the storm shutters (*amado*) this morning, the sky looked dark and ominous, as though washed in *sumi* ink, but it soon cleared. I hoped it would rain, which we need badly.

This is the sixth-day celebration (*muikadare*) by the Eastside family after the birth of their child. Mother and one of our shop-boys have been over there helping them since this morning. According to custom the appropriate gift for a boy is a stack of two rice cakes (*kagami-mochi*), but since it is so hot they decided to send dried red beans (*azuki*) in a lacquerware box together with a piece of dried bonito (*katsuobushi*) instead.

The Eastside family sent us red-bean rice (*seki-han*) and broiled *hamo* for our lunch. We wanted to give them a baby gift but could not come up with a good idea until I finally realized that they have not yet received a single bib. I quickly telephoned Imai Store[1] to deliver some, which were three for 75 *sen*. I took them over right away. While I was talking and joking, the midwife came to visit, so I watched her give the baby a bath.

I went back home when someone came to tell me that Toku-san[2] had come from Tonoshō to visit us. Everybody was in the middle of eating the pears he brought. They are big, beautiful ones called *Jūnirō-nashi* and *Usugumo-nashi*, which are very romantic names for pears.

1. A dry-goods store.
2. Nishimura Tokusaburō.

SEPTEMBER 7 *Wednesday* *Rain*

Since it is raining, today is cooler for a change, and I worked hard from early morning. The untimely rain prevented Toku-san from going out for a while, but when there was a break in the weather, he went to Kyōgoku with Sei-san. I worked fast and made good progress with my sewing.

Narajin[1] came today. His merchandise is so colorful and pretty that I always like everything he has to show. I wished my mother were alive so that I could ask her to buy me some things, and realizing that it cannot be, I became tearful. There is nothing like losing a parent early in your life. Whenever you have something on your mind, there's no one there to listen to you or advise you. I don't know if I will ever be able to forget her. However, I realize that for Eiko and Senzō it must be even harder. Today is our grandmother's monthly memorial day. If only she were still alive, too! I really think I am an unfortunate person and feel very sorry for myself.

There was a violent thunderstorm toward evening with brilliant flashes of lightning. I was terrified, but it stopped after a while.

Hide-san was very upset because he could not find his blueprints. I don't think I put them away anywhere, but if I did, I am very sorry. I just can't remember doing it at all.

I am agonizing[2] over whether to join the calligraphy class or not.

1. A peddler whose wares included cosmetics, hair ornaments, kimono accessories, purses, and the like.

2. Makiko writes *hanmon-chu*, a word popular among young men and women of the time.

SEPTEMBER 8 *Thursday* *Clear, rain later in the day*

Last night's horrible dark sky cleared completely, and it turned out to be a beautiful day.

Toku-san took all the children to the zoo early in the afternoon. He is already 21, but still has a childlike quality and enjoys playing with children nine or ten years of age. His innocence must have something to do with growing up in the country. Today the cuffs of the oversized white shirt he was wearing under his kimono hung way down over his wrists. He looked like a real country bumpkin. As they were leaving, Mr. Moriguchi, known for his sharp tongue, couldn't resist saying, "Toku-san, you are not holding anything in your hands. How about a little toy drum or something?"

Toku-san is really very sweet. He has just finished his military service, and as soon as he was discharged from the army he came to Kyoto to see us. I heard that his parents were jubilant when he was discharged and had a tearful reunion with their precious adopted son. I can understand that. He sent them a postcard saying that he will be a few days late coming home because of the time he had lost on account of the continuous rain.

There was bidding by some contractors on the work planned at the School of Pharmacy that my husband attended.[1]

1. Chūhachi was a trustee of the school.

September 9 *Friday Rain, clearing later*

Toku-san took the children up the hill to Kiyomizu temple after lunch.

My husband left for the office of the Pharmacists' Cooperative around three o'clock. Mr. Matsui telephoned to ask if my husband will be home today, and I told him that I don't know when he'll get back. Indeed, he did not come home for supper.

Toku-san went out again after supper, this time with Sei-san to Kyōgoku to see a movie. They got back after ten o'clock.

Received a letter from Eiko today asking me to come to Nijō, for there seems to be something suspicious about Oasa-han's behavior. I consulted Mother, and she said that since Mrs. Torii had participated to some extent when she was hired, we should inquire of her first.[1] I wrote to Mrs. Torii hoping for a reply tomorrow. Worried about it all day and thought that if only my mother had lived, I wouldn't have to be doing this kind of thing, and on and on and on.

1. The wife of a Nijō pharmacist and the mother of Makiko's friend Yasuko. She seems to have played some role in hiring the housekeeper Oasa-han, but she is not mentioned in the entries for January 8, 17, 18, and 23.

September 10 *Saturday Clear*

Since it is an unusually cool day, I decided to go to the cooking class and left home at nine. The dishes we learned to make today were not very fancy. My husband and Hide-san came to Mr. Matsumiya's house for the tasting, so I came back with them.

Toku-san went home today. My husband had been saying that we should take him to a fish restaurant to celebrate his discharge from the army. But we missed the chance, so instead gave him ¥2 in an envelope on which we wrote "Fresh Fish."

Haven't had any response to my inquiries from Mrs. Torii regarding the problem with the housekeeper at my father's house, and wonder why she hasn't replied yet.

Mr. Matsui has decided to study *utai*, and today he had his first lesson. He is a curious fellow.

Mrs. Fujiwara[1] made a fool of herself in our cooking class today by picking up and dropping a piece of food on the floor. It was supposed to be broiled, but no one had asked her to do it. The teacher was not happy and told her so. She is always acting as though she knows more than anyone else and is so impetuous. She ought to know better, for she is not a young woman—I'd better watch myself!

1. Unidentified.

September 11 *Sunday Clear*

It has been more or less fair all day.

My father came to see me this morning about nothing other than the "Oasa-han incident." Apparently she has the reputation of being a troublemaker and is a follower of the *Konkō-kyō*.[1] He has been told that she is not to be trusted. My father said that he is willing to give her the advance on her wages that she has asked for, but he doesn't understand why she is asking to have her annual wages raised from the initially agreed upon ¥48 to ¥50, which he cannot agree to. As a matter of fact, he said that he is confused about whether she is asking for more money or whether she is after something else. At any rate, he wants me to come to Nijō and find out what's going on. I promised to go there tomorrow, and we left it at that. It was almost noon, so Mother prepared something special for his lunch, which I appreciated very much.

Starting yesterday it began to cool down. It was 79° today.

1. *Konkō-kyō* is one of Japan's many syncretic "New Religions." Founded in 1859 by a peasant in what is now Okayama prefecture, it spread quickly along the coasts of the Inland Sea among farmers, merchants, and artisans. In 1890 it was officially designated a sect of Shintō and became increasingly identified with nationalistic causes. The "New Religions" are often viewed with disdain or distrust by nonmembers, as this passage suggests was the case here.

September 12 *Monday Clear*

I went over to Nijō this morning while it was still cool. First, I went to see Mrs. Torii to find out what she had to say. It's hard to put on paper, but I'll try to summarize the story. Oasa-han wants an advance of ¥30, to be paid now, and an increase in her monthly wage to somewhere around ¥6 or ¥7. Although she made these requests in an indirect and clever way, that is what they amount to. Knowing that my father could not pay that much, Mrs. Torii said that she had told Oasa-han that it would be impossible for him to do. She also told her that even if my father agreed to raise her wages from the initially agreed upon ¥48, he could not pay more than ¥50. When she asked her if that would be all right, Oasa-han said that figure would be fine with her. Mrs. Torii asked her once again if ¥50 will satisfy her, and she said yes. So the negotiation has been successfully completed, leaving both parties satisfied. I could not help thinking that if we had known that the negotiation would be so simple, we wouldn't have involved Mrs. Torii in this matter. However that may be, I still think that Oasa-han has made us all very anxious for no reason at all.

When I came home in the evening I went over to see Omiki-san[1] and told her the whole story. She said, "Please don't do anything until I check with Okō-san."[2] She is going home to Uji the day after tomorrow anyway, so now it looks like we will have to wait for her letter from Uji to tell us what we should do.

I am exhausted from this complicated, unpleasant experience. No wonder I am so sleepy tonight and cannot stop yawning.

Hide-san moved out of his boardinghouse into another one today.

1. Shirakawa Omiki, who formerly worked for the Eastside Doctor and helped out whenever they needed the services of an experienced person. In this instance, she was called in because of the arrival of the new baby. It is she who found Oasa-han, the troublesome housekeeper, apparently with the help of Mrs. Torii.
2. Unidentified.

September 13 *Tuesday Rain*

It has been a gloomy, rainy day. I had a rush order from my father who asked me last night to finish sewing the light wool kimono that he will need for his trip to Toyama[1] tomorrow.

This morning I got the idea of using the sewing machine[2] to make the kimono, which might have been a mistake because I'm not thoroughly familiar with its operation. While I hovered over the machine, which made a sound like *chikon-chikon*, slowly working its way as though it were a wheel laboring to pull a heavy load up a hill, the thread broke. Then I misjudged the stitching, but after all sorts of other troubles finally finished my machine-sewn kimono—my first such endeavor! The sewing was not very neat, but the tightness of the stitches should guarantee that the seams will not come apart easily.

Then I wrote a letter to my father wishing him a good trip and a safe return home. I said that I will be anxiously awaiting his return and sent a shop-boy to deliver the letter with the finished kimono. He came back with a message that my father is still planning to leave for Toyama tomorrow. It rained constantly.

1. A prefecture northeast of Kyoto on the Japan Sea coast, famed as a center of the Chinese medicine trade. Toyama's itinerant herbalists marketed their wares throughout most of the country well into the middle of the twentieth century.

2. Manually operated.

SEPTEMBER 14 *Wednesday Rain*

The rainfall persisted all day, and it turned really cool. My father plans to leave for Toyama today regardless of the rain, and I only pray that there won't be any troubles during his trip.

Mr. Tanaka came to see my husband in the morning. He is going to South America in November and said that he is not doing anything at all these days. He was really excited about his trip and talked about it a lot. Stayed here until the end of the day, but went home while I was taking my bath.

Shortly afterwards, my husband went out after receiving a telephone call from Mr. Kimura. Soon after he had left, Mr. Matsumiya and Mr. Matsui came to the house to see him. Fortunately, my husband returned home right away, and the three of them had a wonderful time together, as usual. Mr. Matsui's performance of *utai* was greeted with loud applause.

When the time came for them to leave, they noticed that Mr. Matsumiya was wearing an unusual hat today, and it got a big laugh from everyone. Naturally they all had to try it on themselves. When he did so, Mr. Matsui looked like a teacher of some sort of traditional art.[1] My husband looked like a Buddhist priest. We decided that Mr. Matsumiya looked best—after all, it is his hat. The funny thing was Mr. Matsui looked so much older with the hat on that I couldn't stop laughing!

1. The tea ceremony, flower arrangement, music, or poetry.

September 15 *Thursday Clear*

There was nothing in particular to write about today. My husband went to the School of Pharmacy, which he frequently does, and following that went to a *kyōgen* performance by the Shigeyama Sengorō troupe. He said that the audience was larger than usual, perhaps owing to the good weather, and that he enjoyed the performance.

Take-chan, Tada-san,[1] and Sei-san went out somewhere to play in the afternoon.

Mr. Tanaka also came to visit in the afternoon and ate quite a lot of the sushi snack we served him. It must have filled him up, for he stayed until nine o'clock without eating anything more.

1. Takeo, the Taniis' eight-year-old son, who had remained with the Nakanos since August, and Tadao, the Eastside family's six-year-old son.

September 16 *Friday Rain*

It was a gloomy morning, and sure enough it started to rain again. We have had enough rain, so I hope it will clear up tomorrow when I go to the cooking lesson.

The workmen who have been laying the underground water pipes have reached our neighborhood and are making all kinds of commotion. At present they are trying to install the pipes under the Otowa Bridge,[1] which explains the huge piles of dirt in the street. This not only made trouble for pedestrians, but vehicular traffic[2] also has been inconvenienced. It is not unusual to see a cart overturned on the streets. Just the other day I saw the greengrocer's cart overturn and the taro and eggplant go rolling out into the street—I felt so sorry for him!

Having piped-in running water will be wonderful, but unless they hurry up and finish the work soon our daily life will continue to be very difficult. When I stepped outside about ten o'clock at night I was startled by the sight of a big charcoal brazier left out on the street.[3]

1. The bridge over a creek running along the south side of the Nakano house.
2. Mostly *rikisha* and carts drawn by men.
3. Probably left there by the work crew. Makiko leaves the sentence unfinished.

September 17 *Saturday Clear*

I was expecting more rain, but it turned out to be a beautiful, sunny day.

Today is my cooking class. I left home about nine, hurrying on my way, since we had been told that we would start early. However, the teacher arrived late, around 9:30. First we took notes as he told us how to make soup stock, and then we started to cook. Today's dishes were all easy to prepare, and there was only one guest for the tasting, whom we served upstairs. I came home a little before two. It has been a rather warm, sunny day.

Our lunch was the Western-style dishes I cooked this morning and for dinner we had our monthly beef sukiyaki. Hide-san came home today. There was some talk about going out for moon viewing, but it didn't materialize. For a change the moon is bright and clear tonight. It uplifts and cleanses my soul to see the beautiful face of the moon, but at the same time I feel somewhat forlorn. My mood must have been brought on by the autumn scene.

Received the letter from Omiki-san regarding the Oasa-han affair that I have been waiting for. Apparently her story that she desperately needs money is a fabrication.

September 18 *Sunday Clear*

Today was gorgeous, even sunnier than yesterday, but it clouded up toward evening and spoiled the *imo-meigetsu* events.[1]

Fusako-sama came over in the afternoon for her first visit since she gave birth. She looks fine now and stayed about three hours, but we didn't serve her anything special.

Mr. Akazawa Manzō also visited briefly. He brought a return gift of a *furoshiki*[2] for the *kōden*[3] we had given. He said that they will have a memorial service for his mother on the 24th at the Jihō-in.[4] He left almost immediately, saying that he has many other calls to make.

Mr. Matsui came again later in the afternoon. He was supposed to go to the moon-viewing party at Kyōraku-kan tonight, but he stayed on and we had to serve him dinner. He left soon after, but Mother made a comment that he always stays too long. He seems to be a truly happy-go-lucky man.

Correspondence in: A postcard from my father saying that he arrived in Toyama safely.

1. In this case, *imo* refers to taro and *meigetsu* means "beautiful moon." On the evening of the fifteenth of the eighth month by the lunar calendar (which falls roughly in mid-September), people make offerings of steamed taro to the moon. It is supposed to be the optimum time to observe the full moon. Today it is called *Jūgoya* (Eve of the Fifteenth).
2. A square wrapping cloth, in this case probably of silk.
3. Money given the bereaved family at a funeral or memorial service.
4. An unidentified Buddhist temple.

September 19 *Monday* *Clear, later rain*

Since Mother suggested that I visit Nijō,[1] I decided to go in the afternoon. Just as I was planning the visit, Elder Sister Kōshima called to say that she wants to visit the family in Nijō, but because there's no one in particular to talk to there she was wondering what to do. When I told her that I will be there this afternoon, she said she would come over, too.

Mother bought a box of sushi for ¥1 and gave it to me to take along as a gift, so I left early in the afternoon to find that Elder Sister had already arrived. We talked a lot without noticing how fast the time was passing. It began to rain late in the day. When I realized that it was about time to leave, it was nearly ten o'clock. We felt we still hadn't finished talking, but promised that we will visit some temples together for the autumnal equinox on either the 24th or 25th.[2]

I hurried home worrying about my late return, only to find that my husband was not back yet. I was surprised to learn that he, the Eastside Doctor, and Mr. Moriguchi had gone to see the Soganoya comedy troupe perform instead of moon viewing, as they had planned to do originally.

Today I was happy to see Mrs. Hiraoka, whom I haven't seen for some time.

1. To see if everything is all right during her father's absence.
2. Both the vernal and the autumnal equinox are occasions for important Buddhist observances directed particularly toward the spirits of the ancestors. See entries for March 18, 21, and 24.

September 20 *Tuesday* *Clear*

Yesterday's rain must have disappointed lots of people who were expecting to see the moon. Mr. Moriguchi for one was feeling low today from disappointment. However, the moon tonight is more beautiful than ever—it makes me wonder why most things don't turn out the way you expect.

My father returned from his trip to Toyama and brought us *ayu*[1] sushi, Kutani chinaware, and some toys and postcards as gifts—all from places he had visited. Apparently it was so cold there that people were wearing lined winter kimono already.

1. A small trout-like fish.

September 21 *Wednesday Clear*

Mr. Moriguchi did not come to work, since he drank a lot of *sake* while moon viewing last night to make up for the night he missed.[1]

The grandfather of the Okunos[2] in Takatsuki, Osaka, died and the funeral was held at two o'clock this afternoon. The Eastside Doctor went there last night, and my husband took the 1:27 P.M. train in order to attend the funeral. He said that his timing was good, so that he made it to the services and got home just after nine o'clock.

The moon tonight is not at its brightest, but is still beautiful, so everyone in the family except me went to view the moon at Hokō-ji[3] where the big image of the Buddha is. I stayed at home holding the fort, sitting all alone in the house feeling very lonely, and could not help remembering my mother, for today is her monthly memorial day. Today is also the beginning of the week of the autumnal equinox, and I am wondering how my family in Nijō is getting along.

1. Drinking *sake* and viewing the moon are closely associated activities. Moon viewing gives Moriguchi the perfect excuse to overindulge.
2. Probably a relative of Fusako, wife of the Eastside Doctor.
3. A Buddhist temple in the northern part of the city.

September 22 *Thursday Rain*

It rained all day, starting in the morning, and was cold and damp.

Today is Shina-san's birthday. Unfortunately, we could not find good fish for the occasion, so we went Western and had beef sukiyaki.

My husband went to hear a talk at the primary school that started at seven o'clock this evening and came home after eleven.

I admit that my curiosity to try anything new has struck again. Brother Tanii sent me a calligraphy book from Tokyo published by

Sokuseikai,[1] which I have started on, but I have a hunch that I might not last long.[2]

In the early afternoon Mrs. Tanii Onui came to see us. It seems that she came to find out what would be an appropriate wedding gift for Okuni-san, and so she wanted to see what she has already received. She didn't stay long and went over to the Eastside family to see the new baby and offer her congratulations, apparently another purpose of her visit.

1. Literally "Quick Acquisition of . . ."—the equivalent of "Calligraphy in Ten Easy Lessons" or "Calligraphy Made Simple."

2. Makiko wrote with brush and ink in what is unquestionably an accomplished style, which indicates that, considering her youth and limited education, she was a skilled calligrapher. Obviously she not only enjoyed calligraphy, but wanted to improve her hand.

September 23 *Friday Clear*

Since it was a bright, sunny day, we aired the summer quilts and mosquito nets before storing them away.

My husband was called out by Mr. Matsui, who telephoned to say that he had bought a used piano for Dōda Primary School for ¥170, and urged him to come and take a look at it and give him a hand with setting up an exhibit at the school. I was puzzled, since he left home around two o'clock and didn't come home for dinner, for I knew that he was planning to go to the school reunion at Shūdō Primary School tonight. But when Sei-san got home from school, he said that my husband had gone to the reunion directly from Dōda Primary School. He got home soon after that.

September 24 *Saturday Clear*

Since it was a crystal clear autumn morning, and is the middle day of the week of the autumnal equinox, there must have been a mob wherever you went.

Elder Sister Kōshima telephoned in the morning and we decided to pay the equinoctial visit to Nishi Ōtani mausoleum[1] that we have been planning. This afternoon my husband went to the first annual memorial service for Mr. Akazawa Manzō's mother at Jihō-in, and I left to meet Elder Sister. I got there first and was arranging flowers and cleaning up the place when she arrived.

Later, we met up with the Akazawa party at Maruyama Park.

Fuku-chan[2] was all dressed up in her best, looking like a young lady of a wealthy family. However, we learned that this young lady had a cold and that after they had visited the Nishi and Higashi Ōtani mausoleums and Kiyomizu, she had got feverish and sick as they were walking through the park.

We took a short rest at a tea shop and had some sweet dumplings. I bought a pair of gloves at Ikematsu Store. When I got home before eight o'clock, I found that the sushi that had been offered at our neighborhood association's equinoctial service had been divided up and our share delivered to the house. Since I was hungry, I really enjoyed it. My husband is attending a party at a restaurant for members of his primary school association.

Note: It is the national holiday of the autumn Imperial Ancestral Festival.[3]

1. See entry for January 7.
2. A little girl, probably a granddaughter of the deceased.
3. The Meiji government adapted the traditional observances associated with both equinoxes, formerly primarily family affairs, and made them into national holidays linked to the imperial institution.

September 25 *Sunday Clear*

I was convinced that it was going to rain, but it has been a nice day. Tenjin-san[1] must have been very happy.

Since tomorrow will be grandfather's monthly memorial day as well as *o-hachigan*,[2] we were planning to make *o-hagi*[3] then, but suddenly decided to make them today instead. We also changed the furnishings back from the summer screens to the regular sliding doors. All of a sudden the rooms look wintry, but at the same time rather cozy.

We distributed the *o-hagi* to the Matsumiyas, the Matsuis, and the Hiraokas—both the main and branch families. Hide-san arrived with two college friends; they had gone to see the Crown Prince,[4] who is visiting Kyoto. I was glad that we had just the right amount of *o-hagi* on hand to serve three more people.

My husband went with the Eastside Doctor to offer our condolences on the death of the grandmother of the Obata family.[5] We were notified by telephone yesterday.

Ingredients for *o-hagi*: 3 *shō* 8 *gō* rice (one-half regular and one-half glutinous rice) and 1 *shō* 8 *gō* red beans. When cooking the rice, put some salt in the water, reducing the amount somewhat from that used in cooking regular rice.

Correspondence in: A letter from my brother Manzō, whom I haven't heard from in a while.

1. See entry for January 25.

2. *O-hachigan* is the first day of a week-long series of memorial services held by members of *kō* of the Jōdo Shinshū sect of Buddhism. A *kō* is a group of worshippers who gather regularly, usually at the home of one of its members, for a religious observance and socializing.

3. Rice cake covered with sweet red-bean paste, a snack eaten on festive occasions.

4. Later the Taishō emperor who reigned from 1912 to 1926.

5. Distant relatives of Chūhachi II.

September 26 *Monday Clear*

It has been warm and humid, perhaps because the rain we have been expecting for some time hasn't yet come our way.

My husband left home in the morning to see the opening of the exhibit at the Dōda Primary School, and to attend the funeral for the grandmother of the Obata family at one o'clock this afternoon. After that he went to the office of the Pharmacists' Cooperative and came home about 7:00 P.M. Mr. Suzuki Kichinosuke came over in the evening to discuss arrangements for the meeting of the Otogi Club to be held tomorrow in conjunction with Kurushima-sensei's visit.

We received the sad news from the Hiraoka branch family that Sannosuke-sama had just died.[1] How sad that he had to die so young after being ill so long—his parents' grief is beyond my imagination. I wonder why people die. How I wish we didn't have to deal with death in this world.

At last the rain we have been waiting for started unexpectedly in the evening, but stopped again about ten.

1. Sannosuke was the youngest son of a related family. One of the major changes in Japan since 1910 is in public health. In the diary, Makiko mentions cholera, typhoid, and tapeworm, all virtually unknown in Japan today. It is also noteworthy that many of the deaths and funerals were those of children and young people; today Japanese have extraordinarily long life expectancies.

September 27 *Tuesday Rain*

It was a dark morning, so dark, in fact, that it looked like evening inside the house. On top of that, the thunder started to roll across the sky and the rain began. This means trouble, for Mr. Matsui asked us several times yesterday to come and see the school exhibit. We cannot possibly go in this rain! Unfortunately, the rain kept falling without let-up, so we ended up not going at all. Actually, my husband saw the exhibit yesterday and didn't seem very impressed.

Yesterday I caught cold, which has made my nose runny and gave me a headache. I haven't had a cold for a long time! I was delighted to have a visit from my father. He brought me a bolt of heavy crepe silk in pastel colors to make a winter kimono that I asked him for the other day.

Kurushima-sensei is not staying with us this time, but with a family who owns a pharmacy in Sanjō. He has never done this before. No wonder it has been raining so hard! He is speaking at the Shūdō Primary School at seven o'clock tonight.

There was a private funeral at the Hiraokas that Sei-san attended as the representative of our family.[1]

A telegram arrived from Brother Tanii saying, "Arriving tomorrow. Tell Takeo to expect me," which means that Take-chan, who has been living with us for a long time, is going home at last.

1. It is not unusual to send a surrogate for the household head when schedule conflicts arise. However, given the importance of the Hiraokas (see Introduction), it at first seems odd that her husband's 13-year-old brother would be asked to represent the Nakano household at a major event such as a funeral. The explanation is to be found in the entry for October 2, when the formal funeral was held, attended by the heads of households closely related to the Hiraokas. See also entry for July 20 for another "private funeral."

SEPTEMBER 28 *Wednesday Rain*

Rained all day. Brother Tanii returned from his trip to Taiwan, arriving at Kyoto Station at 7:10 A.M. Luckily Take-chan was home because it is a school holiday. Brother brought gifts to each of us. He gave me a modern handbag with a white peony design on it that I can hardly wait to carry when I go out. Although someone teased me, saying, "Oh, look, there's a piece of tissue sticking on your bag!" I said, "It's not tissue paper. Can't you see? It's a white peony decoration!"

Brother Tanii went out to see his new house near the Nanzen-ji[1] in the morning, and came home before noon, stopping to see the Matsuis, who live not too far away. The Eastside Doctor came over to see him and joined in our conversation. Later Brother Tanii took the 3:58 P.M. train, this time to go home to Dairi.

Kurushima-sensei gave a talk again at Shūdō Primary School today and dropped in to see us afterwards, but he didn't stay when he found that we were busy with Brother Tanii's visit. At seven o'clock this evening there is to be an assembly of the Otogi Club at the prefectural government's assembly hall to which my husband, Sei-san, Chūji-san, Shina-san, Take-chan, the Eastside Doctor, Yuri-san, and Tada-san all went together, looking very happy. I hear that Mashimo-sensei is also speaking tonight.

1. A large Buddhist temple on the eastern side of Kyoto, about three miles north of the Nakano store.

September 29 *Thursday Clear*

It was a perfectly beautiful sunny day. There wasn't a single cloud in the sky, and somehow it seemed very tranquil. I don't see how we could ask for a better day than this, but I didn't go out anywhere.

Today the Crown Prince visited the girls' middle school that Shina-san attends. When she came home from school, our family got all excited and everyone had a story to tell.

Hide-san came home just before dinnertime. In the evening the Eastside Doctor came over, and those who attended the Otogi Club assembly last night told us about the stories they heard. Their comments were as follows: Mashimo-sensei's talk was very interesting; Kurushima-sensei charmed the audience with his storytelling as he always does; Mr. Suzuki Kichinosuke's speech was awful.

Just before ten o'clock, Mr. Tanaka dropped in and stayed until past midnight, talking about this and that.

Tomorrow will be the last day of September.

September 30 *Friday Rain*

Naturally it rained today just because yesterday's weather was too good to be true! In fact, it rained all day long. It makes me think that there must be an endless supply of moisture up there in the sky.

My husband and Mr. Moriguchi went to the Taniis' new house in Nanzen-ji early in the afternoon to meet a delivery man from the furniture store. Their rented house is not far from the Matsuis, which will be very convenient for them.

Tomorrow is the day for my cooking lesson. However, I wondered if I should go since it is the first day of October, when we expect many of our business branch-families to visit. After consulting with Mother and my husband, I decided to go. Both said, "It would be better if you go, since there may not be many people attending the class tomorrow."

OCTOBER 1 *Saturday Rain*

It rained again today. There is definitely a chill in the air in the early mornings and evenings, and especially on rainy days I feel cold even in my lined kimono. It amazes me how quickly time passes. Here we are at the beginning of October already! The branch-families came to pay their first-of-the-month calls beginning this morning.

Having decided to attend the cooking class today after all, I rushed to get there, only to find that I was the last one to arrive. Everyone was already busily taking notes. However, Mr. Matsumiya came over to tell me that he was glad to see me. How kind of him![1] I started to take notes at once about how to prepare *shitafu*,[2] and we learned to cook it. Today's dishes were not fancy, so I left a little after two.

On my way home I stopped by Nijō to see how they are getting along. My father was not in, but both Eiko and Senzō soon came home from school. They said that the Crown Prince had visited the First Middle School today and that on his way back he would pass through Nijō Avenue, so I went out to the street to see the procession. When the carriage came in sight, I found myself bowing deeply with my eyes down.[3] In his noble presence the air was hushed as a gentle rain fell.

Returned home around six.

1. Mr. Matsumiya, the host, knew how hard it was for her to leave the house on this particular morning.

2. An unidentified dish.

3. It would have been considered unseemly at best for her to look directly at him as he rode by.

October 2 *Sunday Clear*

The sky was cloudy in the morning and it looked as though it might rain, but as the clouds gradually lifted the sun's face peeked out. It was so nice to see the sun in a blue sky again after all the rainy days we've had. Since Sunday comes around only once a week, children must greet sunny ones like this with great joy!

It seems that this is the time maids change their jobs, so our maid Otake-don went to the employment agency this morning.[1]

Mr. Kataoka came to see us regarding arrangements for Kuni-san's wedding. Apparently he chose to pay the visit today because it is an auspicious day.[2] He is superstitious, as usual.

There was a formal Buddhist funeral at the Hiraoka's at nine this morning to which my husband, my father, and Mr. Nakano Chūbei went. They came to our house afterwards. There was another funeral at a later hour for Mr. Takagi Bunpei,[3] to which all of them went together.[4] My husband and my father went to the general assembly of the pharmacists at the Nijō Club from there. My husband came home around seven.

Our kitchen maid, Moto, seems to have gone home[5] without asking our permission. We waited till ten, eleven, and even twelve o'clock, but there has been no word from her. I think it's terrible the way kitchen maids behave these days!

1. What Makiko wrote here is not entirely clear, but apparently this was a time of year when maids did change jobs, and she was anticipating that they would have to find new ones. See entries for October 3, 5, and 7.

2. Makiko has referred to "auspicious days" in several entries—March 1, 23, 27, and April 29 among them. In making marriage arrangements, auspicious days as reckoned by the almanac are still overwhelmingly preferred for the wedding ceremony.

3. Unidentified.

4. Note that both funerals were held on a Sunday. Like Makiko's mother's 100th-day memorial service, they probably had been scheduled for the most convenient non-work day for mourners and families alike. See Introduction and entry for February 21.

5. It is not clear whether she had gone to her family's home or to that of her guarantor. When servants came from distant rural areas, as many of them did, they had local guarantors who acted as surrogate families.

October 3 *Monday Rain*

The good weather didn't last. The rain started again last night and it has been raining steadily since.

Laying water pipes in Hanamikōji Street, north of Gojō Avenue, October 24, 1910. (*Shashin shūsei*)

Kyoto Canal, ca. 1920. (Long Ago and Far Away Image Bank, Tokyo)

(*Above*) Kyoto Station, ca. 1912.
(Kyoto Prefectural Archives)

(*Left*) Tanii Senjirō and Yae with their daughter Toshiko, 1910.
(Nakano Takashi)

Wedding portrait of Matsui Jisuke and Kuniko; see entry for October 14.
(Nakano Takashi)

The brother of our shop-boy, Shigekichi, came to express his gratitude for our taking in his "humble and immature" brother and taking such good care of him, and so on, and so on, using extremely polite language. I didn't know how to respond to such an excessively ornate greeting!

The employment agent, Narita, brought a young girl this morning. We were not impressed by her, for she has never worked as a maid and looked really green. However, we decided that we'd better have someone rather than ending up with no one at all, and hired her.

Received a telegram from the Taniis saying: "Arriving at nine tomorrow morning." They are all coming! We were so excited in anticipation of their arrival that it seemed that time was passing very slowly. Take-chan was unable to go to sleep from the excitement. I felt unsettled all day. Could it be that I was also affected by the excitement?

October 4 *Tuesday Clear*

It was as though the weather was celebrating the arrival of the Taniis. It was a perfectly beautiful day, something we haven't seen for a long time. They arrived around 9:30 A.M. looking very well. Toshiko has grown so much, and although she cannot walk yet, she can stand by herself, and when I pointed to his photograph on the wall and said, "That's your grandfather," she said, "Ah, ah, ah," pointing her tiny finger toward it. She is truly adorable!

In the afternoon around three, Sister Tanii went to visit Mr. Matsui and Mrs. Yamada Osei.[1] Brother Tanii was visiting the home of someone who works for Sumitomo Bank. They both came home before supper time.

While they were gone, Elder Sister Kōshima came to visit, bringing the wedding gift for Okuni-san. However, her daughter, Fumichan, was so restless that she had to take her home right away.

After dinner the Taniis demonstrated their talent by singing *utai*. Together they sang *Kogō*, Brother Tanii did *Kanawa* solo, and Sister Tanii sang *Yuya*.[2] Although the lyrics were rather difficult to understand, I enjoyed them and felt like trying some myself by groaning and moaning.[3]

1. Tanii Senjirō's half-sister.
2. *Kogō* and *Kanawa* are among the many *nō* plays depicting the destructive ef-

fects of a woman's jealousy, which transforms her into an evil spirit. *Yuya* is a very moving piece that contains many references to Gojō, Kiyomizu, the Inari shrine at Fushimi, and Gion, all of which figure prominently in Makiko's daily life and are repeatedly referred to in the diary. Yuya, mistress of Taira no Munemori, receives word that her mother is ill and asks his permission to visit her. He refuses and instead orders her to accompany him to view the cherry blossoms at Kiyomizu temple. As she dances there, a sudden shower causes petals to fall, inspiring her to compose a poem comparing the fragile blossoms to human life. Munemori is so moved that he gives her permission to go to her mother. For further details, see Muraoka and Yoshikoshi; Nippon Gakujutsu Shinkōkai.

3. This is precisely how *utai* sounds to the untrained ear, Japanese and Western alike.

October 5 *Wednesday Clear*

Another gorgeous day! Brother Tanii went to Kobe by the 8:10 A.M. train. Sister went over to their new house to meet the man who is delivering the furniture.

As I looked out on the street this morning, I spotted a woman who seemed as though she might be seeking employment. I reported this to Mother and she sent out a shop-boy to ask her in. She came in to be interviewed, and as a result she agreed to stay and try working for us in the morning; if all goes well she will bring her belongings and move in this evening. We are happy about the arrangement.

Both Sister and Brother Tanii wanted to have dinner somewhere out with the Eastside Doctor, but he was very busy seeing patients so they stayed home for dinner. Since Brother expressed an interest in having hot noodles, we all[1] decided to join him. While we were sipping the hot broth and eating noodles, we were saying that it is best to have hot cooked food these days as the cholera epidemic is spreading. We laughed as we sprinkled raw chopped green onions over the noodles chanting, "Cholera, cholera," and eating them with gusto.

Today is accounting day, and we have been busy. It was one o'clock in the morning when we got to bed.

1. Including the store employees.

October 6 *Thursday Clear*

We have been very lucky that there has been nothing but good weather since the Taniis started to move into their new home.

Before noon Mrs. Hiraoka Okoma came to visit us, bringing a wedding gift. While Brother and Sister Tanii and Mother were all gone to the other house early in the afternoon, Mrs. Tanii Onui also brought a wedding gift. On her way back, she went on to see them at the new house, and I heard that while she was there they took photographs of the whole family together.

After Mrs. Tanii's visit to our house Mr. Nakano Chūbei came, but left almost at once.[1] Next, a wedding gift was delivered from the Kakemi family in Nijō. Shortly after that everybody came home at once, including Hide-san from his boardinghouse.

We all had chicken sukiyaki for dinner, including the Eastside Doctor and Mr. Moriguchi. Brother Tanii left soon after, taking the 8:20 P.M. train to Tokyo. Sister Tanii took Take-chan back to their house and spent the night there for the first time. Tomi-don[2] also stayed over, in order to help her start unpacking tomorrow and checking the contents of the 73 boxes they shipped.

1. Presumably he also brought a wedding gift.
2. Tomikichi, one of the store clerks.

OCTOBER 7 *Friday Clear*

It looked like it might rain this morning, but luckily it still hasn't. We must be doing something right.

Sent a shop-boy to the Taniis' house with breakfast and some prepared food. He is also going to help them with the unpacking. A new housemaid came to work for us today, so we sent Otake[1] to the Taniis' house to help them.

When the boys came home, they reported that there is so much to do that they will have to go back again tomorrow. Tomikichi said that Sister Tanii works so hard herself that he was very impressed, but didn't know what to do with himself at times. My heartfelt admiration goes out to her.

Mr. Tanaka Hozan came over in the afternoon and stayed for dinner.

1. The same maid who was sent to the Taniis when they lived in Kyushu. See entry for April 13.

OCTOBER 8 *Saturday*

Nothing special happened today. We continue to send someone back and forth at least once a day to the Taniis' house.

October 9 *Sunday*

Went to see the Taniis' house with Okuni-san this afternoon. When we got there we found that Mr. Noguchi was also visiting, so we all engaged in conversation and were treated to a snack of noodles. It is a very nice house, better than I had expected, and I thought that it would be nice to live in a house like that just once, quietly and neatly, all by myself.[1]

After the visit we went to Kyōgoku and Shijō for some leisurely shopping and got home after seven. We found a lot of small gift items such as toys and accessories.[2]

1. Makiko is contrasting the Tanii home with the busy, noisy, and sometimes chaotic household into which she has married. Her words are *Hitori de sumitai to omou.*

2. The accessories in this instance are *han-eri*, silk neck-bands, which are attached around the collar of the under-kimono, thus showing a strip of contrasting or matching colors and designs around the neck. Contemporary ones come in mostly white or pale colors, but in the Meiji, Taishō, and early Shōwa periods, dressy ones of heavy silk with hand-embroidered designs came in all colors. Women sought good and interesting *han-eri* much as women in the West might look for scarves or necklaces. All this shopping is in connection with Kuniko's forthcoming wedding.

October 10 *Monday Rain*

The rain that started last night continued to fall all this gloomy day, but in our house things are picking up as the wedding day approaches. We have been busily filling the chests with the bride's trousseau putting things in and taking them out, trying our best to do a good job. I was assigned the task of finishing a kimono, and while I was hard at my sewing upstairs, I heard someone arrive. It was Mrs. Yamada Osei, who brought a wedding gift. Sister Tanii also came. Many other wedding gifts arrived today. We finally finished packing the chests by the end of the day.

I imagine it will be quite lonely after Okuni-san leaves in a couple of days. Mr. Matsumiya came to visit in the evening.

October 11 *Tuesday Rain*

It rained all day again and was very oppressive.

Went shopping in the morning to find *o-aisō-mono*.[1] Bought lots of little things, such as hair ornaments, and got home before noon. My husband had already gone to a meeting of the school board.

My sister Eiko came partly to see the wedding preparations and to congratulate the bride. She was also going to visit the Taniis' new house afterwards.

Tomorrow is the day to ship out the bride's furniture and the trousseau at last! I was busy wrapping gift-money in white paper[2] for tomorrow and feeling somewhat nervous and unsettled. It feels as though a big lump is pressing against my chest.

1. Small gifts for deliverymen, servants, and young adults and children, to be presented in connection with the wedding.
2. Gifts for those helping out with delivering the bride's furniture and trousseau.

October 12 *Wednesday Rain*

The bride's trousseau is to leave the house tonight. I have been looking at the rainy skies ever since this morning and worrying about the weather.

In the morning we wrapped more gift-money and the little gifts for all the children in the families. Finally finished all the preparations, had dinner early, and waited for the go-between to arrive.

Mr. Hiraoka, who is our go-between, came on time. My father and the Eastside Doctor also arrived for the occasion. *Sake* was served with side dishes of broiled fish,[1] dried shellfish, gingko nuts, side dishes of vegetables and fish, and clear soup before the departure of the go-between, who is to accompany the procession of the bridal trousseau. Arrangements had been made to have Hiranoya[2] serve *sake* to the men who would carry the trousseau when they passed by it.

The party departed without incident, and we were informed by telephone that they had arrived at the groom's house safely and that all was well. Soon after, Mr. Kataoka came to our house with the official receipt.

To those who stayed behind—the guests who waited at our house, and Mr. Moriguchi and Mr. Yamada—we served *sake* with dried shellfish, dried cuttlefish, and a soup of *hamo*. About 10:30 the people who had carried the trousseau returned. They were all drunk and some of them looked sick.

The weather was perfect, and everything went very well. We are all very happy tonight!

1. Probably sea bream; like the other dishes listed in this entry, this was considered an auspicious food.
2. See entry for March 21.

OCTOBER 13 *(actually Friday, October 14) Clear*

Unlike yesterday, it has been a beautiful day. This being Kuniko's wedding day we have really been busy. Among other things, the hairdresser came in the afternoon, so that at least our hair is done beautifully.[1]

Towards evening the woman who is to dress the bride arrived. She is the younger-sister geisha[2] of Itchan, whom we ordinarily use when we have occasion to call upon her services.[3] Starting with the makeup, she worked rapidly and dressed the bride in no time at all. Apparently she is the expert makeup artist for the dancers of the Miyako-odori troupe. The hairdresser came and finished the bride's hair. She was beautiful!

In the meantime the go-between arrived, then the families, and finally the relatives, but they left immediately, for they were expected at the groom's house before eight. There was a chaotic moment outside when so many people crowded into the street that the *rikisha* could not get through. However, later we were notified by telephone that everyone had arrived without incident.

After the party had left, those of us who stayed behind and those who came to help had a party. It became quite a drunken affair, and Mr. Moriguchi especially got very drunk. About ten o'clock Osuyan[4] left when someone came to fetch him. Mr. Moriguchi got louder and drunker as he caught Ohama-han[5] and made her his drinking partner. When she said that she would have to leave, he insisted that he would take her home, but having become alarmed by his condition, Mr. Yamada went along with them.

They had not yet returned when the clock struck three. Even the store clerks were laughing about how the two of them, who were supposed to hold the fort while everyone was at the wedding, got so drunk. Mr. Yamada came back at last about half-past three, and Mother and my husband returned home around five o'clock in the morning. They said that the wedding ceremony was beautiful and that they are happy that the celebration went so well. We all went to bed, even though for a very short time.

I used the space for the thirteenth in the diary to record what happened on the fourteenth, the wedding day, for there was so much to write about, and nothing special to write about for the thirteenth.

1. Implying that although their hair is done, they've not yet been made up and so their faces are still very plain. The remark is typical of the occasional self-deprecating tone Makiko adopts.

2. That is, they are registered and live in the same house (*oki-ya*) from which they operate.

3. It was important that an active merchant household like the Nakanos' maintain a continuing relationship with a geisha, whose services might be required on a variety of occasions, such as weddings or entertaining guests at a tea-house (*cha-ya* or *age-ya*) or restaurant. For more information, see Dalby.

4. One of the helpers.

5. The hairdresser.

October 15 *Saturday Clear*

Another beautiful day. Slept soundly until 7:30, since we had gone to bed very late. I was shocked to see the time.

Today's big agenda is *o-heya-mimai*.[1] I was nervous about it at first, but learned that Mrs. Hiraoka Okoma will also be there, and all I have to do is to follow what she says and does.

I left home about three o'clock, having had my hair touched up by Ohama-han and changed into a good kimono. Upon arriving, each of us had to exchange formal greetings with each family member of the groom, which took such a long time that I found it rather boring. Then we were treated to a fabulous dinner around five o'clock. Okuni-san seemed to be in good spirits, and I was very impressed by the ladies of the groom's family. As we were leaving I met my father and Brother Tanii at the gate of the Matsuis' house. It seems that they had gone somewhere together.

1. A formal visit paid to the groom's household by female members of the bride's household.

October 16 *Sunday*

Good weather again. Mrs. Hiraoka came to call. She is as good a conversationalist and as elegant as ever.

October 17 *Monday*

Another beautiful day. Went to Senbon in the morning to visit the Kōshimas. Their little girl, Fumi-chan, insisted on following me home. I was afraid that she might get naughty, but she was rather well-behaved once she got to our house. Her father came over later, but went out somewhere with my husband, apparently to look into the possibility of buying a house.

I telephoned the Kōshimas to see if anyone could come to fetch Fumi-chan, and her mother came over while we were having our sukiyaki dinner with the Eastside Doctor. She didn't stay, but left with Fumi-chan right away.

OCTOBER 18 *Tuesday Clear*

This is the day the bride is to return for a visit to her natal home.[1] I have been anxiously waiting for Kuniko's return since seven o'clock this morning. She finally arrived with her mother-in-law and a maid. We entertained them by serving *sake* with sushi, broiled fish, and a clear soup. I liked her mother-in-law very much. She is wonderfully cheerful and fun to be with, and looks remarkably young with her healthy complexion. She must be a nice person. She gave each of us a gift, which must have been quite an expense for her. She left after a while, leaving Okuni-san behind.

The weather has been beautiful every day since the wedding, which is wonderful! I heard that Brother Tanii is going to Tokyo today.

1. *Satogaeri*, the occasion of the bride's first return visit to her natal house, is marked here on the fourth day after the wedding.

OCTOBER 19 *Wednesday Clear*

The weather has been pleasant again today. Just before noon Kuniko's new husband, Mr. Matsui, came over, had lunch, and went out with my husband to Okazaki to pay a visit to Mr. Nakano Chūbei to thank him for attending the wedding.

While they were gone (they were not out long), Mother and I tidied up the storehouse and were trying to start on the parlor next. Just as our work was getting under way Uncle Akazawa came to see us. We stopped what we were doing to entertain him. We talked and listened to him, and he had a bath and dinner before he left. He thanked me profusely, which made me very happy.[1]

I don't do anything useful at night these days, but just idly pass the time.

My husband went to the Hall of Youth tonight to attend Shibata Tamaki's concert,[2] which he said he enjoyed very much. He got home after ten.

1. See Makiko's Social World and entry for January 1.

2. Shibata Tamaki (1884–1946) later divorced her first husband and remarried. Under the name Miura Tamaki she became a famous operatic soprano and one of the handful of Japanese singers whose names were widely known in the West before World War II. She was celebrated for her performances of Chō-Chō-san in *Madama Butterfly* in North America and Europe, but she did not perform the role in Japan until 1936 at the astonishing age of 52. See Groos, pp. 182–86.

October 20 *Thursday*

It has been a cloudy day. Sister Tanii telephoned this morning to say that she won't be able to go to the meeting of *Ebisu-kō* today.[1] It was my fault that she cannot make it, for I completely forgot that she told me yesterday that there would be no need to send anyone to her house to help because she was planning to go out. However, since I forgot and had already sent a helper there, she had no choice but to stay home and work, and as a consequence missed the chance to attend the meeting. I felt terrible and apologized a thousand times, but the facts cannot be changed. It started to rain, and I felt even guiltier. Not being able to contain my guilt, I wrote a postcard to her. To think that tomorrow I am going to visit my friend, Uta-sama,[2] makes me feel somewhat happier, though.

I heard that the maid at the Eastside family took the day off yesterday and, without notifying them, didn't return, which is extremely bad manners.

We delivered our return gifts with our thank-you notes to those who sent gifts for Okuni-san's wedding.[3]

1. For the deity Ebisu, see entry for May 16. The most common day for meetings of *Ebisu-kō* is November 20 by the lunar calendar, but in some districts, January 10, January 20, or October 20 was favored. For an explanation of *kō*, see entry for September 25.

2. Kakemi Uta, whose married name is Takayama.

3. It is the custom to return gifts for those received in connection with weddings, childbirth, funerals, memorial services, and so forth.

October 21 *Friday Clear*

The rain began yesterday, and it looked like it might continue today, but fortunately, it cleared up. Sister Tanii telephoned in the morning to say that she'll be over to see us today.

Since the weather is good I was planning to go with Okuni-san[1] to call on Takayama Uta-sama, who now lives in Shirutani.[2] We thought we would do it before Sister Tanii got here, but she arrived just as we were about to leave in the early afternoon. We excused ourselves and went anyway. Since it was quite far, it was a great relief when we finally arrived at the gate of the Takayamas' fine, large house.[3] Upon entering, we noticed how quiet and clean the place was. We did spot one peculiar thing in the parlor, however, where there were four or five men's ties hanging from a shelf. We stayed a little while and left early to hurry home.

Went out to Kyōgoku with Sister Tanii after having a snack of sushi at home. For the first time I tried pushing a baby carriage with Toshiko-chan in it and discovered that it is not easy to steer. I walked all the way to their house, finally. She gave me some fruit to eat, and I returned home.

We finished writing and mailed all the thank-you notes for the wedding gifts that we received from out of town.

1. Following custom, the new bride is still visiting her natal house.
2. A neighborhood in Kyoto.
3. The typical residence is surrounded by a wall, fence, or hedges, and has a gateway entrance. Houses like Makiko's, which are combined residence and place of business, open directly on the street and have neither fence nor gate.

October 22 *Saturday Clear*

We took a gift of a big, fresh sea bream today to the Hiraokas and Okamotos[1] to express our appreciation for their having attended the wedding.

It seems too soon to go back to the regular Saturday cooking class after the wedding,[2] but Okuni-san and I decided to attend it anyway because I wanted to go very badly.

Another new person has joined the class. We had told the family that we would take the dishes we cooked today to Sister Tanii's house and eat them there. We all three thought they were quite good. We brought Take-chan and Toshiko-chan back home to Gojo. After they had taken their baths, Take-chan wanted to stay overnight, since it is Saturday. He was overjoyed when we told him that he can join tomorrow's mushroom-hunting expedition that all the children in our family are going on, together with visiting Sazanami-sensei and Numata-sensei.

Tonight Okuni-san was due to return to her new family, so Mother accompanied her, taking as a gift some hard candy called *mame-hei-tō*[3] from Kansendō.

1. Relatives of the Hiraoka family.

2. The meaning of this passage is not entirely clear. It may be that Makiko hesitated to leave the house because she and Kuniko had gone out to visit their friend just the day before.

3. Made of sugar and roasted soybeans, this old-fashioned hard candy is still sold in Kyoto.

OCTOBER 23 *Sunday Clear*

It was a perfect day for the mushroom-hunting expedition for the visiting Otogi Club dignitaries. The sky was clear in the morning, and it was very pleasant. They all gathered at our house about nine o'clock and departed. Mr. Matsui remembered that his family went mushroom hunting just about this time last year on October 22. The party consisted of Sazanami-sensei, Numata-sensei, Mashimo-sensei, and Mr. Suzuki Kichinosuke, Mr. Tanaka Hozan, Mr. Kimura Osamu, Mr. Matsui, my husband, Seiichi, Chūjirō, Shinako, Takeo, and Mr. Suzuki's younger sister. They were in a happy picnic mood when they left and didn't get back until about eight o'clock in the evening.

We received a very elaborate five-tiered lacquerware food box from Mr. Matsumiya today. The first and second boxes contained sardine sushi, the third one had mushroom sushi, the fourth had broiled wild birds and pickled turnips cut in the shape of chrysanthemums, and the fifth contained a sea bream stuffed with seasoned tofu. They were all delicious.

OCTOBER 24 *Monday Clear*

Today was the funeral of the Nabeshimas' child, who died from cholera. I heard that the doctor tried everything to keep him alive and that he had lingered in critical condition for four days, but, alas, he did not make it. It was a very fine funeral.

OCTOBER 25 *Tuesday Clear*

It was a beautiful day again. The continuous fine weather makes me happy and light-hearted.

Brother Tanii left from Kyoto Station at 8:45 P.M. for his new assignment in Taiwan. Mother went to their house this afternoon. Many members of the family went to the station to send him off. I heard that Mrs. Yamada Osei, her husband Genzaburō, and Mrs. Tanii Onui were there, among others. Mr. Matsui, who also went to the station, stopped by here for a while on his way home. It occurred to me that, although he is one of our family now, when I really think about it, it doesn't feel that way at all! How strange!

OCTOBER 26 *Wednesday Clear*

What a magnificent autumn day!

My husband went with Mr. Matsui to a memorial service at the Yakushijis' at ten o'clock this morning. After my husband came home, he had planned to bathe before going out to a funeral in the afternoon, but Mr. Kimura came over unexpectedly to tell him that he should hurry to City Hall at once because they are debating the revision of the land price,[1] so he rushed out without taking his bath. Since he was scheduled to attend a temple-style funeral for the Okamotos at the Daiun-in,[2] he decided to go there directly from City Hall.

Later Mr. Koizumi[3] telephoned to ask my husband to come to the School of Pharmacy. I told him that my husband was out and hung up. When he came home, I told him about the telephone call, and he was very angry and demanded to know why I had not called him at City Hall. I was terrified by his sudden outburst, but said nothing. I have noticed that when he is too busy, he gets angry and scolds me.

1. See entry for June 20. Chūhachi clearly had some interest in the outcome.
2. Apparently most funerals were held at home rather than at a temple.
3. A pharmacist and fellow trustee of the School of Pharmacy and the Kyoto German Academic Society, the latter founded in February 1910.

OCTOBER 27 *Thursday Clear*

Sister Tanii came to visit us this morning with her children. Since Take-chan has not been feeling well ever since he and Toshiko-chan were exposed to a lacquer plant, she and Mother took the children to Dr. Kitawaki's office. Apparently the doctor said that he is going to be all right, and that although Toshiko-chan seems fine now, she should avoid bathing for a while because she may develop an allergic reaction. We were relieved at the doctor's words.

Mr. Matsui came over and had lunch with us. Then he and my husband went to Shūdō Primary School to see the principal about some Otogi Club activities.

Mother went to Sister Tanii's house to help her out.

Imai Store delivered a feather comforter that cost ¥10. This is a farewell gift for Mr. Tanaka, who will be leaving for Brazil soon.[1]

My husband and Mr. Matsui came back once but went out together again—my husband on business at the School of Pharmacy, and Mr. Matsui on business at Dōda Primary School.

1. Japanese emigration to Brazil began in 1908 and peaked in the mid-1930's. By the outbreak of war in the Pacific in 1941, almost 200,000 Japanese had emigrated there.

October 28–31

[No entries]

十一月

November 1 *Tuesday* *Clear*

It was an especially beautiful day. Since it is the first day of the month many faithful people went to shrines and temples of their choice. The streets seemed somewhat crowded with young weavers from Nishijin who have the day off.[1]

Mr. Ōkita Toyosaburō came early in the morning for the customary first-day-of-the-month visit. Mr. Yamamoto Matsu, who always comes early, didn't come at all.

A lady from Demizu[2] who once visited us came with her cute little girl, apparently in order to have her eyes examined at the Eastside Doctor's office. It was close to noon when they arrived, so we served them lunch and talked. She had some interesting stories to tell. Sister Tanii stopped by on her way to visit her mother-in-law.

There was a meeting of the Otogi Club tonight to which I wanted to go very much, so I persuaded Mother to go along with all of us. The talks were all very interesting. I particularly enjoyed listening to Sazanami-sensei's, entitled "Laughing Hell," which was not only delightful but also told in good taste. I listened to Mr. Suzuki Kichinosuke's talk, "Bubbling Water," feeling sorry for the fate of the hero, but was disappointed by the grammatical errors in the synopsis.

1. See entry for March 23.
2. A district in northwest Kyoto.

November 2 *Wednesday*

An unusual rainy day, for it hasn't rained for a long time. Now I am worried about tomorrow's *Shinnō* festival in Nijō.[1]

1. The festival of the deity of medicine, Yakusoshin, the protector of pharmacists. The festival was organized by the pharmacists in Nijō, where the wholesale and retail establishments were concentrated, and was scheduled to coincide with the Meiji Emperor's Birthday, November 3. Originally, it was celebrated privately in every household of pharmacists. The stores competed in displays of famous historical figures or scenes, created with medicine bottles or cans and Chinese herbal medicines, by the store owners and their employees. Vendors, who were invited to set up stalls among these displays, sold cotton candy, sweets, and children's toys. It was a very popular event that drew big crowds.

November 3 *Thursday* *Clear*

Last night's rain stopped and it has been a perfectly beautiful, sunny day, a most appropriate one for today's festivities celebrating the Emperor's Birthday. The national flags decorating each house lined the streets, waving in the warm breeze. At our house we began the day by singing the national anthem—a little ceremony we started in our household.

Since it is also *Shinnō* festival day in Nijō, I went there in the morning. The themes of the decorations in our neighborhood this year are a sacred palanquin and a sacred sword. Some of them are very well made—I was really impressed. The children, who are on school holiday, came to join us in the afternoon. At one point the streets were so crowded that there was no need to walk because just the sheer force of people was enough to push you along. It happens every year!

Stayed in Nijō until almost 10:00 P.M., having paid no attention to how time had flown, so had to rush home.

November 4 *Friday* *Clear*

Today was even sunnier than yesterday and very pleasant.

My husband went to the barbershop only to find that it was closed, so he went to his favorite bookstore and bought an album of prints by Takehisa Yumeji[1] and a print of Mt. Tsukuba done by Nakamura Fusetsu.[2]

Okuni-san came over at night and brought us lots of eggplant pickled in *sake* lees (*narazuke*).

1. Takehisa Yumeji (1884–1934), at the time a very popular poet and artist, known for his portrayal of delicate female figures. Reproductions of his works are still popular today.

2. Nakamura Fusetsu (1866–1943), a well-known painter in the Western style, studied in France, Italy, and England. Mt. Tsukuba lies north of Tokyo.

November 5 *Saturday Clear*

Sunny, but suddenly it turned cold. My husband announced that this is the day to replace the contents of the chest of drawers with winter clothing. Because it was the day for my cooking class, I was getting ready to go out, and although I felt sorry to leave it to Mother to help him, I went nevertheless.

The teacher came so late that we did not finish until around one o'clock. I visited Elder Sister Kōshima, went on to the Matsuis' house and had lunch there, and got back home after three. My husband had gone out.

Since Fusako-sama is visiting her family in Takatsuki, Mother asked the Eastside Doctor to come and have lunch with her, because it was our customary sukiyaki day.

November 6 *Sunday Clear*

Since it was a beautiful Sunday and is the memorial day for grandmother Nakano, Mother stopped by to visit the family grave with Sister Tanii, Take-chan, Shina-san, and Chūji-san on their way to see the fall colors in Shin-Takao.[1]

My husband also left early in the morning with Mr. Suzuki Kichinosuke for Mino-o[2] to view the maple leaves with a party organized by the people they met on a tour of Manchuria and Korea.[3] He said that they will also attend the performances at the Imperial Theater in Osaka[4] on the way back.

I waited up for everyone to return, but no one came home for a long time. At last Mother came in just before ten, saying that she had stopped at the Taniis' house and that Chūji-san is staying there tonight and will go directly to Nijō tomorrow. At eleven I was still up waiting and getting very sleepy. Finally, not being able to control my drowsiness I lay down, intending to take a short nap. However, I was sound asleep when my husband came home at last around one o'clock and was startled by the sound of his footsteps coming through the parlor. I suddenly found myself blinking my eyes. Apparently he was let in by a shop-boy who unlatched the door for him.

1. "New Takao," an excellent spot for maple viewing in the compound of the Kiyomizu temple. It is named after a place outside Kyoto called Takao, celebrated for its glorious autumn foliage.

2. Another locale, north of Osaka, famous for its autumn foliage.

3. This appears to have been a reunion of the tour group.

4. Designed to rival the Imperial Theater in Tokyo, which had opened only a month before. The actor-producer Kawakami Otojirō opened his new Imperial Theater in Dōjima in Osaka in March 1910. Kawakami fell ill after only six productions had been staged and died on November 11, 1911. See Salz, p. 70, and entry for April 5.

November 7 *Monday Clear*

How fortunate we are to have such beautiful weather day after day! This year the *Jidai-matsuri*[1] has been postponed because of the cholera epidemic, but they are holding it today at last.

Without paying much attention to the housecleaning, I rushed to Nijō in the morning. When I got there the streets were already lined with spectators. In time there came a long procession in which there was a group portraying the Yamaguni-tai,[2] new this year, complete with the corps of flutes and drums playing their famous tunes.

We took turns watching the parade, so I worked in the kitchen while the maids went out to enjoy themselves. We had visitors. Fumiko came to join us, we all had lunch together, played games, and generally had a good, festive time. We even beat the confident Mr. ?[3] at the games we played, so that he ended up miserably defeated.

I came home about six, having had a wonderful time running around playing all day long. Now I must settle down and concentrate on my domestic duties. My husband came home around midnight after attending another meeting at the school.

1. The Festival of the Ages, today one of Kyoto's major annual events, ordinarily held on October 22, at the Heian Shrine. It features a parade of people in period costumes from the Heian period to the Meiji Restoration.

2. The Yamaguni-tai were royalists from the mountains of the Tanba district, near Kyoto, who had fought against the shogunate prior to the Meiji Restoration.
3. An unidentified visitor.

NOVEMBER 8 *Tuesday Clear*

It suddenly turned cold today. I was still wearing only my lined kimono and feeling brave, but since Mother scolded me, I finally changed into my winter padded kimono. It is thick and heavy, and I feel like a fat *sake* barrel wrapped in straw matting.

Tanii Toshi-chan seems to have an intestinal disorder and is not feeling well. Her mother brought her to our house to be examined by Dr. Kitawaki, who is paying a house call at the Eastside family's. Fortunately it seems not to be serious, and they left about four o'clock.

My husband went to a meeting at the school again, which started at seven o'clock tonight.

NOVEMBER 9 *Wednesday Clear*

Nobuo-chan[1] apparently is better today. His parents are happy because he has no fever. Where babies are concerned, even the slightest illness makes you worry, for the situation is so unpredictable. Omiki-san told me today, when I went over to the Eastside family, "You are a remarkably free-spirited person, like a dragonfly, but if you had children you would have to be worrying about their welfare all the time." I guess she is right, for I do flit around a lot like a free-spirited dragonfly[2] almost every day! I should listen to my elders.

1. The Eastside family's baby boy.
2. The expression she uses, *gokuraku tonbo*, means literally "paradise dragonfly."

NOVEMBER 10 *Thursday Clear*

Another sunny day. However, for some reason, everyone stayed home all day.

NOVEMBER 11 *Friday Clear*

It was mostly sunny, but we had quite a shower at one point.

Elder Sister Kōshima telephoned to ask if I could go to Ohara[1] with her tomorrow, since she received a letter requesting her to call there around noon. Considering that I am going to a performance of *nō* plays with the family tomorrow and the fact that I have been out on many occasions recently, I declined her invitation as politely as I could.

In the evening my husband suddenly got the idea of papering the inside walls of the closet! When he decides to do something, it must be done at once. Luckily, we finished up before ten o'clock, but since I always fill the role of his assistant in whatever he does, it was not easy for me.

Our store manager, Mr. Moriguchi, took Tomi-don to view the maple leaves in Mino-o, and they have not returned yet.

1. It is not clear here whether Makiko is referring to a surname or to the district called Ohara northeast of Kyoto. See entry for November 13.

November 12 *Saturday Clear*

The hairdresser came early in the morning for this is the day we all were going to attend a performance of *nō* by Katayama Kurōsaburō.[1]

Mother hurried off first, and then my husband. Sister Tanii also went. Kuniko-san and I had canceled our cooking class when we decided that we would go to the *nō*. I was so happy that I could hardly wait for the clock to strike three—I was the last to leave. The house was completely empty![2]

When I got to the theater they had just finished performing *Ohara Gokō*,[3] but I was able to see *Hōgetsu* and *Momijigari*.[4] I had always wondered what *nō* is all about and discovered that not only are the plays beautiful to watch but they are also very interesting. They are indeed elegant, and I thought that I would like to see more.

Afterward my husband and I stopped by the Taniis' house and had dinner there. Also dropped in at the Matsuis' on the way home and got back around 10:30. I could still hear the sound of the drums and the chanting of the *nō* after we got home. I should add that the *kyōgen* entitled *Utsubozaru*[5] performed by Shigeyama Sengorō was very amusing.

1. Their theater was located in Yanagi-no-banba, south of Nijō.

2. Except for the servants, of course. This is one of the rare occasions when the entire family was out. Ordinarily, Makiko would have been the one designated to stay home.

3. Based on a chapter of the great military epic, *Tale of the Heike*, the play con-

The street leading to Kiyomizu temple. (Winkel, *Souvenir from Japan*)

Kiyomizu temple. (Collection of Ukiyo-e Books)

Makiko and Kuniko, ca. 1911. (Nakano Takashi)

A vegetable vendor. (Asian Collection, Herbert F. Johnson Museum of Art, Cornell University)

(*Below*) The Shintō shrine at Miyajima; see entry for November 22. (Asian Collection, Herbert F. Johnson Museum of Art, Cornell University)

cerns a visit by the cloistered emperor Go-Shirakawa to the nunnery Jakkō-in in the Ohara district to commiserate with the former empress Kenreimon-in, who has vowed to spend the rest of her life there praying for the soul of her son, the child-emperor Antoku. See Muraoka and Yoshikoshi.

4. I have not identified *Hōgetsu* (Treasure Moon), but *Momijigari* (Maple Viewing) is a popular favorite. Like *Ataka* (see entry for March 19), it is a staple of both the *nō* and the kabuki repertoire. It is a demon play. Taira no Koremochi has come to Mt. Togakushi to view the autumn foliage. He and his party encounter a beautiful princess and her retinue. She invites him to join them, entertaining him with *sake* and dance. He is half dozing when a messenger sent by the local deity of the mountain appears to warn him that a powerful demon dwells there. Koremochi, realizing that the princess is the demon in disguise, determines to kill her. She appears in her true form to do battle, and he runs her through with his sword. See Nippon Gakujutsu Shinkōkai.

5. *Utsubozaru* (The monkey-skin quiver) is a touching play involving a monkey trainer and his animal. The close relationship between the two as they are threatened by a nobleman out on a hunt is extremely affecting, made more so because the roles of the trainer and the monkey often are taken by a father and son. See McKinnon.

November 13 *Sunday Clear*

I had planned to go to Ohara with my Elder Sister Kōshima this morning, but my husband told me not to go to such an uninteresting place, so I stayed home.

It was a beautiful, warm and sunny day.

I had a dream early this morning that might have something to do with the good time I had last night. The dream was about my Elder Sister ascending into heaven. It seemed at first that a kind old lady arrived as a messenger and carried my sister away on her back. Suddenly, a sharp cry rang out, my sister's body was tossed up in the air, and the old lady's face changed into that of a horrible demon. Hearing the *nō* chorus singing, "What a glorious wonder! What swift action!" and so on, all at once I was awake. What I had heard was the clatter from the kitchen where things were being set up for breakfast. I jumped up thinking, "I've overslept again!" and indeed it was 7:30!

I learned today that Tahara Yuka-san[1] died at long last on the tenth of this month at three o'clock in the morning. What sad news. She will be missed. I cried quietly.

1. Possibly a school friend.

November 14 *Monday*

The carpenter came today to put up some shelves, which we needed badly. They were quite spacious, but as soon as he had finished, we started piling them up with things and ended up filling every inch of space in no time at all. This house is full!

November 15 *Tuesday Clear*

The carpenter came again today. This time he worked on the organ, cutting off the ornament around the edge as we had asked. It was quite a production, but now we can use it as a place to work on the account books.

November 16 *Wednesday Clear*

A terrific wind that rattled the house blew all the leaves off the paulownia (*kiri*) tree in the back garden today. Mother said that this is known as an *inoko* storm[1] that comes around at this time of the year. I wonder what it would be like if you were at sea. It suddenly got very cold, making you long for the warmth of the *kotatsu*.[2]

1. *Inoko* is the name of the day that marks the transition from fall to winter according to the old calendar; it falls somewhere in mid-November in the new calendar.
2. See entry for January 17.

November 17 *Thursday Clear*

Since today is *inoko* we made *o-hagi*[1] and distributed them to the Matsuis, Taniis, Nakaos, Matsumiyas, and the Eastside family and to Hide-san. Everybody was pleased to receive them. We sieved the sweet red-bean paste, which turned out smooth and delicious.

We bought twenty bundles of radishes from a street vendor today to make *takuan* pickles for the winter.[2] Mother said that the ratio should be 2 *shō* 5 *gō* for one cask and 2 *shō* 8 *gō* for the other, and I asked "What do you mean by the ratio?" She replied, "The ratio of the salt, of course," and I realized how ignorant I am.

In the evening Sister Tanii and Okuni-san came over and had some more of the *o-hagi* we made. They are very popular, and I even had four myself.

I prepared a small *kotatsu*[3] for myself before going to bed tonight. Tomorrow we are definitely going to open up the pit for the big *kotatsu* by removing the floor mat.

1. See entry for September 25.
2. A bundle would contain five or six of the long, white radishes. See entry for March 3.
3. A portable one, rather like a foot-warmer.

NOVEMBER 18 *Friday Clear*

It has been a cold day. I wonder what caused this extreme chill.

I thought that Mr. Matsui would show up this evening, but he didn't. Mr. Tanaka Hozan came instead. Hide-san also came home so I made a snack with sweet potatoes and the left-over sweet red-bean paste. However, my intention of making *chakin-shibori* produced nothing but pressed cakes![1] Obviously I don't know how to twist them properly.

A year ago tonight my mother and I returned home from a visit to her natal family in Hikone.[2] She was in fine spirits then, but she is no longer with us.

1. *Chakin-shibori* are made by putting a paste of mashed sweet potatoes in a cloth and twisting it tightly. The result is supposed to be a nicely rounded cake, with a peaked swirl pattern on the top.
2. A castle town northeast of Kyoto. Makiko's mother was from a samurai family.

NOVEMBER 19 *Saturday Clear*

Hurried to the cooking class in the morning and arrived just on time. The dishes we learned today were all delicious! Okuni-san and I had planned to go shopping for a shawl in the afternoon, so we excused ourselves and left a little early. Before embarking on our shopping trip, however, we first had lunch at Sister Tanii's house.

Mr. Matsui and Hide-san have gone to the Ōe *nō* theater. My husband attended the graduation ceremony at the School of Pharmacy and afterward went on to a class reunion party in the evening.

It's been a cold day again. Saw frost this morning. I must go to Nijō tomorrow. Just remembering last year's incidents makes my eyes fill with tears. "Hail, Amida Buddha."[1]

1. See entry for May 7.

November 20 *Sunday Clear*

It's been another cold day, almost as cold as yesterday or colder. We even had frost again this morning.

Went to Nijō with my husband to attend the memorial service for my mother marking the first anniversary of her death. A year ago this morning I ran to Nijō to see her, but when I got there she was already gone; I could only hear her breathing faintly. I realize how fragile our life in this world is, and memories of her brought on a flood of tears.

The service started at ten o'clock. After lunch we went to the Nishi Ōtani mausoleum where her ashes are and offered our prayers. My father, my sister Eiko, Elder Sister Kōshima, her daughter Fumiko, and I were in the party. We stopped by Shin-Takao briefly and then had dinner together at Kyōraku-kan before going home.

I cannot believe it has been a year already since my mother has gone. It seems nothing but a dream.

November 21 *Monday Clear*

Today is my mother's real memorial day.[1] I am very sad.

At Sister Tanii's invitation, Mother took Chūji-san and Yuri-san to the Taniis' house in the afternoon. Apparently Brother Tanii is to arrive at Kyoto Station around midnight tomorrow. The two children came back about eight o'clock, but Mother stayed overnight as she had planned.

My husband ate his dinner in a hurry and went to hear Dr. Matsumoto's lecture at the university with several friends, including Mashimo-sensei and Mr. Suzuki. I have just finished sewing a kimono and am writing in my diary while waiting for him to come home.

Note: Ordered ten bolts of material from Daichū Store in order to have gift towels with the designs we specified made from them.[2]

1. The memorial service was scheduled a day early, on a Sunday. See Introduction and entries for May 7 and October 2.

2. Daichū was a dry-goods store that handled a variety of textiles and dyed fabrics to order. Distributing towels bearing the name of a store as a gift to its regular customers is still a common practice. Ten bolts of cloth would have made hundreds of towels.

NOVEMBER 22 *Tuesday* *Clear*

I learned that Brother Tanii is not coming home tonight after all, but will stop over at Miyajima[1] first and will be here around nine tomorrow morning.

Mother came back home around four o'clock this afternoon. While she was gone the house seemed empty and cold. I missed her very much, feeling cold and chilly, just like the weather has been the past few days. I am glad that the house has come alive once again!

1. An island in the Inland Sea, famed for its large Shintō shrine, whose great red gateway stands in the water at high tide.

NOVEMBER 23 *Wednesday* *Clear*

Today is the national holiday of *Shūki kōrei sai*[1] and all the houses have the national flag out in front, which makes the streets look colorful and gay.

We had been told to expect a visit from Brother Tanii as well as Mr. Matsui some time this morning, but they didn't come until late in the afternoon. First Sister Tanii arrived with her baby daughter, and Brother Tanii came with Mr. Noguchi. While we were having our sukiyaki dinner, Mr. Matsui and Kuniko arrived and joined us. The parlor was overflowing with all these people, and things got very lively.

After dinner the Taniis and Mr. Noguchi left, and the rest of us continued to talk. It started to rain, so the Matsuis had to hire a *rikisha* to take them home. It often rains when Mr. Matsui visits.[2]

1. Autumn Imperial Memorial Day.
2. She refers to him as *ame-otoko* ("rain man"), meaning that he and rain are closely associated. There are also *ame-onna*, women who seem to bring rain when they visit or plan any kind of outing.

NOVEMBER 24 *Thursday* *Clear*

My husband took Chūji-san to the Children's Exposition in the afternoon. They had dinner at the Matsuis' house and stayed on until almost one o'clock in the morning. I wonder why they get along so well?

November 25 *Friday Clear*

Went to Nijō briefly. Stopped by the Matsuis' and also at the Taniis' place to thank Brother Tanii for the gift he brought me. I love the rubber-soled sandals[1] that he gave me. Mrs. Tanii Onui was visiting them and I heard him scolding her loudly about the newspaper incident.[2]

I got home around two o'clock after taking care of several errands and found that Brother Tanii was just arriving. The Eastside Doctor came over to see him, since Brother is leaving for Tokyo again tonight. He is always busy and never seems to rest.

1. *Gomu-zōri*, thonged sandals with rubber soles, then very rare; not the all-rubber *zōri* sandal that has achieved worldwide distribution since the end of World War II.

2. What incident and why he is angry about it, are not explained.

November 26 *Saturday Clear*

The gardener came back early in the morning and finished up by noon.[1]

Today is grandfather's[2] monthly memorial day, so a shop-boy was sent to the Enjū-ji[3] to pay the fee for the service. Also sent someone to the *Ōtani-kō*[4] meeting place at ten o'clock with 50 two-*sen* round pieces of fried bean curd[5] and five bundles of *mizuna* for their lunch. The fried tofu should be purchased in advance, the night before.

Grandmother Hiraoka came to call. She is a gracious old lady, and I like her a lot. Take-chan came to play with our children. He brought lots of sweet steamed buns for us from his mother.

My husband went to a party at the school to welcome a group of returning soldiers and afterwards came home with Mashimo-sensei.

1. At this time of year, the gardener would probably be covering the trees and shrubs in the back garden with straw mats to protect them from the winter cold.

2. Chūhachi V.

3. The Nakanos were parishioners of this Buddhist temple, which is located a short distance southwest of the store.

4. The *Ōtani-kō* is a religious association that customarily meets twice a month. After listening to a sermon by a Buddhist priest, they prepare food and dine together.

5. *Hiryōzu*, a round patty of fried tofu containing chopped vegetables. It is called *ganmodoki* in Tokyo.

November 27 *Sunday Clear*

Take-chan, who stayed over last night, woke up, and he and Chūji raised a ruckus early in the morning. They were severely scolded by my husband and were so startled that they pulled the quilts over their heads and kept quiet!

Chūji-san and Tada-san went out somewhere in the afternoon. I heard that Yuri-san wanted to go with them and gave her mother a hard time. My husband seems to enjoy having these children in and out of the house on the weekends. They came back around nine o'clock, happy at having received some big persimmons.

November 28 *Monday Clear*

There was a funeral for great-grandmother Kunitomo,[1] which started at ten o'clock. My husband was supposed to attend, but upon hearing that it was a temple funeral, he moaned and groaned like a baby and said he didn't want to go, but finally went anyway. He came home after eleven and said that he made it just in time for the funeral.

In the afternoon he went to Okazaki to see an exhibit of paintings, which is being sponsored by the Ministry of Education, with Mr. Matsumiya and Mr. Matsui. He had dinner at the Matsuis' house once again and came home late, around one o'clock. It seems to me that he has acquired a bad habit lately of staying too late when he visits the Matsuis' house. Okuni-san must be sleepy, having to stay up so late. I am equally sleepy and cold waiting up late at night. If I lie down, I always go to sleep without knowing when he comes home, and that leads to leaving him standing at the door for as long as a half-hour.[2] If only he would come home by midnight, I would have no problem. He should realize that I am frightened to stay up all alone late at night.

1. A distant relative of the Akazawas in Sakai.

2. The front door would have been latched at night, so that he must wait for someone to open it. A servant could easily have let him in, as happened on November 6 when Makiko did not hear him knocking, but it was considered primarily the duty of a wife to stay awake until her husband returned. Since external, keyed locks were not yet common in Japan, there was no question of letting one's self in.

NOVEMBER 29 *Tuesday Clear*

It is wonderful that we are having this run of good weather.

My father came to pay for the merchandise that we had ordered for him. He also asked my husband how much he should pay Mr. Matsumiya for the two paintings of Manchuria he has commissioned him to do. They discussed the fee and came up with the figure of ¥10, so he left the money to pass on to Mr. Matsumiya.

My husband went to a trustees' meeting at the School of Pharmacy again in the evening with Mr. Koizumi, but got home early about ten o'clock. That's because he came home straight without stopping to see Mr. Matsui.

NOVEMBER 30 *Wednesday Rain*

It rained today for a change, and I cannot help feeling gloomy.

Nothing special happened today. Tomorrow is the first day of December, so the merchants are all busy running around today trying to finish their accounting.

It's frightening to realize how fast time goes. It's as though time were chasing us from behind. Just to think that I'll be 22 in a month makes me feel terrible.[1]

1. In the system of reckoning ages used in Makiko's time, everyone gained a year on New Year's Day. See entries for February 4 and July 5, however.

DECEMBER 1 *Thursday Clear*

Finally the last month of the year has come! I feel very pressed and agitated.

My husband got up early and went to Fushimi with some other people from the neighborhood association to send off the Odagakis' son to the army barracks, and came home about ten o'clock.[1]

Since it rained all last night, I expected it to continue today, but it was nice and clear. Perhaps the weather cooperated because today is the first day of the month, which is the customary visiting day for our business branch-families. As one of the visitors said, "*Oyakata biyori*."[2] As usual, Mr. Yamamoto Matsu was the first to arrive. Even

Fusako-sama came. The only one who didn't show up was Mr. Ōkita Toyosaburō.

While Mr. Kimura was visiting us there was a strange telephone call. The caller said it was from Mr. Kimura and had something to do with the school. I was puzzled, but it turned out that he had arranged to have someone else make the call from his home. It was his way of letting us know that he had got a telephone line hooked up![3] He wanted to show off his new acquisition in a mischievous way. How unusual for a man to do such a thing!

My husband went to greet Shimoyama-sensei who is in town. There was a party for him at Nakamura-rō, which my husband attended. He came home late, at 12:30 in the morning. Of course, because Shimoyama-sensei is such an important man,[4] I cannot blame him.

1. When a young man went into the army, representatives of the neighborhood association participated in ceremonies sending him off at a train station or barracks with his family and friends.

2. The expression carries the flattering implication that the weather has cleared up *because* the main house is receiving visitors.

3. Telephones were not at all common in ordinary homes in Japan until well after World War II. It is clear that they were installed in places of business very early, however, for Makiko reports any number of telephone calls to and from the store.

4. However important he may have been in his day, I have been unable to identify him.

DECEMBER 2 *Friday Clear*

I have been looking forward to seeing the art exhibit with my husband,[1] longing for this day to come, but he said that he has to go to the School of Pharmacy this morning. I asked him, "How about this afternoon?" and his answer was that he has work to do, which is to mark the reserved tickets with a rubber stamp.[2] He left home to get started on the job. By then I realized that I had to give up.

Mr. Nakamura[3] came to the house to see my husband, so I sent a shop-boy to get him. In the meantime Mr. Tanaka Hozan came to say good-bye. He is leaving for South America at last, the day after tomorrow. It's hard to believe that he is going so far away, even leaving his father behind, but I must say that I admire his decisiveness and courage. Modern men have to be brave sometimes. We will miss him. Since this may be the last chance for him to have a meal at our house for a long time, we served broiled fish, vegetables cooked in seasoned broth, and soup.

While we were talking Mashimo-sensei came and joined us. He stayed until eleven o'clock, obviously enjoying the lively conversation.

1. Chūhachi went to see the exhibit on November 28 and apparently promised Makiko that he would go again with her.

2. What the "reserved tickets" were for is unclear.

3. Unidentified; possibly a son of Nakamura Satoru, Makiko's mother's brother. See entries for July 22 and 23.

DECEMBER 3 *Saturday Clear*

Today's cooking class ended early, around two o'clock, and when I came home, the soybeans to make miso were already cooked. I expected that the taro would be cooked today, too, but was told that they will be boiled and mashed tomorrow morning.

The gift towels that we ordered the other day were delivered. The amount of the order this year is ten bolts of material, and the cost comes to a little over 6 *sen* for each towel.

While my husband was out attending the reunion at Shūdō Primary School after dinner, Mr. Tanaka came to see him. He said that this is his last visit to our house, which made us feel melancholy. He didn't know about the reunion and left right away to go there.

DECEMBER 4 *Sunday Clear*

Nothing but good weather on Sundays lately.

Made it to the art exhibit today, at last! Mother, Hide-san, Sister Tanii and Take-chan, Chūji-san, Toshiko-san, Sue,[1] and I all went together. An enormous number of people were pushing and shoving in the exhibition hall trying to see the paintings, so that we could hardly see anything at all. Besides, since we didn't buy the program, I couldn't tell who the artists are or get any kind of information about the paintings. I was able to see the Japanese paintings quite well because Hide-san helped me, but we had to run through the sections of oil paintings fast, as the closing bell was ringing. Obviously, we had arrived too late to take in the whole exhibit. After we got home and started talking about what we had learned, I realized that I had missed a great deal. Now I must go back and take a good look at the paintings that I missed.

Mr. Tanaka left from Kyoto Station tonight by the 10:50 train.

My husband said that about 30 people came to see him off, including Mr. Matsui, Mr. Matsumiya, and classmates from the Shūdō Primary School. I wish him a safe, successful trip and hope he will return to Kyoto as soon as he can.

Note: We made miso this morning.[2] For 4 *shō* 5 *gō* cooked soybeans add 4½ sheets of rice yeast and 1 *shō* 5 *gō* of salt. For 3 *shō* 5 *gō* soybeans add 3½ sheets of rice yeast and 9 *gō* of salt.

1. A maid.
2. The ingredients listed here are mixed in two huge casks, stored to ferment, and used throughout the year primarily to season soup.

DECEMBER 5 *Monday Clear*

Although it's been very cold, it was a beautiful day.

Since I hardly remember seeing any of the oil paintings yesterday, I asked my husband if I could go back to see them today. His reaction was cool, and he said, "Going once should be enough, but if you want to go, I don't care." I knew that it is a rather unusual request, but he should have understood how much I wanted to see the paintings. I was sad, however, and got permission from Mother to go with Okuni-san. It was a sudden decision, and we were joined by Mrs. Yamada Osei, who was visiting the Taniis at the time and wanted to go, too.

At the art exhibit we ran into Mr. Matsumiya Hōnen, his brother Yūnen, and Mr. Hirai Baisen,[1] and as we left the place together we discussed the paintings. Some of their criticism was very harsh. I was generally impressed by the oils, particularly Kōhei's[2] figure in a flannel kimono which looked very real!

I felt so happy and liberated after I saw all the paintings. I must remember to go early next year so that it will not take two days to see them all. It is much too soon to plan for next year, of course. Nevertheless . . .

1. All are artist friends of Chūhachi.
2. The name of either the artist or his model.

DECEMBER 6 *Tuesday Clear*

A nice sunny day again, but I feel I haven't accomplished very much. Since this morning we have been talking about nothing but the paintings—every time we got a chance to get together, we talked and talked! On top of that Yasu-san, the salesman from the kimono shop who dropped in to show us some beautiful materials, kept us from our work. I realized that once you engage in idle activity, there is no end to it. I regret that I wasted a lot of time today when I should be doing so many things that need to be done at the end of the year.

I must clean the house tomorrow. Hope it will be a nice day.

December 7 *Wednesday Clear*

It was not as cold as yesterday—perfect weather for housecleaning. Starting with Mother's quarters, the upstairs, the sitting room, and the parlor, we steadily worked our way through the house and finished before the end of the day, even though the days are short lately.

Luckily we have Asakichi[1] working for us this year, so he prepared a bath for us. After the bath and supper Sister Tanii came with her two children. She said she had hoped to come before noon and have lunch with us, but was held up. We laughed and told her that her timing was perfect for us, for we had just finished cleaning the whole house.

Sister has trouble with a boil on her hand and eczema on her face and nose, which must be really irritating. She left about nine because Take-chan got sleepy. I am sorry that we didn't do very much to make her feel welcome.

1. A male domestic servant, whose duties would have included heavy work such as carrying water from the well to fill the bath tub, chopping wood, cleaning the garden and the area in front of the store, and so forth. Such servants were usually older men.

December 8 *Thursday Clear*

It's getting colder by the day.

Late in the afternoon, while my husband was at a meeting of the cooperative,[1] Mr. Matsui telephoned to ask him to come to the Minami-za theater where he was calling from. Apparently he was there with Mr. Suzuki.[2] I called the Matsuis' house, which is located near the office of the cooperative, and asked them to give my husband the message. Luckily, he got it in time, finished his business there, and went on to the theater. I was urging Mother to go join them, but she said that she'd rather stay in the *kotatsu*[3] at home this year.

My sister Eiko stopped by to see me on her way home from visiting Sennyū-ji where her school attended the first memorial service for Prince Kaya.[4] She left about eight o'clock since she has an examination tomorrow. I learned from her that Oasa-han[5] is away again, and that my father is suffering from a severe toothache. All this news troubled me very much.

My husband came home after midnight and said that he particularly enjoyed *Ōboshi Yuranosuke*.[6]

1. *Baiyaku dōgyō kumiai*, which means literally Cooperative of Dealers in Patent Medicines.
2. They were anxious to have her husband join them for the special year-end kabuki performances.
3. See entry for November 17.
4. This princely branch of the imperial family no longer exists. For Sennyū-ji, see entry for January 30.
5. The housekeeper; see entries for September 11, 12, and 17.
6. Yuranosuke was the leader of the group of masterless samurai known as the "Forty-seven *rōnin*," whose young lord had been disgraced by one of the great villains of Japanese drama and forced to commit *hara-kiri*. Vowing to avenge his death, under Yuranosuke's leadership they pursue an intricately plotted campaign that ends in an assault on the villain's residence and his murder. They are convicted of pursuing an unauthorized vendetta and allowed to commit *hara-kiri*. The full-length account of their exploits, as told in the kabuki play *Chūshingura*, requires about ten hours to perform. The performance referred to here probably is a segment of the play.

December 9 *Friday Clear*

[Makiko mistakenly repeats the same events that occurred the day before. The following is the only additional entry.]

It looks like I will be able to go to the Minami-za theater on the twelfth, which makes me very, very happy!

December 10 *Saturday Clear*

A cooking class day. I got there early with the intention of leaving early, but since it was my turn to serve and wait table, it was three o'clock when I finished.

The Matsuis called ahead to say that they plan to come over tonight. They arrived at last around nine o'clock. My husband got home a little later, having attended the celebration for the completion of the second tunnel for the canal.[1] The event took place in Miho-noura in Ōtsu, and that led to their singing *utai*.[2] They also did some monologues from famous kabuki plays. We had such a good time that we didn't notice how quickly time passed. When the clock struck two, we were all startled and the Matsuis left at once. Even our shop-boys had already gone to sleep after starting to clean the store[3] and finishing their late-night snack of sushi as a special treat. I really enjoyed tonight!

1. The canal runs from Miho-no-ura on Lake Biwa to the eastern part of Kyoto. Construction was begun in 1885 and completed in 1890. The digging of the canal and the "Incline," designed to haul boats from Lake Biwa over the hills to the Kamo River, were projects conceived in 1881 by the governor of Kyoto prefecture with a view to providing the city with water for irrigation, navigation, and manufacturing in hopes of reviving its fortunes.

2. They would have been moved to sing *utai* because the setting of one of the most famous of all *nō* dramas is a place called Miho in Suruga province. The play, *Hagoromo* (The cloak of feathers), closely resembles the European folk tale of the swan maiden.

3. They had already started the year-end cleaning in preparation for the New Year.

December 11 *Sunday Clear*

The shop-boys were up at four o'clock this morning to resume their end-of-the-year cleaning, banging around and making all sorts of noise, and they finished their work earlier than expected. For lunch we served them broiled salmon and miso soup, and for dinner cooked sea bream and turnips accompanied by *sake*. They were very happy.

I am going to bed early tonight.

December 12 *Monday Clear*

Woke up at six o'clock, which is unusual for me, and was unable to go back to sleep, so got up at 6:30 and began the preparations for today.[1] I was so excited that I could not eat breakfast—everyone thought it was amusing!

Mother and I went to the kabuki in the morning. Okuni-san and Mr. Matsui came to join us. We were able to see the much-talked-about *kao-mise*,[2] which I found very interesting. We saw three plays, *Sangokushi*, *Narihira Azuma Kudari*, and *Ranpei Monogurui*.[3] I noticed that the theater was not full, though. We came home after six o'clock.

In the evening we prepared small return gifts, putting a towel and a bundle of rice paper in each package, to be handed out tomorrow when the business branch-families bring the gifts of ceremonial rice cakes for the New Year.

1. Getting dressed, putting on her makeup, doing her hair, and so on. When women went to the kabuki theater, it was an occasion for dressing their best.

2. Literally "face-showing." In the last month of the year, all the famous kabuki actors appear on stage together. It is a special, gala performance that no fan of kabuki would miss.

3. I have been unable to identify the first play, but it bears the Japanese title of the great collection of Chinese tales called *The Romance of the Three Kingdoms* in English. The period is the third century A.D., and the stories of heroism, moral rectitude, and conquest have been popular in Japan for centuries. The second play also remains unidentified, but the title, *Narihira Leaves the Capital*, indicates that it concerns Ariwara no Narihira, one of the six sages of poetry of the Heian period. Celebrated in innumerable ballads and dramas as the most handsome man of his time, he was as renowned for his romantic exploits as for his poetry. The third, *The Madness of Ranpei*, is a bravura piece whose plot is largely submerged by its emphasis on exhibiting the skill of a category of actors called *tate*, whose talents include acrobatics and complicated, stylized fight scenes.

DECEMBER 13 *Tuesday Clear*

It has been very cold today. The frost on the roof looked like a thin layer of snow. My hands and feet are so cold that sometimes I don't feel anything at all.

Today we begin official preparations (*kotohajime*) for the New Year's celebration with the delivery of the *kagami-mochi*[1] to the main house by our branch families and the business branch-families. Mr. Yamamoto Matsu was the first to arrive, then one by one, they all came. We literally had no break all morning talking to them.

Early in the morning we sent a set of *kagami-mochi* to the Matsuis' house by messenger. It was ordered ahead of time from a special shop and is made from 3 *shō* of glutinous rice.[2] The other day when Mr. Matsui came to see us, we made an agreement that we will send *kagami-mochi* to them this year, and next year they will send one to us, so that we will take turns each year.[3]

Received a telephone call notifying us that the grandmother of the Inui[4] family has died and that the funeral is scheduled for one o'clock tomorrow.

Bought a bundle of turnips (*aze-kabura*) for ¥1, and some dried shredded radish (*kiriboshi*).

1. See entry for January 8.

2. The quantity of rice used to make the cake, 5.4 liters, indicates that it was much larger than the ordinary variety.

3. It appears that since neither this recently married couple nor the Nakanos wished to institute a traditional junior-senior relationship, they devised a neutral arrangement in which they would take turns making the presentation.

4. A distant affinal household.

December 14 *Wednesday* *Clear*

Since this is the memorial day for the 47 loyal, brave samurai who attacked and killed their master's enemy and committed *hara-kiri* in 1703, there were numerous meetings in schools all around town to tell their story.[1] My husband went to the one at the Third Higher Primary School that started at six.

Mr. Matsumiya and Mr. Matsui came to see him and waited for a while, but decided to leave before he got back. No sooner had they left than my husband came home, and he went after them to bring them back. When they all returned we made *o-zōni* as a snack in clear broth with chicken and fish cake, using pieces of the *kagami-mochi* in it. They said they liked it very much, for it's lighter than Kyoto-style *o-zōni*.[2] When they finished eating, the clock struck midnight, which prompted them to leave apologizing for "eating and running." We all laughed, because that literally is what they did!

Today is *kagami-biraki*.[3] Sent a set of two to the Eastside family and one to the Taniis. When Uncle Akazawa came to visit he was also given one.[4] The rest were cut into small pieces, to be used mostly for cooking and eating. We cut some into tiny pieces to be made into rice crackers (*arare*) later—a trayful should be enough.

For lunch it is our custom to have *mizuna no o-zōni* on this day.[5]

1. See entry for December 8 concerning the kabuki play *Ōboshi Yuranosuke*. Because the Tokugawa censors were extremely sensitive about dramas with political content, playwrights used pseudonyms (often quite transparent) for the main characters. The real name of the leader of the 47 *rōnin* was Ōishi Kuranosuke; he and his followers are held up as shining examples of high moral character and conduct.

2. Since taro is the main ingredient in Kyoto-style *o-zōni*, it is quite thick. Today *o-zōni* is not served until New Year's Day and after. See entry for January 1.

3. "Opening the ceremonial rice cake." After having been displayed in the *tokonoma* (the alcove in the parlor) for two days, they are ready to be eaten. This custom, too, is practiced after New Year's Day in contemporary Japan.

4. Customarily, the day after the branch and business branch-families brought a set of *kagami-mochi* to the main family, one of the two rice cakes was returned to them.

5. See entry for January 8.

December 15 *Thursday* *Clear*

It is getting colder day by day.

My father came over in midafternoon and stayed until after dinner. He told us about the plays he had seen recently. He seemed lonely.

My heart ached to see him so lonesome, and I longed to go to Nijō to be with him but could not bring myself to ask permission to leave here. I wish I had someone to turn to for help, someone to depend on. Having no one, all I can do is calm my emotions.

Tonight we made *o-zenzai*,[1] using the rice cake before it gets moldy, and served it to the store staff. Sister Tanii, who happened to drop in for a visit, joined us for the special snack, and bathed before she left since it is our day to prepare the bath.[2] My father went back to Nijō shortly after she left.

1. See entry for January 22.
2. See entry for February 25.

DECEMBER 16 *Friday Clear*

It has been a cold day; the sky looked like it might be snowing. I was not able to work very effectively at all today and instead have been huddling over the charcoal brazier off and on since this morning. I shouldn't have done that, for this is an especially busy time of the year.

We made turnip pickles today. They have been dried for a couple of days, and when the leaves are shriveled up, they are ready to be processed. Wind the leaves around and tuck them under each turnip, place them in a vat, and sprinkle a little more than one *shō* of salt over them. While she was showing me how to make them, Mother said that these are quick pickles that will be ready in February.

DECEMBER 17 *Saturday Clear*

The first snow of the season fell this morning, creating unseasonable blossoms on the bare branches of the trees. It was beautiful everywhere one looked. Even a sleepyhead like me opened my eyes and leaped from bed upon hearing the word "snow!"

Because of the snow and the extremely cold weather, I skipped the last cooking class of the year. I was glad to find out that I didn't miss much, for the dishes they prepared today were not that great.

Take-chan came to play with the children from Imazato[1] and had a good time running around with them. The children left when they were sent for to come home, but Take-chan decided to stay overnight.

My husband came home at 2:30 in the morning from the year-end celebration party of the pharmacists in Nijō.

1. A place name, but it is not clear who these children were.

December 18 *Sunday Clear*

A sunny day again. The hairdresser came in the morning and, since she was planning to go somewhere, did my hair quickly, but it was unsettled for a while, as it perched right on the top of my head.

I dressed quickly and went to Nijō, taking as *o-seibo* gifts[1] two sea bream that Mother gave me. Since it is Sunday, Eiko and Senzō were home. Elder Sister Kōshima came to join us and on the spur of the moment we decided to go and see a comedy, leaving home around seven in the evening. Unfortunately, it was not at all interesting, so we left without seeing the last scene.

1. The generic term for any year-end gift. As subsequent entries show, *o-seibo* gifts were extremely important, as indeed they are in contemporary Japan. Surprisingly, today's equally important midsummer counterpart, *o-chūgen*, is not mentioned at all in this diary.

December 19 *Monday Clear*

Another nice day, but the thermometer has been hovering around 42–45° and hasn't budged at all.

This morning we made envelopes containing *o-seibo* money to pass out. In the afternoon I took a basket of 30 eggs (cost: ¥1) to the Matsuis' as *o-seibo* from us. That's all I did today.

My husband attended a meeting at the School of Pharmacy that started at six o'clock. He got back home around eleven.

We received a box of tangerines from the family in Tonoshō.

December 20 *Tuesday Clear*

Uncle Nishimura from Tonoshō came to visit us. Rather than taking the train, it seems that he walked all the way, leaving his house at nine in the morning and arriving here after two o'clock in the afternoon, carrying a big plum-tree branch![1] When I arranged it in the *tokonoma* temporarily, it filled the whole place, suddenly transforming it into a plum forest.

I was amazed at what country people can do, carrying such a heavy burden on their shoulders and walking miles and miles without minding! We served him a nice dinner with *sake*, which he enjoyed so much that it took him a long time to finish. The Eastside family gave us sea-bream *sashimi*,[2] cooked shrimp, and bamboo shoots to serve him, so we ordered *chawan-mushi*[3] from the fish shop and served trout fry as well. He went to bed early.

1. The plum blossom is one of a trio of auspicious plants known as *shō-chiku-bai* (pine-bamboo-plum). He had brought the branch expressly so that the Nakanos would have an appropriate flower arrangement for the New Year.
2. Thinly sliced raw fish, a delicacy.
3. Egg custard with shrimp, fish cake, mushrooms, spinach, gingko nuts, and so forth.

December 21 *Wednesday Clear*

Uncle Nishimura had *sake* with his breakfast. I bought some fish cake last night and served it with a salad of mixed grated radish and trout fry to accompany the *sake*.[1] Late in the morning he went to the outdoor market at Tō-ji.[2]

While he was out, we prepared the *o-seibo* gifts for him to take back to his family. For his wife and son each, we made up an envelope of money and a box of dried bonito (cost: ¥1), and added a box of white sugar for the family and one of brown sugar for their relatives in Taga.

I arranged the plum branch in the *tokonoma* so that he could see it for himself while he is here. It looks gorgeous, filling the whole place with blossoms!

1. It is not uncommon to serve *sake* at the morning meal, especially when the guest likes to drink.
2. On the 21st of every month, an open market is held at this great Buddhist temple. The last one of the year, on December 21, is still known today for the enormous number of stalls and the variety of merchandise offered. See entry for January 25.

December 22 *Thursday Clear*

While I was cleaning around the *tokonoma* with the duster this morning the plum branch fell over. As I was picking it up, water spilled from the big jar in which it was arranged and down onto the floor, flooding the whole place. I was startled and cried out for someone to bring something to mop it up with, but no one responded. At last Omiki[1] and the shop-boy heard me and came to my rescue. We mopped it up as fast as we could, but by then the water had seeped between the tatami mats, so we had to take out the heavy mats and remove the wet paper underneath. I was horrified at the mess I had created!

Just about dark Mr. Matsumiya came over with a bottle of sherry and some salad oil as *o-seibo* gifts.[2] He had dinner with my husband and left around nine o'clock.

Note: Ordered 4 *shō* of small rice cakes and a 1-*shō kagami-mochi* from the Yoshikawa *mochi* shop today. Later I was told that 4 *shō* will not be enough and that I should have ordered five.

1. One of the maids, not Shirakawa Omiki.
2. Note that both items were probably imported from the West. It was in the Matsumiya home that the cooking lessons were held.

December 23 *Friday Clear*

Today is the winter solstice.

We had our customary *o-zenzai* for lunch.[1]

This is the day that Mr. Nishimura Sada[2] visits us every year, bringing the customary annual codfish to serve for snacks tonight.

Mr. Matsumiya, Mr. Matsui, and Okuni-san came over, and Take-chan, too. The house was filled with people. The Matsuis brought a duck, which we cooked for dinner.

After dinner we performed the annual event called *o-hitaki*.[3] The children from the Eastside family joined our children, and they all sat around the iron charcoal brazier. Each held a piece of thin wood and chanted, "*Ta-a-ke, ta-a-ke, o-hi-ta-a-ki, nō-nō. Mi-i-kan, manjū, hōshi-i-ya, nō-nō.*"[4] Then, while chanting, they thrust the slips of wood into the fire in the brazier, and trays of tangerines, steamed buns, and candied popped rice were passed around. Later on, trays of the same food were sent to the store, and all the members of the staff enjoyed them.

Next, sushi and a clear soup of codfish were served to everyone. The store staff had their *sake*. All the events were completed, and everyone left about ten o'clock. After they left, it seemed as though a big tide had swept out, leaving behind only silence.

1. See entry for January 22.
2. Unidentified.

3. This is the winter solstice. *O-hitaki* means literally "lighting a fire" to warm the earth and invite spring back early. In pharmacists' houses, it is also the day to honor Yakusoshin, deity of herbal medicine. Professor Nakano reports that on this day portrait scrolls of Yakusoshin and Hippocrates were displayed in his house, to indicate that the pharmacy dealt in both traditional and modern medicines. See Introduction.

4. "Burn, burn, god of spring! We want tangerines and steamed buns!" The duplicated *nō-nō* is a children's word for deity, in this case the one who ushers in the spring season, reckoned to begin very soon after the beginning of the new year. See Introduction.

December 24 *Saturday* *Clear*

The last day of school, a happy one for students! Hide-san came home from his boardinghouse. He will go to Ōtsu tomorrow to train with his crew.

Elder Sister Kōshima telephoned to ask if I want to see the Soganoya comedy troupe with her. I felt that I should say no, as I have been out a lot recently. On the other hand, if I turned her down again, she might think that I am being difficult. So I asked Mother if I could go, and she said, "Yes, you may," and that was that!

December 25 *Sunday* *Clear*

Since the school holiday started today, the children are home.

Mother had planned to take *o-seibo* gifts to the Hiraokas and Matsuis today, but decided not to because I was going out to the theater. I left home before five o'clock feeling guilty, for this is the busiest time of the year.

When I arrived at the theater, I was glad to see Elder Sister Kōshima already there waiting for me, but I also ran into Mr. Matsumiya and his brother Yūnen. That was bad enough, but on top of that, on the way home I also ran into Mr. Matsui unexpectedly. I should have known better than to go out![1] However, the plays were good and quite funny, and as usual the place was packed.

At last I was able to buy the doll that "somebody" has been talking about so much.[2] She closes and opens her eyes and is adorable. It cost ¥1.20.

Note: The 27th is our *mochi-tsuki* day.[3] In preparation, 3 *shō* of rice[4] are soaked in water the day before.

1. In this entry we see the conflict of Makiko's feelings and expectations of herself. She wishes to please her Elder Sister and appreciates her mother-in-law's understanding. Indeed, Mine is more compassionate than might have been the case had Makiko not lost her own mother. I think that she is making every effort to treat Makiko

as she would treat her own daughter. But Makiko clearly is very embarrassed at having been caught in what surely was highly irregular behavior for the wife of a household head at one of the busiest times of the year.

2. I have put "somebody" in quotation marks because the reference is clearly to Makiko herself. Still childless, she seems to have been slightly embarrassed at admitting to wanting a doll so badly.

3. The day to pound glutinous rice, using a mortar and mallet, for rice cakes for the New Year.

4. The rice is half regular, half glutinous.

DECEMBER 26 *Monday Clear*

Nothing in particular happened this morning. After cleaning the sink and well area in the kitchen, we washed the rice and transferred it to the big cask to be soaked overnight. Since we and the Eastside family are combining our *mochi-tsuki* work, their maid came to help. The children are anxiously awaiting tomorrow's big event.

DECEMBER 27 *Tuesday Clear*

For the *mochi-tsuki* this evening a lot of preparation was done in the morning. First, we washed the steamers, tub, and casks. The tub had to be filled with water for a while so that the wood would expand and the hoops would tighten.

So we could start the operation immediately after dinner, the fire under the big iron pot was lit before dinner. Putting a cloth lining around the edge of the steamer is a must, so that the steam will not escape.

When the time had come to pound the *mochi* in the courtyard in the back of the house, it was overcrowded with people who had come to help; there must have been more than twenty altogether.[1] Someone was joking, "Watch your wallet!" and a joyful air permeated the yard. There were Mrs. Ōkita,[2] who is a skillful *mochi* turner,[3] a worker from the Usagiya *mochi* shop who came to help, and Zen-san,[4] who always shows up when we need extra hands. In addition, the nurses from the Eastside clinic came to help make numerous small round *mochi* cakes because the Eastside family gets their share of *mochi* from this operation.

There were a great many people moving around in the yard, pushing and shoving, but the work was completed by ten o'clock because there were so many helping hands. While everyone was gone to the public bath-house,[5] we prepared for the party. We had *sake* and for side dishes, a big Spanish mackerel that we received as an *o-seibo* gift from Harisei,[6] cooked with turnips, and radish pickles that were opened and served for the first time today.

For the tasting of the fresh *mochi*[7] we had cooked 1 *shō* and 3 *gō* of red beans to make a sweet paste to go with it, but there was not enough to go around.[8]

It was after one o'clock when we went to bed.

1. Including their own servants, the store clerks and shop-boys.
2. The wife of Ōkita Toyosaburō.
3. A mass of hot steamed rice in the mortar is turned by hand between strokes of the large wooden mallet.
4. Zen-san is *de-iri-mono*. See entry for May 9.
5. Since the bath in the Nakano's home could not accommodate so many people, they were given money to go to the public bath-house.
6. It is still the case that places of business such as this restaurant send year-end gifts to their regular patrons.
7. The last batch, while the rice cakes are still warm and soft.
8. In the Nakano household, it was the custom to serve fresh *mochi* with two kinds of sauce: one of sweet red beans and the other of grated radish with soy sauce.

December 28 *Wednesday Clear*

Take-chan, who has been staying with us, went home this morning because he heard that his father had sent him a parcel from Tokyo.

Mother went to the Taniis' house after lunch, saying that she is also going to pay her *o-seibo* visit to the Matsuis. She came home around nine o'clock, having learned that Brother Tanii will be home on the 31st.

Starting tonight we serve broiled *uru-mochi*[1] for our evening snack.

1. A half-and-half mixture of regular and glutinous rice, shaped into a loaf, then sliced and broiled.

December 29 *Thursday Clear*

The end of the year is approaching fast.

Tonight's event is the grinding of the miso beans.[1] First, the mortar and pestle[2] should be got out and made ready before dinner time. Start working immediately after dinner and the dishes are done. Bring the miso cask into the kitchen and put some in the *suribachi* bowl. When the beans have been ground into a heavy, smooth paste, put it in large lacquerware boxes. If the paste is too thick, thin it with *sake*.

As was done the night before, broil *mochi* and serve to the store staff as a snack.

Uncle Akazawa came to visit. He promised to come back on New Year's Day to have lunch with us.

I was reprimanded this evening[3] for not working when there is so much to be done. Was told that I depend too much on Mother where housework is concerned, and that if I don't work myself, at least I should direct the servants. It is true that I have been crocheting,[4] totally unaware of what was going on around me.

I was startled, but at the same time, I have to admit that I was wrong. To show my sincerity I worked so hard at grinding miso that it was all done before nine o'clock!

1. To be used in the preparation of New Year's dishes, such as *o-zōni*.
2. The mortar in this case is a ceramic bowl with a striated interior, called *suribachi*.
3. Probably by her husband.
4. A handicraft newly imported from the West.

DECEMBER 30 *Friday Clear*

I am supposed to polish all the brass fixtures in the household Buddhist altar today,[1] but I was unable to get to it because there were so many other things to do.

After lunch went shopping for New Year's food. Bought 45 large taro (*kashira-imo*) for 30 *sen*, a bundle of burdock for 9 *sen*, two carrots, to be added to 5 *gō* of black beans, for 1 *sen* 5 *rin*, and five pieces of fried bean curd to be wrapped in the *kobu-maki*.[2]

Cooked the black beans today. Peeled the taro and the radishes, which will be cooked tomorrow in the water the rice is washed in.[3] Made the rolled kelp tonight by wrapping it around the burdock and the fried bean curd. The white beans are cooked without dried bonito stock (*katsuobushi no dashi*), but are soaked overnight in simple seaweed stock (*kobu-dashi*) to flavor them.

Went to bed at 2:30 A.M., since it is the day before the big accounting day,[4] and lots of preparation had to be made.

1. Caring for the household ancestral altar is the responsibility of the wife of the household head.
2. Rolls of kelp. One of the classic New Year's dishes. The Nakano household used fried bean curd with burdock stuffing.

3. It is believed that cooking certain kinds of vegetables, such as these and bamboo shoots, in water in which rice has been washed will reduce their tendency to create surface scum while boiling.

4. December 31 is the final day to clear all payments and debts for the year.

December 31 *Saturday*

Unexpected snowfall this morning, which should have come a day later. At about 4:30 this morning it apparently rained hard so that the streets turned muddy like miso paste,[1] which made it difficult for the bill collectors to make their rounds. Our store clerks and shop-boys were complaining about it.

I cleaned and decorated the family altar in the morning. Hung the portrait of Shinran Shōnin.[2] Took the individual trays, lacquerware bowls, lacquerware food boxes, the guest charcoal braziers, and the folding screens from the storehouse and got them ready.

For lunch we use lacquerware bowls for the family, and the menu for this day is always broiled sardines and miso soup with green, leafy vegetables.

Cooked the big taro in a large pot today in the white water left from washing rice. The small taro and the radish should be cooked the day before, as needed.

Made salad of cooked burdock with white sesame sauce, candied small fish, and sweetened black beans, and arranged them in the lacquerware food boxes.

The rolled seaweed is cooked in the morning and again in the afternoon to enhance the flavor.

For dinner we had clear soup with tofu, as we do on the last day of every month.

Heated the bath water after four o'clock, bathed, and went over to the Eastside to exchange greetings, saying, "*Okotō-san de gozaimasu.*"[3]

Finished the final accounting, which took a long time this year. When we were done, we had our customary noodles,[4] and by the time my husband finished writing individual names with a brush and *sumi* ink on the envelopes of the New Year's chopsticks,[5] it was already six o'clock in the morning.

It seems to me that the year of Meiji 43 has gone by in a flash.

1. Brown in color and thick in texture.
2. Founder of the Buddhist sect Jōdo Shinshū.
3. "It is a busy time. Can we help you?"

4. In southern Japan *udon* noodles made from wheat flour are eaten, but in northern Japan, including the Tokyo area, *soba* noodles made from buckwheat flour are preferred. Noodles symbolize long life, and the custom of eating them at New Year's continues today.

5. The names are always written by the head of the household. This type of chopsticks envelope (*hashi bukuro*) is prepared only for use at the New Year. The chopsticks are new, made of unfinished wood, and are used only during the festive period.

EPILOGUE

Makiko's diary is only a thin slice called "1910" out of the 88 years of her life, and a much thinner slice out of the more than 200 years of the history of the Nakano household. Apparently she kept diaries from time to time later in her life, but none as complete as this one. I found myself wishing that she had continued at least a little into 1911, for I felt I had come to know her so well that I was reluctant to leave her at the end of the year.

What happened to Makiko and her family?[1] Childless when the diary was written, Makiko and Chūhachi eventually had four children, a son Yasuo in 1913, a daughter Hisako in 1918, a second son Takashi in 1920, and a third son Hiroshi in 1923. The joy at Yasuo's arrival must have been short-lived, however, for in 1915 Chūhachi's mother Mine died of blood poisoning, leaving Makiko to assume the duties that Mine had trained her to and care for her two-year-old. By then, however, it seems safe to assume that she had been so thoroughly schooled in the ways of the house that she was able to take up the direction of the domestic side of the household affairs with confidence. Makiko as the 25-year-old mother of a little boy would have been very different from the carefree young wife whose diary we have read.

With growing responsibilities and the arrival of three more children, Makiko would have had little time to spare for art exhibits and the theater for many years—and none at all for jump-rope! The re-

1. Most of the information that follows was obtained directly from Professor Nakano Takashi and from two of his publications, *Chūgakusei no mita* and *Shōka dōzokudan*.

sponsibilities of her position were manifold, for now she alone supervised the domestic help and looked after her husband, the younger members of the family, and her own four children, deciding what food to serve to the guests and on what special occasions, determining what gifts to present to whom when they were required, and arranging for the weddings of her sister Eiko and all her husband's younger siblings. I like to think that when it came time to oversee the making of pickles and miso, she consulted the notes she had made in her diary. She was a loving mother, and she and Chūhachi enjoyed the frequent visits by the ever-expanding number of children of relatives as well as members of their extended family.

Over the years, her adventurous spirit never dimmed, and I find it entirely fitting that she was the first member of the Nakano family to fly—from Tokyo to Nagoya in 1936. She reported to her family, eager to hear all about this momentous event, that it was very much like being on board ship. The only difference, she told them, was that because the tremendous noise of the propellers made it impossible to carry on a conversation, each passenger was provided with ear plugs and paper and pencil to write out messages.

In 1918, the store was expanded and reoriented to face on Gojō Avenue and continued to operate there much as it had eight years before. That is, one half of the business was in pharmaceutical items and cosmetics, the other in sugar, processed foods, soft drinks, and imported liquor. The front of the new store was almost twice as wide as the old one had been and was equipped with four windows for displaying merchandise, on whose back panels were hung paintings done by students from the Kyoto School of Arts and Crafts. This unique art show changed every month and became quite well known. The two store managers, one the familiar figure of Mr. Moriguchi, whose rudeness so upset Makiko, eventually retired and were replaced by men from two other commuting business branch-families. Makiko and Chūhachi's eldest son became a licensed pharmacist and took charge of the prescription section, succeeding the pharmacist who had been employed by the store up to that time. Makiko does not mention it in the diary, but her husband, although licensed himself, apparently had always employed a pharmacist. Instead of practicing his profession in his own store, Chūhachi chose to lead a very active life as the chairman of the Kyoto Pharmaceutical Association and participated in a great many public activities.

The Nakano family, ca. 1913: (*from left*) Makiko with her first son Yasuo, Hidesaburō, Tadao(?), Chūhachi, Mine, Chūjirō, Seiichi, and Shinako.
(Nakano Takashi)

Makiko's family, ca. 1924: (from left) Makiko with youngest son Hiroshi, Hisako, Chūhachi, Takashi, Yasuo.
(Nakano Takashi)

Makiko with daughter Hisako and eldest son Yasuo, ca. 1918. (Nakano Takashi)

Makiko, ca. 1930. (Nakano Takashi)

Shijō Avenue Bridge, ca. 1920. (*Me de miru Taishō jidai*)

There seems to have been no let-up in the stream of visitors to their home, and eventually a wooden floor was installed in the sitting room, creating a kind of Western-style room that served as the place for informal social gatherings. There Chūhachi would sit in his chair with his back to the European-made desk and entertain his close friends and relatives who now sat on chairs, for all the tatami mats had been removed. The kitchen and dining areas remained in the same place, as did the parlor containing the ancestral altar. Following the death of Chūhachi's mother Mine, her quarters in the back of the house were used both as guest room and sick-room, and it was there that Makiko gave birth to her four children. Eventually, a formal Western-style parlor was put in on the second floor, along with rooms for the children above the new store building. The live-in store clerks and shop-boys continued to live above part of the new store in much improved quarters whose higher ceilings and larger windows let in more light and air.

Makiko's father, who had given his son Manzō permission to pursue a scientific career rather than succeed him in the business, eventually closed the store in Nijō and lived out his retirement years in the Tōfuku-ji district of Kyoto. Manzō became an internationally known Sinologist, contributing to the scientific study of herbal medicine and publishing widely on the history of ancient Chinese ceramics and porcelain. He and Yukiko had one daughter. He worked in Manchuria and China until his resignation from the position of Acting Director of the Shanghai Research Institute of Natural Science at the time of the Shanghai Incident in 1932, then returned to live in Kyoto, where he died of cancer in 1936. His collected works were published in 1981. Makiko's younger sister Eiko, about whom Makiko was so concerned, married a colleague of Manzō's in Dairen. They had two children and eventually moved to Tokyo. Her younger brother Senzō died at the age of nineteen while visiting Manzō in Dairen on holiday.

Hidesaburō (Hide-san), Chūhachi's brother who was still in college at the time the diary was written, married a daughter of Kurushima Takehiko, the children's storyteller whom we have encountered many times. Hide-san went as an adopted husband and so changed his name to Kurushima; he and his wife had four children. He became a geologist and was the general manager of the mining department of the Anshan Steel Mill in Manchuria. However, he resigned his position following disagreements with his superiors over the new policies the company was being pressured to adopt by the Japanese Kwantung Army in Manchuria. He returned to Japan and started what eventually proved to be a very successful business in Tokyo.

Chūhachi's sister Kuniko, who married Matsui Jisuke in 1910, had no children. Eventually they adopted one of the two younger daughters of the Eastside family. After her husband's death from tuberculosis in 1929, the *sake* distillery continued to operate under a manager for a while, but eventually closed. Kuniko married a second time, to a professor at Kyoto Imperial University. As for Chūhachi's two other younger brothers, Seiichi became a professor in a college of agriculture and taught in Japan and later in Manchuria; the youngest, Chūjirō, graduated from the Naval Academy and became a pilot in the Imperial Japanese Navy. He engaged in air combat over China but, strongly influenced by what he learned of Japanese actions while he was stationed there, became an ardent pacifist. He died from tuberculosis shortly after the war ended. Shinako, Chūhachi's youngest sister, married a banker and lived in Kyoto.

The Eastside family continued to operate the eye clinic at the same location. The Eastside Doctor and his wife had nine children in all, six sons and three daughters. Their eldest daughter, Yuri, who appeared in the diary frequently, married an ophthalmologist who took over the practice when her father died. He did not take the family name as he would have done had he been an adopted husband. As mentioned above, one of the two daughters born after 1910 was adopted by Matsui Jisuke and Kuniko. None of the six sons had any immediate interest in succeeding to the family business, apparently, and consequently pursued quite varied careers. The eldest son, Tadao, first became a judo expert, then took up chicken farming, and only late in life went to a medical school and became a licensed ophthalmologist. The second son, Takao, became a movie producer; Kyoto was developing a movie industry on the outskirts of the city in Uzumasa. The third son emigrated to Brazil; the fourth, Nobuo, whose birth is recorded in Makiko's diary, also became an ophthalmologist and appears to have established his own practice elsewhere in Kyoto. The fifth son became an army doctor and was killed in World War II; the sixth became a surgeon. When Yuri and her husband moved into the Eastside family house, the Eastside Doctor's widow and the remaining unmarried children moved to a section of northern Kyoto.

The Taniis, Chūhachi's elder sister Yae and her husband Senjirō, had two more children after Takeo and Toshiko. Senjirō became executive director of the sugar company for which he was working in 1910.

The Hiraokas became one of the leading ceramics dealers in Kyoto. In 1994, when I was searching out places mentioned in the diary, I found Hiraoka Manjudō at the same address as in Makiko's time. It was a modern building in whose large plate-glass show windows fronting Gojō Avenue were displays of exquisite ceramics. Only two years later the Hiraokas fell victim to Japan's severe economic recession, sold the building, now a funeral parlor, and relocated to Ohara.

The Nakano's country relative in Tonoshō, Nishimura Tokusaburō, who appeared in the diary as an innocent young man of 21 who loved children, remained close. Members of the Nakano family continued to visit Tonoshō, often sending the children there to enjoy the country life. Their Uncle Tokusaburō was a frequent visitor to Gojō, and Professor Nakano remembers that one fall he walked all the way pushing a cart on which he had loaded a huge branch of a persimmon tree, laden with fruit. Everyone in Gojō was impressed and delighted with the gesture, just as Makiko had been so many years before when Tokusaburō's adoptive father walked from Tonoshō carrying a branch of a blossoming plum tree for the New Year's decorations.

Chūhachi continued to develop his interests in Western music and became manager of a group called *Kashiopia Gakudan* (the Cassiopeia musical group). Among his many interests, he particularly enjoyed his work with the Japanese Boy Scouts, which had been founded by his old friend Kurushima Takehiko. In 1915, Chūhachi established the *Kyōto shōnen giyūgun*, the first troop in Kyoto, and eventually became chairman of the board of trustees of the Boy Scouts of Kyoto. Chūhachi realized his dream of going abroad and made two extended trips. In 1924 he attended the International Jamboree of the Boy Scouts in Copenhagen as one of the representatives from Japan and spent some months traveling in Europe. In 1931 he participated in international meetings of the scouting movement in Vienna and Geneva, but the high point of his trip was a training institute for scout leaders in England where he received direct instruction from Baden-Powell himself. For the next ten years he worked ceaselessly for scouting until the outbreak of war in 1941, when the Japanese authorities ordered the "enemy" organization disbanded.

After the war ended in 1945, Chūhachi's health deteriorated rapidly, primarily from the effects of malnutrition, which was widespread in Japan at the time. Nonetheless, he served as trustee of the Kyoto Private School of Pharmacy, which had been elevated to the status of college, and devoted his remaining energies to reestablishing the Japanese Federation of Boy Scouts. It was his passion until his last moments, and it is a bitter irony that when he received the invitation to go to Tokyo to receive appointment as Chief Scout of Japan, he was on his deathbed and too feeble to make the journey. In 1949, five years after Japan's surrender in World War II, he died of typhoid. As we know, Makiko survived her husband and lived with her children until her death at the age of 88 in 1978.

During the time of Chūhachi VII and Makiko, both the business and its associated families underwent many drastic changes. When Chūhachi became head of the Nakano household, the family business was in severe decline owing to an unfortunate combination of outright mismanagement and bitter family disputes. The young new head, with the help of the dedicated store staff and with the guidance of a skillful adviser, brought the business through the crisis and was able to expand the enterprise. The successful negotiation of this difficult period was made possible in part because Japan was experiencing a period of rapid economic growth and in part because Chūhachi was alert to the increasing demand for modern medicine and food products.

At the same time, however, all traditionally organized enterprises were facing the challenge of adjusting to major changes in employer-employee relations. We know that Chūhachi was trying to modernize the business, an effort that eventually brought about significant changes in the relationship between the main house, its branch-families, and the business branch-families. Among many other problems encountered by the main house was the difficulty of raising enough capital with which to establish new business branch-families. Furthermore, up to Chūhachi's time the authority of the head of the main house was seldom subject to challenge, but people's view of the employment system was changing rapidly.

In the years around the time that Makiko's diary was written, the Nakano household was able to create only a few new business branch-families, some of which did not last. The major problem was that it simply was no longer financially feasible to provide them with enough capital to open a new store. As a consequence, the store clerks and shop-boys, who had once worked long hours for very low wages with the prospect of having their own business one day, came to realize that such jobs no longer held much promise. In the Nakano pharmacy, as a way of signaling a more democratic relationship between employer and employee, Chūhachi had decreed that shop-boys were no longer to be called *detchi*, but *shō ten'in* (literally "little clerks") instead. But such reforms came too late, for in rapidly industrializing Japan other jobs, such as factory work, paid better and required less adherence to older ideals of hierarchy and obligation. The abandonment of traditional employment practices accelerated as Japan pursued increasingly expansionist policies in mainland Asia. With the invasion of China in 1937 and the outbreak of World War II in 1941, the old customs were breaking down as the growth of the military-industrial machine demanded more and more efficient organization of the labor force. All these changes had a major impact on the pharmacy in Gojō as the Nakanos attempted to adjust to the new social order.

The most devastating change in the lives of the Nakanos occurred in 1945, however, just before the end of World War II when the government ordered the clearing of fire-breaks through the city. The Nakanos' house and store, which had stood at the southwest corner of Gojō and Yamato-Ōji Avenues for more than 200 years, was razed. The leveling of structures along one side of the narrow streets, which was done in many cities, was designed to widen them with two aims in view. First, the authorities believed that in the event of incendiary raids on Kyoto, the move would facilitate the work of firefighters and thus greatly lessen the danger of the spread of fire. Second, they foresaw the day when tanks and heavy artillery would need room to maneuver in defense of the cities in the event of a landing by an Allied invasion force. Ironically, the destruction served no purpose, for of all of Japan's major cities, only Kyoto was spared incendiary raids.

In any event, the Nakanos and all those who lived on the south side of Gojō Avenue were given four days' notice to vacate their homes and businesses, which were razed within a few weeks without even modest compensation by the government. This was early in 1945, by which time the family already had sent most of its young men to the war. Two of their sons were drafted and fighting in Burma and North China, and the store clerks, drafted one by one, were all gone. Even the women of the family, daughters and maids alike, were called to work in factories or otherwise contribute to the war effort. By the end of the war in August 1945, all the domestic help had gone back to the farms they had come from, where only old people and children were left to work in the fields. When the two Nakano sons returned to Kyoto more than a year after the surrender, they found no trace of the pharmacy but discovered their parents living in a small house not far away.

At the time of the forced move, it had been left to Makiko and Chūhachi to pack and relocate in a matter of days with no one to help them. Many things were lost in the confusion of the move and of the end of the war. But according to Professor Nakano, who was drafted in December 1943 when he was a student at Tokyo Imperial University and repatriated from North China in May 1946, when he returned home, he found that his mother had managed to save many important family papers, including some twenty volumes of the diaries of his great-grandfather, Chūhachi V. It was on these materials that Professor Nakano based the study of merchant *dōzoku* mentioned in the Introduction. Fortunately, among the papers that Makiko had packed away in a tea box were her own diaries. She also kept her children's diaries, among them those of her sons who had gone off to war. It is my guess that, like many Japanese mothers of the time, Makiko treasured them particularly, for she must have feared that she would never see her sons again.

Thus, the pharmacy ceased to exist. Its 200-year history as a business was at an end, and in a way, so was the household. Makiko's eldest son Yasuo, a licensed pharmacist, had returned from Burma in the fall of 1946, a year after the war ended. As the eldest son, he would have become Chūhachi VIII, but there was no hope of reviving the business. Eventually he found a position in the Kyoto prefectural government. Even though the store had been demolished, the business branch-families continued to call on the first day of the month, just as Makiko reported they had done before the war, until Chūhachi VII's death in 1949. Old habits and long-standing relationships die hard, and Professor Nakano says that as late as 1963, on the first of the month, two of the heads of business branch-families came all the way to Yamashina (east of Kyoto) to pay their respects. The remnants of the family had moved into a small house there, and like so many Japanese in the immediate postwar period, were facing the challenge of putting together a way of life radically different from anything they and their ancestors had known. Makiko's diary gives us a glimpse of their vanished world.

BIBLIOGRAPHY

Brandon, Reiko Mochinaga, Barbara B. Stephan, Enbutsu Sumiko, and Ian Reader. *The Japanese New Year: Spirit and Symbol.* Honolulu: Honolulu Academy of Arts, 1994.

Dalby, Liza. *Geisha.* Berkeley: University of California Press, 1983.

Groos, Arthur. "Return of the Native: Japan in *Madama Butterfly / Madama Butterfly* in Japan." *Cambridge Opera Journal* 1, 2 (1989): 167–94.

Ichihara, M., comp. *The Official Guide-Book to Kyoto and the Allied Prefectures, Prepared Especially for the Eleven Hundredth Anniversary of the Founding of Kyoto and the Fourth National Industrial Exhibition by the City Council of Kyoto.* Nara: Meishinsha, 1895.

Iwaya, Sazanami. *Waga go-jū nen* (My fifty years). Tokyo: Tōadō, 1920.

Kai, Miwa, trans. *The Diary of a Japanese Innkeeper's Daughter.* Edited and annotated by Robert J. Smith and Kazuko Smith. Ithaca, N.Y.: Cornell University East Asia Papers No. 36, 1984.

Kurabayashi, Shōji, ed. *Nihon matsuri to nenjū gyōji jiten* (Dictionary of Japanese annual festivals). Tokyo: Ōfūsha, 1983.

Kyōto shomin seikatsu shi (History of the common people of Kyoto). Kyoto: Kyōto shinyō ginkō, 1973.

McKinnon, Richard N. "Utsubozaru." In *Selected Plays of Kyōgen*, pp. 105–21. Tokyo: Uniprint, 1968.

Morris, Ivan, trans. and ed. *The Pillow Book of Sei Shōnagon*, vol. 1. New York: Columbia University Press, 1967.

Muraoka, Daiji, and Yoshikoshi Tatsuo. *Noh.* Tokyo: Hoikusha, 1969.

Nakano, Takashi. *Chūgakusei no mita shōwa jūnen dai* (1935–1945 through the eyes of a middle-school student). Tokyo: Shinyōsha, 1989.

———. *Meiji yonjūsannen Kyōto: Aru shōka no wakazuma no nikki* (Kyoto in 1910: The diary of the young wife of a merchant house). Tokyo: Shinyōsha, 1981.

———. *Shōka dōzokudan no kenkyū* (A study of merchant dōzoku organization). Tokyo: Miraisha, 1964.

Nippon Gakujutsu Shinkōkai. *Japanese Noh Drama: Ten Plays Selected and*

Translated from the Japanese, vol. 2. Tokyo: Nippon Gakujutsu Shinkōkai, 1959.

Nolte, Sharon, and Sally Ann Hastings. "The Meiji State's Policy Toward Women, 1890–1910." In Gail Lee Bernstein, ed. *Recreating Japanese Women, 1600–1945*, pp. 151–74. Berkeley: University of California Press, 1991.

Salz, Jonah. "Intercultural Pioneers: Otojiro Kawakami and Sada Yakko." *The Journal of Intercultural Studies* 20 (1993): 25–74.

Shimizu, Hajime, and Shibata Minoru. *Kyō no minka* (The houses of Kyoto). Kyoto: Tankōsha, 1962.

Tōyō Keizai Shinpōsha, eds. *Meiji Taishō kokusei sōran* (Meiji-Taishō national census). Tokyo: Tōyō Keizai Shinpōsha, 1975.

Tsurumi, E. Patricia. *Factory Girls: Women in the Thread Mills of Meiji Japan*. Princeton, N.J.: Princeton University Press, 1990.

NAME INDEX

In this index "f" after a number indicates a separate reference on the next page, and "ff" indicates separate references on the next two pages. A continuous discussion over two or more pages is indicated by a span of numbers. *Passim* is used for a cluster of references in close but not consecutive sequence.

GENERAL INDEX

In this index "f" after a number indicates a separate reference on the next page, and "ff" indicates separate references on the next two pages. A continuous discussion over two or more pages is indicated by a span of numbers. *Passim* is used for a cluster of references in close but not consecutive sequence.

NOTE ON ILLUSTRATION SOURCES

Unless otherwise indicated, most of the photographs of Kyoto were taken before 1910, the year of Makiko's diary. Exact dates are often unknown, but the consensus among experts is that the majority of these photographs were taken in the later nineteenth or very early twentieth century. I have used these earlier photographs because they show the city as it still was in Makiko's time. Those taken after 1910 that I have been able to find usually show a more modernized city. The widening of avenues began in 1911; streetcar lines spread throughout the city; and a significant increase in the number of Western-style buildings, such as hotels, banks, department stores, and municipal buildings greatly altered the central district.

Scenes of Kyoto and Japanese life were provided by several sources. I wish to thank the Asian Collection, Herbert F. Johnson Museum of Art, Cornell University, Ithaca, New York; the Kyoto Prefectural Archives; Long Ago and Far Away Image Bank, Tokyo; the Peabody Essex Museum, Salem, Massachusetts; Ukiyo-e Books, Leiden, The Netherlands; and the Yokohama Archives of History.

The following published sources also provided photographs. These are cited in short form with the appropriate illustrations.

Ketteiban Shōwa shi: Shōwa zen shi. Nichiro sensō Meiji 34–45 [Final version: History of Shōwa, vol. 3. Pre-Shōwa history, 1901–1912]. Tokyo: Mainichi Shinbunsha, n.d.

Kyōto fu shi, I [History of Kyoto prefecture]. Kyoto: Kyōto fu, 1919.

Me de miru Taishō jidai, 1 [Viewing the Taishō period, vol. 1]. Tokyo: Kokusho-kankōkai, 1986.

Shashin shūsei: Kyōto hyakunen panorama-kan [Pictorial collection: The panorama of Kyoto in the last one hundred years], ed. Yoshida Mitsukuni. Kyoto: Tankōsha, 1992.

Winkel, Margarita. *Souvenir from Japan: Japanese Photography at the Turn of the Century*, London: Bamboo Publishing, 1991.

Photographs of the festival at Kitano Tenman-gū (facing p. 75); primary school class and girls dancing in schoolyard (facing p. 116); spectators at the Aoi-matsuri procession (facing p. 135); and Kyoto Station (facing p. 185) by Iwai Yukimasa. Deposited in the Kyoto Prefectural Archives.

Photographs of Gojō Bridge (facing p. 93); Shijō Avenue after a rain (facing p. 113); cherry blossoms in Maruyama Park (facing p. 124); and Gion-matsuri procession (facing p. 157) by Kurokawa Suizan. Collection of the Kyoto Prefectural Archives.

Library of Congress Cataloging-in-Publication Data

Nakano, Makiko, 1890–1978.
[Meiji yonjūsannen kyōto. English]
Makiko's diary : a merchant wife in 1910 Kyoto / Nakano Makiko ; translated with introduction and notes by Kazuko Smith.
p. cm.
Includes bibliographical references and index.
ISBN 0-8047-2440-7 : — ISBN 0-8047-2441-5 (pbk.) :
1. Kyoto (Japan)—Social life and customs—1868–1912. 2. Nakano, Makiko, 1890–1978. 3. Kyoto (Japan)—Biography. I. Smith, Kazuko. II. Title.
DS897.K85N3313 1995
952'.1864031'092—dc20
[B] 94-39864
CIP

∞ This book is printed on acid-free recycled paper.

Original printing 1995
Last figure below indicates year of this printing:
07 06 05 04 03 02 01 00 99 98